Physics Teaching in Schools, 1960–85

Studies in Curriculum History Series

General Editor: Professor Ivor F. Goodson
University of Western Ontario, Canada

1. Social Histories of the Secondary Curriculum: Subjects for Study
   Edited by Ivor F. Goodson, University of Sussex

2. Technological Revolution? A Politics of School Science and Technology in England and Wales since 1945
   G. McCulloch, E. Jenkins and D. Layton, University of Leeds

3. Renegotiating Secondary School Mathematics: A Study of Curriculum Change and Stability
   Barry Cooper, University of Sussex

4. Building the American Community: Social Control and Curriculum
   Barry Franklin, Kennesaw College, Georgia

5. The 'New Maths' Curriculum Controversy: An International Story
   Bob Moon

6. School Subjects and Curriculum Change
   Ivor F. Goodson, University of Western Ontario

7. The Formation of the School Subjects: The Struggle for Creating an American Institution
   Edited by Thomas S. Popkewitz, University of Madison–Wisconsin

8. Physics Teaching in Schools 1960–85: Of People, Policy and Power
   Brian E. Woolnough, University of Oxford

Studies in Curriculum History 8

Physics Teaching in Schools 1960–85: Of People, Policy and Power

Brian E. Woolnough

 The Falmer Press

(A member of the Taylor & Francis Group)
London, New York and Philadelphia

WILLIAM MADISON RANDALL LIBRARY UNC
AT WILMINGTON

UK	The Falmer Press, Falmer House, Barcombe, Lewes, East Sussex, BN8 5DL
USA	The Falmer Press, Taylor & Francis Inc., 242 Cherry Street, Philadelphia, PA 19106-1906

© Copyright B. E. Woolnough 1988

All rights reserved. No part of this publication may be reproduced, stored in a retrieval system, or transmitted in any form or by any means, electronic, mechanical, photocopying, recording or otherwise, without permission in writing from the Publisher.

First published 1988

Library of Congress Cataloguing in Publication Data is available on request

ISBN 1-85000-202-9
ISBN 1-85000-203-7 (pbk.)

Jacket design by Caroline Archer

Typeset by Alresford Typesetting & Design, New Farm Road, Alresford, Hants

Printed in Great Britain by Taylor & Francis (Printers) Ltd, Basingstoke

Contents

Acknowledgements		vi
Frontispiece		viii
General Editor's Preface		ix
Chapter 1	Preparing the Way—Setting the Scene	1
Chapter 2	Years of Plenty, Years of Draught—National Development	23
Chapter 3	More Precious than Rubies—The Teachers	65
Chapter 4	Streams in the Desert—The New Courses	85
Chapter 5	In the Courts of the Mighty— Institutional Influences	117
Chapter 6	Marshalling the Troops—ASE Influences	137
Chapter 7	Making Bricks with Straw—School Influences	159
Chapter 8	Tightening the Net—Central Policy	181
Chapter 9	Labouring in the Fields—School Cameos	195
Chapter 10	The Coat of Many Colours—Of People, Policy and Power	223
Index		259

Acknowledgements

In writing this story of the development of physics teaching I am conscious of two things; my gratitude to so many people and my inadequacy in doing justice to them. For, at the heart of this story are people, remarkable people, people who are still alive and people many of whom I would dare to call my friends. I hope that they will not feel that friendship has been betrayed or that others will not feel that it has distorted my judgment. Inevitably, I will do scant justice to many of the personalities involved, I will interpret certain actions in a way that the people involved would not have done for themselves, and I will not be able to give recognition to many of the other people who have been important in shaping these developments. I hope that they will accept my apologies in advance, and put such failings down to incompetence rather than malice. My only defence is that it is a tale, a remarkable tale, that deserves to be told, and that my own professional history has put me in an unusually good position to write it.

Having been involved and committed to so many activities in physics education through this period, my own insights will inevitably have been influenced and shaped by them. Different commentators would have seen the action differently. I hope that my own position, as both a sympathetic, privileged insider and as a detached, 'licenced ruminator', will have maintained some degree of balance in the analysis of the developments. In the final resort, however, this must be seen as the interpretation of one individual, and for that I do not apologize.

My first acknowledgement must be to all those who have made this story possible; to the thousands of physics teachers and others involved in physics education over this period. They have produced a remarkable success story, over and above the call of duty. My own personal indebtedness must be to the countless, unnamed colleagues and friends with whom I have had the joy of working. Each, in their own indefinable way, has contributed to this story and to my own appreciation and enjoyment of it.

Though it might appear invidious to name specific people, I would want to acknowledge in particular those who have given time to discuss aspects of this work as I have been researching for this book: Tim Akrill, Fred Archenhold, John Baker, Brian Chapman, Ron Cockerill, Maurice Ebison, Maurice Elwell, Keith Fuller, Ivor Goodson, Don Harlow, Maurice Holt, John Howson, Jim Jardine, Harvey Johnson, Gron Jones, John Lewis, Norman Lilley, Wilfred Llowarch, Wilf Mace, Beverley Madge, Edith McLean, Sir Nevill Mott, Jill Nelson, Nicholas Perrin, John Poole, John Robards, Graham Verow and Cathy Wilson.

I am also most grateful to the heads and science staff at King Arthur's, Riverside, Camford and Windmill Hill schools, and Brunel College, for allowing me to share their time and experience, to enable me to develop some of the themes in the context of their reality. I hope that, if they recognize themselves, they will not feel that I have so simplified the situation as to have distorted the essential truth.

Many others, whose brains I have picked during informal encounters, but without warning of my ulterior motive, I felt would not wish to be named here. But to them too, as to the many who have influenced me by their written and spoken words, I would acknowledge my gratitude.

I am grateful to the Director and staff at the Department of Educational Studies at the University of Oxford for allowing me the sabbatical term in Michaelmas 1985 which inspired me to get started on, if not to complete, this book. But my final, and fullest, acknowledgement must be to my wife Peggy, not only for reading and correcting drafts of this book, but for sharing and bearing with me throughout so much of this period in physics education.

I have been conscious while writing this book of two possible audiences: physicists and teachers of physics on the one hand, and social historians of the curriculum on the other. The former may not be fully conversant with the thinking of social scientists, the latter no more conversant with the ways of physicists. In trying to outline some of the background in each area to give a grounding for readers from the other, I am conscious I may have been guilty of oversimplification. I hope, however, that the story will prove comprehensible and meaningful to both groups, and that in bringing the two approaches together, a greater understanding of the complexities of the development of physics teaching in its social context will be obtained.

Brian E. Woolnough,
Oxford, 1987.

Dedicated to all teachers of physics who through their example have encouraged others to continue with and enjoy their physics.

Secretary of State at Hatfield

'This photograph, taken when the then Secretary of State for Education visited ASE headquarters in June 1977, shows not only some of the central characters in our story but also represents nicely the different constituencies that were important in shaping physics teaching in schools. (HMI, the UDEs, the ASE, Industry, the DES, the Nuffield foundation and the physics teachers themselves)'.

John Whinnerah HMI, Dick West, Brian Atwood, Sir Alastair Pilkington, Mrs. Shirley Williams, John Lewis, Alan Hall and Maurice Savory.

General Editor's Preface

Brian Woolnough's sub-title 'of people, policy and power' deserves to be taken very seriously for it summarizes the wide ranging approach he has adopted. In particular, it shows the emphasis he places upon individual agency. This agency, however, is always related to and located within a clear notion of structure. This embrace of individual agency is indeed almost celebratory. 'Inevitably and thankfully, fundamental to the developments in physics education are the people themselves. In the creation of schemes in their development and discrimination, and in their execution, ideas and practices are mediated through individuals.'

But some individuals are more powerful than others, and some individual's ideas are taken up and other's ideas resisted. Agency as always bumps into structure 'men make their own history but not in circumstances of their own choosing'. I believe Woolnough gets this balance about right where he says 'we will be looking at the people involved and consider how far their individuality was significant'.

The balance between people, policy and power, of course, changes during Woolnough's time-span, from 1960–1985. In this situation the capacity for individual action may itself be constrained for as he argues: 'By the end of our period it was no longer a question of who had the power to control the curriculum: the government had clearly established its claim to decide'.

Of course this doesn't mean that the triumvirate of 'people, policy and power' is dissolved — not at all — merely that the 'arenas' where this triumvirate works are starkly relocated. The arena moves away from schools, from teachers, from subject groups — towards the 'hidden sanctums of government bureaucracy'. This is a working tendency if Woolnough is correct in asserting that Britain is a 'country whose government seeks passive acquiescence in a hierarchically structured society'.

Yet this book is itself testimony that passive acquiescence is not entirely possible. In his critical scholarship Woolnough points to the vitality of emerging new directions in curriculum research. This is a welcome addition to the *Studies in Curriculum History* series.

Ivor Goodson
The University of Western Ontario

1 *'Preparing the Way'* — *Setting the Scene*

Introduction

This is the story of the place of physics in the school curriculum, and the way that the subject has developed in the twenty-five years from 1960 to 1985. Yet, while focussing on a single subject over a relatively short period of time, it illustrates much wider issues relating to the way that subjects develop in a changing school context. For physics is, arguably, the archetypal academic subject in the school curriculum and its development exemplifies the tensions and the change agents acting when an educational system is changing from a largely hierarchical structure of grammar/secondary modern schools to a more egalitarian pattern of comprehensive schooling. Changes which paralleled, and which were influenced by, the enormous changes in peoples' attitudes and expectations in society at large. For physics is, at one and the same time, a vocational and an educational subject, it is both useful and cultural. And so the arguments about the relative importance of these issues, as justifications for including a subject in the curriculum and for determining the nature of learning within that subject, are well illustrated through physics. The story of physics is, in sharp relief, the story of the development of the comprehensive school curriculum. It illustrates the battles and conflicting pressures exerted by many different agencies and individual people who, consciously and unconsciously, influenced the shaping of the subject.

The choice of period over which a continuous process is to be studied will, inevitably, be an arbitrary one, and yet the twenty-five years straddling the early seventies suggests a natural and manageable time span through which quite dramatic changes were occurring. It was the period of curriculum revolution and of comprehensivization, and of an unparalleled expansion in school population and resourcing followed by a sharp tightening of the educational purse strings and falling school rolls. It moved from the conservative, stable values of the late fifties, through the permissive, swinging sixties, to the secular, materialistic seventies and into the reactionary, utilitarian world of the eighties. It started with hope and idealistic optimism that education would change society and bring both individual fulfillment and national prosperity; it ended with that hope sorely dented as a cold sense of realism and accountability forced schools onto the defensive in an increasingly unsympathetic, hostile and demanding world. It started with schools providing the hope for society's well-being; it ended with them being the scapegoats for society's ills. In the early sixties there was a general consensus that schools should provide a liberal education for all, by the early eighties such aspirations were to become politically unfashionable, soft uneconomic naivities, in a world where vocational demands and economic productivity were the prime arbitors of change.

And over this period the status and position of physics itself had suffered similar changes. In the early sixties its position in the curriculum was unchallenged, it stood supremely confident as both the hope for the national economy and the stimulation of the minds of the brightest pupils. By the early eighties, its position, indeed its very existence in the school curriculum was under threat. It had become defensive as the nation's hopes became pinned more on technology than on science and the intellectual stimulation came to be seen as increasingly divisive and irrelevant to the needs of the majority of pupils. In the early sixties, a grammar school head could write that 'physics is now the most important subject in the secondary school. It has no rival for intellectual respectability, for excitement, for basic educational value (in developing the gifts of imagination and analysis) or for economic and social relevance' (Judge, 1966, p. 267). By the end of our period, a professor of science education, himself a physicist, was questioning whether physics should be 'readmitted to the curriculum' (Black, 1985, p. 266). Though both were, perhaps, extreme statements of the changing position, they were in no way atypical and truly represented both the status and the mood surrounding much of physics teaching at the two ends of our period. Clearly there was much that had happened in schools and in physics teaching over these twenty-five years, and it is this that our story is about. Whether it will be a wake or a celebration is, of course, still an open question for, while the earlier air of self-confidence may have been ingenuously optimistic, it is in no way certain that the latter pessimism is any more realistic. The words of Mark Twain on reading his own obituary, 'the announcement of my demise is premature', could well apply to physics in school. I suspect that it will still be possible to write of the development of physics teaching in schools over the next twenty-five years; but that will be another story told, I suspect, by another author.

Setting the Scene

Who's Driving the Bus?

The changes in school physics teaching from 1960–1985 will be considered in the context of England and Wales alone, and will exclude Scotland. For though there has often been a strong interaction between developments in Scotland and England (often schemes developed in Scotland have been exported south into England a year or two later) the much more centralized and consequently more homogeneous educational system north of the border means that their institutions behave quite differently. In our study we will consider how physics teaching in schools has changed and what factors have affected those changes. We will consider those factors in the educational system that have had to be changed, those factors which have been acting on the system to try to make it change and those factors which have been influencing the way in which those changes have come about.

We will be considering developments at both the macroscopic and the microscopic levels, at the national and at the school level. In a sense it is easier to consider the bulk effects that have occurred by considering the overall developments across the country; to consider the changing school patterns, the supply and training of physics teachers, the activities of the Association for Science Education (ASE), the Royal Society and the Institute of Physics, the changes that have occurred in school text books, in apparatus manufacture and the examination system, the involvement of HMI, the DES and the science advisers, the development and uptake of the different curriculum packages; and this we will do. It is easier, because the data, the sources of information and indeed the activities themselves take place and are accessible at the public level. But we know, especially from the work of Brown and MacIntyre (1978) and Egglestone (1976), as they have studied the ways that teachers have implemented curriculum innovations, that there is a considerable difference between the teaching schemes that are developed by central teams of curriculum developers and the way that they are implemented by real teachers in real classrooms with real pupils. Consequently, to get a fuller insight into the way that physics teaching has developed in practice we will consider how it has changed in some typical schools. Typical is, of course, a dangerous word to use of schools, especially those in the English system where each school has so much autonomy and is so distinctive. Nevertheless, five representative schools will be chosen and cameos produced of each. These cameos will, hopefully, typify the different types of schooling and illuminate the way that the national developments have been translated, or not translated, into the classroom and laboratory. For the fundamental question concerns not what schemes and activities have been developed nationally, important and significant though they are, but what experience of physics teaching pupils actually receive in the laboratories from their physics teachers. Thus, in considering the developments at both the national and the local level, we will see that the overall trends mask a considerable variation between different schools. Though each has been influenced, to a greater or lesser extent, by the various national initiatives.

When we consider the developments in physics teaching that have occurred over our twenty-five years, we find many different inputs from many different people and organizations. Each of them, in their quite separate ways, have sought to improve physics teaching in their own area of influence, through their own resources and with their own perspectives on the needs. As we consider the overall influence of such inputs we are faced with the question 'who's driving the bus?'! With so many different influences and conflicting demands, it would be good to know who is actually in control, who has their hands on the steering wheel of physics education, indeed who decides where the bus is trying to go, and what characteristics of the bus, of the road, and of the surrounding traffic determine the performance of the bus. Of course, it may well turn out that noone is driving the bus, or — a rather disturbing picture — that a whole collection of would-be drivers are fighting for control in the driver's cab in an attempt to hijack the bus to where they want to go! Perhaps this picture will be less alarming when we consider the massive inertia and stability of buses! It could be argued that the whole process is less deterministic, and more randomly mechanical. More like the Brownian movement, where the apparently erratic, visible, movement of the smoke particles is caused by the incessant, random bombardment of many, invisible, air molecules. Which ever is the more appropriate model, and there may well be more useful ones, we will be looking at what can be seen and detected in the development of physics teaching in schools and try to make sense of it, to try to explain why such changes have taken place. In the event, we will find that no simple model or explanation is adequate in itself to describe such a highly complex system. Yes, there are individual people who have had a very considerable influence on what has happened, idiosyncratic influences which no one else would have made in quite the same way. There are policies which, through the conviction of their appropriateness and through expediency, have influenced what has happened. And there have been underlying power struggles determined to shape the school curriculum and society itself through the type of science that is taught. But none of these interpretations is, in itself, adequate to explain what has happened to physics teaching over this period. In the best English tradition we will find that the overall direction has come about through an amalgam of people, policies and power struggles, each of which we will consider in turn.

Of People

Inevitably, and thankfully, fundamental to the developments in physics education are the people themselves. In the creation of schemes, in their development and dissemination, and in their execution, ideas and practices are mediated through individuals. At both the national level, where curricular are developed, resources provided and policies established, and at the local school level, where the teachers are teaching their physics to their students, the personality of the individual is paramount. We will be looking at the people involved and consider how far their individuality was significant. Physics teachers are, almost with out exception, physicists. At school they enjoyed and were successful in physics, they went to university to study physics and increasingly thought like physicists, then they entered the teaching profession and spent much of their working life with other physicists, talking, demonstrating and teaching physics to their students. Most were still to think of themselves as physicists who went into teaching, rather than teachers who happened to teach physics, though there was to be an increasing shift from the former to the latter through our twenty-five years. There are those who would argue that scientists in general and physicists in particular are a distinctive group, with distinctive personality traits, and this would clearly affect the way that they perceived and taught physics. Hudson (1966) in his study of the sixth form student characterized the scientist as unusually conservative, industrious and convergent, and suggested that these would carry through into adult life. Physicists are often considered to be much more interested in things and ideas than people, being absorbed with inanimate objects, technical gadgets and toys but disinterested in the human and social issues. Such generalizations are commonly accepted, indeed often caricatured. We will see that, though they have had a significant influence on the development of physics, they are gross oversimplifications and many of the most influential people involved are far removed from such stereotypes. Others have gone further and argued that, consciously or unconsciously, science teachers and curriculum developers have transferred not only their subject expertise and their own perceptions of physics but also their own attitudes and value systems into their work, that much contemporary curriculum material in science carries 'their authors views of social reality and of their social and political aspirations' (Millar, 1985, p. 381). We will need to be aware of both of these aspects when considering the involvement of the many different and varied people involved in the development of physics education.

Of Policy

Statements of policy often arrive with an appearance of impersonal objectivity which belies the reality both of the individuals who wrote them and their underlying perspectives and unspoken assumptions. Policies appear, whether about education in general or about science and physics education in particular, as if driven by an inevitable, intrinsic, logic independent of the school context to which it is applied. Statements of principle and policy often appear with an absolute authority claiming that 'this is right, or better' without acknowledging the relevance of the context or the underlying philosophy; 'right' for whom? 'better' to achieve what ends? And such has been evident in many of the policy statements relating to the place and purpose of physics in the curriculum through our period. We have had those who have started by looking at the nature of knowledge itself, and have distinguished between different types of knowledge. They have made important clarifications concerning the different ways of looking at the world, of different forms of evidence and different ways of knowing. Perhaps Hirst's seven forms of knowledge (1975), first put forward in 1965, have been the most influential. All have included scientific knowledge, (including experimental science), as an important form of knowledge; being an important part of our culture to which all educated people should be, and can be, introduced in a meaningful way. Such classification of knowledge has lead through into the later policy statements of HMI and DES, and other writers on the whole curriculum who have discussed the areas of experience and learning to which all pupils have an entitlement and should be exposed (DES, 1981; HMI, 1985; Lawton, 1983). Implicit in all these is the concept of 'the educated person' who should have received a liberal education in schools. Primarily, for the benefit of the individual, but also benefitting society as 'the best sort of society is one filled with educated people'. Other questions regarding the primacy of education over training, of the appropriateness of 'academic' knowledge for vocational demands, of the merits of an explicit, conceptualized form of knowledge over a tacit, practical form of knowing (Polanyi, 1958 and 1969), have often been ignored. Yet all have direct relevance to the type and purpose of the physics that is to be taught in schools.

Bodies such as the Science Masters Association, the Association for Science Education, the Royal Society, and the professional institutions, have issued policy statements referring to physics and its relationship to science, to technology and to the curriculum as a whole. We will be looking at these to see how far they reflect and how far they determine the prevailing practice and thinking. In each case, we will need to be aware of the context, the priorities and the perspectives of the policy-writing body. We will see that the social, educational and school context have strongly affected the significance of these policies for physics teaching in the schools.

Perhaps surprisingly, in view of the dominance of physics and the other separate sciences throughout our period, is the paucity of policy statements about physics, *per se*. There have been many policy statements about science in various forms, by ASE, DES, RS, SC, HMI and APU, but few have overtly stated distinctive policies for physics.

Policy for physics has indirectly been determined by tradition, by text books, by examination boards and, for those who followed them, by the Nuffield courses. Since the Physics for the Grammar Schools policy statement of the SMA and ASE (1961 and 1963), there was to be no further policy definition of physics until the 1980s with the national criteria from the SEC (1985) and the core curriculum from SCUE and the RS/IoP (1980 and 1984). Few philosophers of science wrote specifically of physics, though it was clear from their exemplars that they were using physics as their paradigms (Kuhn, 1970; Popper, 1959; and Bruner, 1960 and 1966). But even here there was little consensus of opinion, and the little that there was was not to filter down to the thinking or practice of most physics teachers to any great extent. So there was little basis for a policy for physics teaching there. Even leading physicists writing in answer to the question 'what is physics?' (Schofield, 1977; Marx, 1983; Ogborn, 1978) did not find it easy to arrive at a simple, explicit answer. And yet, physicists found no difficulty in recognizing physics when they saw it, and were thus 'able to say without hesitation what in fact counts as doing physics' (Schofield, 1977, p. 65). It was in this belief that physics teachers have denied the necessity of a policy for physics. Physics is what physicists do, and if physicists are doing the teaching of school physics they will, automatically, see that the pupils 'do physics' too. In practice, what has gone on in many physics lessons throughout our period has been far removed from the type of activity indulged in by real physicists.

So, we will see that though seeking a policy for physics teaching in schools, seeking out what is intrinsically distinctive about physics that makes it an important part of the curricular experience of all pupils, could make a useful philosophical argument, in reality the determinants of a subject, and its status in the curriculum, are not established in such a way. It is true that most physics teachers believe that there is an absolute, intrinsic, apolitical worth in physics and that teaching it is an undoubted, neutral benefit to all. No statement of policy would make overt any political implications of teaching one type of physics or another. There are others, however, who have seen the teaching of physics as a distinctly political activity, and would see those who enjoy teaching physics as, at the best, political innocents and, at the worst, agents of capitalist oppression, but that is for the next section.

Of Power

It would not be unfair to say that the majority of physics teachers see no political significance in the subject they are teaching; most physics teachers would be amazed to be told that they were part of a political power struggle for the hearts and minds of their pupils, indeed for the type of social order that should be maintained or overthrown. And yet the whole of education must be part of a political context, being determined by it or being influential in determining it. There are inevitably political implications in the aims of education itself, in the organization of schooling, in the type of curriculum in the schools, and even the way that different subjects are taught. Such implications hold for all subjects, for physics the arguments and ramifications are central. There is a political perspective to the question of whether physics or general science is on the curriculum, of whether that physics is taught as a pure science or as part of technology, and of whether it is taught authoritatively as a transfer of knowledge or heuristically as an individual's personal discovery. The developments in physics teaching since 1960 can, and some have argued should, be seen through that perspective as a key battle ground in which power struggles have been fought.

The political significance of education as a whole is not, of course, a new idea. Lady Bracknell summed it up well when, in defending ignorance against modern education, she was pleased to note that 'in England, at any rate, education produces no effect whatsoever. If it did, it would prove a serious danger to the upper classes, and probably lead to acts of violence in Grosvenor Square' (Wilde, 1895). Most educators and teachers seek to encourage their pupils to be independent, thinking, rational beings, and to live lives which are personally, as well as socially, satisfying. While seeking to encourage them to serve their society they should not be passive, submissive, or exploited by it. Yet this is essentially a political position, especially in a country whose government seeks passive acquiescence in an hierarchically structured society. In the UK we have developed a tradition that, in Lawton's words, 'there should be a system of free education for all young people to enable them to become autonomous individuals in a democratic, industrial society' (1981, p. 62), a tradition of liberal education for all, as a right. Furthermore, such an education should lead not only to personal fulfilment, not just to developing skills and intelligence in the individual, but corporately to 'a society that can use them wisely' (Bruner,

1972, p. 18). And such a tradition has important implications for the place of physics and science in the curriculum as a whole. HMI were well aware of this in 1960 when, in urging that science should find a central place in a liberal education for all, they warned of the dangers of limiting our scientific knowledge to a few specialists or 'we risk becoming a well-fed rabble ordered about by experts subject to a new despotism' (HMI, 1960, p. 1).

In 1960, most of the English people accepted an essentially stratified society, especially when under such a benign, benevolent leader as Macmillan they had 'never had it so good'. Correspondingly they accepted the hierarchy reflected in, and perpetuated by, the tripartite school system which satisfied so well the vocational needs of society. With about 20 per cent of the country's pupils in the grammar schools moving steadily into the 20 per cent of jobs that required professional, clerical and managerial skills, the rest were reasonably content to accept their role as 'the managed' in the factories, shops and farms of the country.

But, with the coming of the Beatles, and the satirical TV programme *That Was the Week That Was*, people were allowed, even encouraged, to question the accepted authority of those in higher positions in society. Soon the hierarchies in every branch of society, in the arts, in the churches, in politics as well as in education, the existing order was being challenged. It was a time of great optimism, and much faith was placed on the schools to make a significant improvement in the whole quality of life. The leading sociologists of the time (Halsey *et al.*, 1961) were quite confident that education could change society and was therefore important and worth spending government money on. On such a tide the move to replace the stratified system of schooling which was seen to reinforce, if not create, the stratification in society by a comprehensive system which would provide equality of opportunity for all, quickly gained acceptance. The mood of the nation had started this bandwagon rolling in some areas of the country even before the Wilson government in 1965 obliged all LEAs to introduce comprehensive schooling with their White Paper Circular 10/65; Manchester and London had abolished the 11+ in 1963. The inertia of the school system was to cause a considerable hysteresis in the introduction of a genuinely comprehensive education for all; initially many new comprehensives were formed by secondary modern schools changing their names while grammar schools remained unchanged alongside (the percentage of pupils in grammar schools had only fallen from 24 per cent in 1960 to 19 per cent in 1975). Nevertheless, the political die had been cast and the political revolution to a more democratic, egalitarian school system was to come inexorably and irreversibly into effect throughout the seventies. By 1980, 83 per cent of the school population was in comprehensive schools and when, in 1983, the

Thatcher government tried to reintroduce grammar schools into Solihull it was the middle class Tory parents who fought, successfully, to retain their popular comprehensive schools. And so, through our period, the political implications of different types of schooling for different types of pupil had been recognized. The political battle had been overtly fought, and largely won, by the left through comprehensivization. The realization that the curriculum too had political implications was arrived at more slowly, and the power struggles for a genuinely comprehensive curriculum were to be fought more covertly. And central to these political arguments about the curriculum was the place of physics and its influence on it.

Just as there are political implications in the way the schooling is oranized, so, it is argued, there are political implications in the way the curriculum is organized, and in the subjects themselves. Throughout the seventies, sociologists were arguing that the effect different subjects had on the curriculum acted as important political determinants on pupils' lives. There were high status, difficult, academic subjects like physics, French and Latin and there were low status, easy, useful subjects like general science, European studies and metalwork. In choosing the high status subjects, as the children from middle class homes did, all roads to future success were open. In choosing the low status subjects, as most children from deprived backgrounds did, pupils were cut off from the opportunity of achieving the academic passports of 'O' levels in these high status subjects and thus were irreversibly prevented from ever achieving a rewarding profession and position of power in society. Thus, having removed the stratification of society by type of schooling, we were left with a stratification of society by type of knowledge through having maintained a stratified curriculum in the new system. This argument was spelt out clearly in the Open University course book *Patterns of Curriculum* (Raynor and Grant, 1972), where different political ideologies were clearly linked with different types of curriculum, in Bernstein's writings (Bernstein, 1975), and, with especial relevance to physics and science, in Young's *Knowledge and Control (1971)* and *The Schooling of Science (1976)*. Young argued that the power to define what counts as knowledge is a discussion about the status of knowledge, and thus the curriculum subjects are established. Changes in the curriculum will tend to be resisted in high status areas, such as physics, and areas which have low status, like technology, will find great difficulty in making significant inroads. In Bernstein's familiar phrase 'how a society selects, classifies, transmits and evaluates the educational knowledge it considers to be public, reflects both the distribution of power and the principle of social control'.

The significance of these arguments was considered so important for the position of physics in the curriculum that, in 1976, the Institute of Physics set up a public meeting at the Royal Institution in London for a public debate between Michael Young and Roy Schofield (Young and Schofield, 1976, pp. 498–503). Young argued that physics was maintaining the distinctions between academic and non-academic science, was overplaying the importance of explicit, theoretical knowledge at the expense of tacit, practical knowledge, was cutting science off from its social roots and thus making it inaccessible to the majority of the pupil population and therefore socially divisive. Science education, he argued, though originally 'envisaged as undermining dogma and leading to social emancipation ... had become almost the opposite — necessarily dogmatic ... in producing technological domination rather than emancipation'. Science teaching, through its separation into a high status physics and a low status general science had become 'a crucial force of production and determinant of the division of labour' (p. 501). If we kept physics as a separate subject we would be maintaining the existing social order, and prevent the social mobility that a more accessible, universally applied, 'science for the people' would allow. When physicists thought that they were debating the neutral virtues of the best way to teach their subject, it was being suggested that they were actually in the centre of a political battle, and furthermore were to be found on the side of reaction and repression! Most teachers continued to be either unaware of, or indifferent to, such arguments and took a pragmatic view of the implications of their subject being more intellectually demanding than others. It was necessarily so, and could not be changed without altering its intrinsic nature or its value for future study and vocational value. For it to be, in Lawton's terms, both 'the disinterested pursuit of knowledge' and 'the producer of the industrial market place', its place in the school curriculum could not be seriously challenged. But the political implications were there, and some educators saw this and fought the curriculum battle to remove physics from the curriculum consciously as an ideological battle for social control.

An interesting illustration of this was seen in the schools of China which, during the cultural revolution of 1966–76, removed all the academic sciences from the curriculum and instead made the learning highly practical and vocational; the science was taught through applications in industry and agriculture. Since the cultural revolution, their science teaching has reverted to the formal, academic teaching of physics and chemistry (and to a lesser extent the lower status biology).

Just as there are political implications in the way the subjects of the curriculum are organized, so, it is argued, there are political implications in the way that these subjects are taught. Physics could be, and usually was, taught in a authoritative, teacher centred, didactic style and this medium carried the covert message that society too was hierarchical and authoritative, with the pupils the passive receiver of accepted wisdom. If physics could be taught in a more individualized, pupil centred, heuristic style with more emphasis and respect given to the pupils own values, the pupil would be encouraged to develop a more self-confident, independent, questioning attitude to society which, in its turn, would liberate him or her from accepting either their role or the authority of others in society. The medium was the message. Young (1976) and Hoskyns (1976) argued this case with exemplars from physical science and physics classes respectively. In both cases they emphasized the liberating effect of introducing investigational project work into the previously teacher directed, passive classroom. Hine also, in his article on the political bias in school physics (1975) argued that 'an integrated approach would allow pupil participation and control to a much larger extent. It could be seen as politically dangerous, no longer would science justify the status quo, serve the idol of industrialization but offer explanations and even possible alternatives . . .' (p. 40).

Nowhere was this more developed than in the ILIS (Independent Learning in Science) movement of the mid-seventies. Ostensibly, it had no political bias, and collected together a large and catholic group of curriculum innovators in science who, for many and different reasons, were developing independent learning strategies. The leadership of the organization, however, Eric Green and, especially, Jack Whitehead were strongly politically motivated and caused considerable frustration and bewilderment, and eventually, detachment by other teachers through the steadily increasing revolutionary rhetoric and politicalization of the group. The ILIS newsletters increasingly spoke of the power struggles and pupil 'alienation in the classroom', of teachers 'using their position of power to impose their will on others irrespective of the basis on which his/her power rests', of demanding 'a commitment to engage in the politics which are always necessary to create and sustain improvements in our social situations', and of the 'wish to unite with the world in the spontaneity of love and productive work. This choice involves a power struggle against those material forces and other persons who would lead us to choose a kind of security by such ties with the world that destroys our freedom and the integrity of our individual selves' (Whitehead, 1976). All this, when most physics teachers thought that they were only concerned with finding better ways of teaching physics to their pupils!

All such arguments were particularly stark and, educationally, dangerous in England. England had an excessively divided culture, where high value was given to knowledge compared to skill, where the academic was more highly regarded than the craftsman, the scientist more than the engineer, and where a distinct hierarchy in acceptable forms of knowledge had long held sway. Though the classics were rapidly losing their popularity they were still considered by many as the peak of academic excellence, followed by the arts, by mathematics, by the pure sciences and then, a long way down the pecking order, the applied sciences, the engineering and the craft skills. In England, for reasons so well argued by Martin Wiener in his *English Culture and the Decline of the Industrial Spirit 1850–1980* (1981), an unreformed society still gave enormous deference to the ability to know rather than to do. Hence a considerable cultural shift was demanded lest the educationally liberated pupils be left stranded, in dissonance from the accepted values in society.

For many the political implications of physics teaching were, if recognized, accepted pragmatically as being inevitable. For others, however, they were tackled directly as part of a greater political battle. Academic physics was attacked or, more publicly, individualized integrated science exposed so that society itself might become more egalitarian and the previously 'oppressed and deprived' sectors might become 'liberated' and improve, if not overturn, the existing social order. By moving towards a common curriculum for all, by changing physics to a form of peoples' science, and by replacing the authoritative teaching style to one which elevated the pupils' own independence and values, it was believed that society would become less stratified and the under-privileged gain more influence and reward.

There was, of course, an alternative perspective which suggested a fundamental flaw in that argument. By removing subjects like physics from the curriculum, one was removing the very means of escape from exploitation that such passports allowed. If all such meritocratic means were removed from the bulk of the population, those in power would find other means of controlling the system, and the underprivileged majority would be all the more helpless without such means of fair competition. And this danger was all the more real in England where the private schools could maintain their high status subjects and, more completely, retain their instruments of power over the products of the state 'folk schools'. Increasingly through our twenty-five years, we will see that such political perspectives for physics teaching were, in a varying degree of explicitness, a matter of active discussion.

Alongside the ideological perspectives of the sociologists in the seventies, themselves the product and expression of the flower power idealism of the sixties, there was developing a harsh wind of political and economic reality that was to have a significant effect on the control and development of the curriculum as a whole and of physics in particular. Accountability was about to raise its ugly head, and central government about to intrude into and trample over the hidden garden of the school curriculum. The sixties had been a period of intellectual and financial expansionism, and teachers had had great freedom in developing their curriculum as they wished. In 1963, following the recommendations of the

Beloe Report in 1960, the CSE exam was introduced, with its Mode 3 allowing the teachers to determine their own curriculum and to assess it. In 1964, the liberal Minister of Education, Edward Boyle, set up the Schools Council for the Curriculum and Examinations. This was to be teacher-led, with teachers having a majority membership of all the main committees. The Council set in motion a plethora of teacher-led curriculum development projects. The scene looked fair for the teaching profession to gain full control of the school curriculum and to develop a national policy for it. But the opportunity was to be missed. In part the reason for the failure of the Schools Council to capitalize on its opportunity was due to internal problems of structure and philosophy, but there were also various pressure groups led by the Black Paper activists who increasingly suggested that the teachers' liberty was developing into licence and that the curriculum was 'too important to be left to the teachers'. This calling to account of the expanding yet unaccountable educational system was brought into acute relief with the oil crisis of 1973. This watershed led the whole western world into financial crisis and a period of recession which was to last through into the eighties, causing massive cuts to public expenditure including education. In 1973 the Heath government cut £200 million from the education budget only a year after the same Secretary of State for Education, Margaret Thatcher, had published its educational policy paper under the title *A Framework for Expansion*. With money for education becoming severely restricted, the opportunity arose for the government to become concerned and increasingly interventionist about educational priorities. This concern was focussed by the William Tyndale affair when, towards the end of 1974, it became public knowledge through the media that at least one primary school in London was providing what was generally accepted by the parents, the governors and the Inspectorate as being a very bad educational experience for the pupils. Furthermore it was not at all easy to see how, in such cases, power could be torn from the hands of the teachers — short of the most drastic disciplinary action, which was in this case applied. Though an individual case, the Tyndale affair provoked and channelled public concern about the state of the educational system as a whole, about the abuse of teacher power and about the direction and content of the curriculum.

The Conservative party in opposition, still smarting under the abolition of the direct grant schools, were making great political capital out of educational standards, but were pre-empted when James Callaghan, then Prime Minister, introduced 'The Great Debate' in 1976. Though many believed that the debate was being used as a smokescreen to hide the sorry state of the country's economy, now the honeymoon was over, and schools were being used as an easy scapegoat for industrial incompetence. It was widely accepted that it was the teacher control that had led to the unsatisfactory state in the schools. The public confidence in the teachers and the schools had gone. From then on it was open season for government intervention into every aspect of the 'secret garden'. The DES had already set up, in 1974, the Assessment of Performance Unit (APU) to monitor, and control, standards in the schools, and soon a multiplicity of reports, recommendations and policy statements were coming out of the DES establishing a position on every conceivable area of the curriculum. Not content with directing attention onto the schools, the DES was also putting increasing pressure on the local education authorities in its long running battle between central and local government control, between Whitehall and county hall (Sampson, 1982, pp. 219–31). With the thinly veiled enquiry of the LEAs about their policies for the curriculum in Circular 14/77 (DES, 1977), followed by various forms of financial constraints, the freedom, the responsibility and the ability of the LEAs to manage the education in their schools became seriously undermined. Under Margaret Thatcher's leadership, and with Sir Keith Joseph as Secretary of State for Education and Science, the monetarist, centralist policies came more and more to the fore. The Schools Council was abolished in 1982 to be replaced by first the well-funded Secondary Examinations Council (SEC) and then, significantly later, by the less well funded School Curriculum Development Committee (SCDC); both directed by the Secretary of State's personal nominees (SEC, 1984). Thus the new national criteria for all the 16+ exams could be enforced and the curriculum controlled by the centrally-controlled exam system. By the end of our period it was no longer a question of who had the power to control the curriculum; the government had clearly established its claim to decide. This backcloth for our period, the first half in an expansionist climate — the second half during recession, the first half with teacher control — the second half the government increasingly influential, will be seen to play a highly significant part in the development and control of the physics curriculum in schools.

A Physicist Looks at Social Science

When a physicist, brought up to think as an experimental scientist, enters the world of the social scientist he needs to do so with caution. He needs to be aware of both the strengths and the limitations of the scientific way of looking at problems in this field of human interactions. This book is very much a social history of a recent period and I am conscious that I will bring to this study the thought processes of a physicist. Scientists want to make sense out of what they see, they believe that there is some rationality in the world they are studying and seek to find patterns in their observations. They are not happy just recording events, they want to try and make sense of such observations by finding relationships and patterns in them. Further, they believe in causality, that they are part of an ordered world governed by cause and effect. Having found patterns a scientist will seek to find underlying causes and, where there is no obvious explanation, will invent theories and conceptual models to help him make sense of what he observes. These models, mental crutches, do not represent absolute truth, nor are they intended to, but are useful to the scientist who will feel happier and more confident in dealing with the different phenomena if he can hold a mental picture of what is going on. He will know that atoms are not tiny billiard balls, but this model will help him to explain, to feel confident in handling, and to enable him to predict the behaviour of gases. When studying the behaviour of light he will first find patterns for its behaviour, how it is reflected, refracted, diffracted, and how it both causes interference patterns and emits electrons from metals. He will then feel happy when he has established a wave model for the nature of light as this enables him to 'explain' many, if not all, of these phenomena. He may need to invent another model to explain other phenomena, a particle model to explain the photoelectric effect, and will accept — because neither model claims to represent the truth — that he needs to hold two apparently conflicting models for the nature of light. All the time he will be seeking for a simpler, more unified theory and conceptual model to explain it all, for he will believe that the simpler theory is always preferable, better, more likely to be correct, than a more complicated one. Scientists were happier accepting Copernicus' helio-centric model of the solar system for to Ptolemy's complicated model of cycles and epicycles for the motion of planets around the earth, not because it was right but because, being simpler, it was more likely to be right. So scientists are always seeking the simplest explanation of events, in an ordered, cause and effect, world.

Social history is not like physics. Scientists need to beware when seeking to make sense of what has happened, seeking to find patterns and causal relationships, that such patterns and simple cause and effect relationships might not, in any absolute sense certainly will not, exist. Historians tell us that there are two distinct interpretations that can be taken on any series of events; the 'conspiracy' theory and the 'cock-up' theory. The former interpretation sees events happening because they were deliberately planned so to happen, the latter interpretation puts a greater significance to the capriciousness and serendipity of events — things happened because things happened, by accident, by chance, no one is actually in control. In reality, I suspect, neither extreme holds a satisfactory interpretation for history, but they do suggest caution when deciding why things happened and who, or what, influenced who. It is easy to see history, to see the history of physics education, in terms of one simple theory or perspective, to see all events as fitting together in a single 'grand design' with one model giving adequate explanation for all that happens, but such a scientific hope will not be appropriate here. We will certainly find different pressures, different social and economic climates, influencing the people involved in the development of physics education but we, and they, will never be able to claim that 'this happened because of this'. Certainly those involved were not conscious, either at the time or in retrospect, of responding to the pressures and influences around them. The curriculum developers themselves saw their work as being themselves, doing their own thing and, in John Lewis' phrase, 'having fun' (Lewis, 1981). Who would ever suggest that the idiosyncratic genius heading up the Nuffield 'O' level physics course, Eric Rogers, would act differently?! Even the Nuffield 'A' level physics organizers were given simply as the brief for their course 'do what you think is right' (Ogborn, 1978, p 11). Though external pressures might well have been acting and influential we, as licenced ruminators, seeking to interpret as well as record such history will need caution in inferring too much of the physicist's causality. But we will still be trying to make some sense of events, to consider what influences were acting and to seek some models, some perspectives, through which the development of physics education can be interpreted.

Dangers for Interpretation

In trying to make sense of the developments in physics teaching over the last twenty-five years I have been conscious of six possible dangers in making such interpretations, dangers concerned with coincidence, correlation and causation, reconstructivism, reliability and validity, reductionism and preconceptions.

I have been struck by the number of coincidences, chance meetings, that occurred at various stages of key developments. People have met each other through 'chance' social occasions, they have taught each other's sons, they have dined together, they were at university together, they belonged to the same London club; it is easy for these chance encounters to acquire an unwarranted significance. Everybody lives through a life full of chance encounters and casual coincidences, but not everyone is able to capitalize on them and to create lasting significance out of them. Chance, as we know, favours the prepared mind and the well trained, successful scientist is the one who takes advantage of it. Medawar (1969 and 1986) rightly decries the interpretation of science progressing by induction: 'it really proceeds by intuition, serendipidy and imagination' but recognizes that this must be followed by rigorous attempts at disproof. Fortunate accidents happen to the mentally prepared and, though we all have random opportunities, it is only Nobel prizewinners who recognize them and pin them down.

A second danger is that of equating correlation with causation in interpreting social history. It is not difficult to show a correlation between two different factors, it does not follow that one caused the other. Two factors may be increasing at the same time, yet they may not be interdependent. The Nuffield curriculum projects were developing at the same time as the social climate was being liberated in the permissive sixties. We can not claim with confidence that it was this social climate of permissiveness that caused the curriculum revolution, or, indeed, that the Nuffield 'O' level physics course caused the moral permissiveness! Though there will inevitably be some interaction of one factor with another, the assertion that one has caused the other because of a correlation between them is a simplistic fallacy, though one strongly favoured by politicians claiming that developments in the school curriculum were causing industrial decline.

A third problem relates to the whole business of reconstruction, of looking back at an event or document and trying to reconstruct how it happened. Even at the time it is often difficult to know exactly why something happened or what thought processes caused or shaped a particular curriculum innovation. Some years later, in a different context from a different perspective, it is even more uncertain. All who have seen their own work or actions reviewed will know the feeling of being misinterpreted and of having sequences of events reconstructed erroneously. In C.S. Lewis' experience, this method of reconstruction 'shows a record of one hundred per cent failure'! (Lewis, 1975, p. 115). How then are we to make any sense of past events? We have first hand evidence in talking with the various people involved and we have second hand evidence by studying the written records and data published. Both sorts of evidence have their limitations; individual memories tend to be unreliable, and naturally influenced by hindsight and wishful thinking, written records tend to miss the flavour, the nuances, the smell of events, all of which are so vital in assertaining why, as distinct from what, things happened. The written records have an intrinsic reliability but we will need to look to the people involved for a sense of validity. We will, in this study, be examining both types of evidence and try to interpret the one with the other in the hope that a useful blend of reliability and validity will be achieved. At the end of the day, however, we will have just one man's interpretation of events, based on an individual judgment, nothing more or less.

A fifth danger concerns reductionism, the tendency to oversimplify issues and reduce them to a single explanation. Because the physics syllabus has political implications, it should not be reduced merely to the status of a political device in a struggle for power. Because those developing the physics curriculum were people with distinctive characteristics, such developments should not be reduced to being merely the self-indulgent outworking of individual personalities. Because the apparatus manufacturers made considerable profits out of the physics equipment, their motive should not be reduced to one of mere commercial gain. Such factors may well be significant, but not exclusively so.

And the final danger which needs to be made explicit relates to the writer's individual preconceptions. We have become increasingly aware in our physics teaching that what a pupil learns depends very largely on what preconceptions he or she brings with them into the laboratory: what a pupil perceives depends very largely on the perspective that is brought to the observations. Such is equally true of this, or any, observer of history; my insights and understandings will be shaped very much by the perspectives that I bring to my observations, and for this reason I have tried to make them explicit in this introductory chapter. I will be looking at the developments through three perspectives; by the contributions made by individual people, by the outworkings of policies and by the implication of political power conflicts in physics. I do not expect any one of them will hold a complete explanation, I hope that each will contribute something of value.

An Horticultural Model

The model we will use to help us comprehend the developments in school physics teaching is an horticultural one. Physics teaching itself is like a plant, a living organism not an inanimate object. It will not be produced in some distant factory and then handed on, like a neatly wrapped Christmas present, to be accepted in its pristine, immutable form. It is a living plant, needing a seed bed, a garden, watering, feeding, cultivating; its growth will depend on the condition of the soil and the climate. There will be gardeners tending its growth, there may be vandals tramping through the flower beds, there will certainly be a tendency for weeds to grow naturally! It may seem a simplistic picture, but it helps some of us both to hold together and to suggest new questions of relevance in this area of curriculum development and dissemination. The questions for physics education follow naturally. Has the growth been natural or cultivated, how much has it been a free profusion of randomly scattered seeds or has it been carefully planted and tended by gardeners? If the latter, what have those gardeners sought to grow? — masses of wholesome cabbages for the whole population or a few exotic orchids for a privileged elite? Who has made the decision about what should be grown? How far has physics been cultivated as an education for all or a stimulus and training for a few? Is it meant to be useful or beautiful? Will the curriculum be developed from seed in the school soil, or will it have its early development started elsewhere, in the Nuffield seed-bed, to be transplanted as a carefully nurtured seedling? How will this seedling survive and develop when introduced into the normal garden, subject not only to the sustenance of the less rich soil but subject to the heat and winds of the prevailing weather? Will the climate in the schools be sympathetic to growth, will the season be right?

And so, with this horticultural model as an 'advance organizer', we will begin on the fascinating story of the development of physics teaching in schools.

References

ASE (1963) *An Expansion and Teachers Guide to Physics for Grammar Schools*, London, John Murray.
BERNSTEIN, B. (1975) *Class, Codes and Control*, Volume 3, London, Routledge and Kegan.
BLACK, P. (1985) 'Could physics be re-admitted to the curriculum?' *Physics Education*, 20.6, pp. 266–70.
BROWN, S and MCINTYRE D. (1978) 'Factors influencing teachers responses to curricular innovations,' *British Educational Research Journal*, 4.1, pp. 19–23.
BRUNER, J.S. (1960) *The Process of Education*, Cambridge, MA, Harvard University Press.
BRUNER, J.S. (1966) *Towards a Theory of Instruction*, Cambridge, MA, Harvard University Press.
BRUNER, J.S. (1972) *The Relevance of Education*, London, Allen and Unwin.
COX, C.B. and DYSON, A.E., (1969) *Fight for Education*, London, The Critical Quarterly.
DES (1977) *Local Authority Arrangements for the School Curriculum*, London, HMSO.
DES (1981) *The School Curriculum*, London, HMSO.
EGGLESTONE, J.F., GALTON, M.J., and JONES, M.E. (1976) *Processes and Products of Science Teaching*, London, Macmillan.
HALSEY, A.H., FLOOD, J. and ANDERSON, C.A. (1961) *Education, Economy and Society*, London, Collier, Macmillan.
HER MAJESTY'S INSPECTORATE (1960) *Science in Secondary Schools*, Ministry of Education pamphlet no. 38, London, HMSO.
HER MAJESTY'S INSPECTORATE (1985) *The Curriculum from 5 to 16*, London, HMSO.
HINE, R.J., (1975) 'Political bias in school physics', *Hard Cheese*, 4–5, pp. 93–6, (quoted in WHITTY, G. 1977) *Schooling and Society* E202, Unit 14–15, p. 40, Open University Press).
HIRST, P.H. (1975) *Knowledge and Curriculum*, London, Routledge and Kegan Paul, (contains HIRST, P. (1965) 'Liberal education and the nature of knowledge'.)
HOSKYNS, A. (1976) 'An experiment in the teaching of physics' in WHITTY G. and

YOUNG, M. (Eds) *Explorations in the Politics of School Knowledge*, Driffield, Nafferton Press.
HUDSON, L. (1966) *Contrary Imaginations*, London, Methuen.
JUDGE, H.J. (1966) 'Teachers of Physics', *Physics Education*, 1.4, p. 267.
KUHN, T.S. (1970) *The Structure of Scientific Revolutions*, Chicago, University of Chicago Press.
LAWTON, D. (1981) *An Introduction to Teaching and Learning*, London, Hodder and Stoughton.
LAWTON, D. (1983) *Curriculum Studies and Educational Planning*, London, Hodder and Stoughton.
LEWIS, C.S. (1975) *Fern-Seed and Elephants*, Glasgow, Fontana.
LEWIS, J. (1981) 'What fun' (one man's view of events in the last thirty years) private mimeo.
MARX, G. (1983) 'What is physics?' *Physics Education*, 18.1, pp. 7–13.
MEDAWAR, P.B. (1969) *Induction and Intuition in Scientific Thought*, London, Methuen.
MEDAWAR, P.B. (1986) *Memoir of a Thinking Radish*, Oxford, Oxford University Press.
MILLAR, R. (1985) 'Training the mind: Continuity and change in the rhetoric of school science' *Journal of Curriculum Studies*, 17.4.
OGBORN, J. (1978) 'Decisions in curriculum development: A personal view', *Physics Education*, 13.1, pp. 11–18.
POLANYI, M. (1958) *Personal Knowledge*, London, Routledge and Kegan Paul.
POLANYI, M. (1969) *Knowing and Being*, London, Routledge and Kegan Paul.
POPPER, K. (1959) *The Logic of Scientific Discovery*, London, Hutchinson.
RS/IoP (1984) *A Reduced-Content 16+ Syllabus in Physics*, London, RS.
RAYNOR, J. and GRANT, N. (1972) *Patterns of Curriculum*, Milton Keynes, Open University Press.
SAMPSON, A. (1982) *The Changing Anatomy of Britain*, London, Hodder and Stoughton.
SCHOFIELD, R. (1977) 'What is physics?' *Physics Education*, 12,2 p. 65.
SECONDARY EXAMINATIONS COUNCIL, (1984), *Annual Report*, London, SEC.
SECONDARY, EXAMINATIONS COUNCIL, (1985) *The National Criteria for Physics*, London, SEC.
SMA/AWST (1961) *Physics for Grammar Schools*, London, John Murray.
STANDING CONFERENCE ON UNIVERSITY ENTRANCE, (1980) *A Minimal Core Syllabus for 'A' level Physics*, London, SCUE.
WHITEHEAD, J. (1976) 'Chairmans remarks', ILIS Newsletter no. 8.
WILDE, O. (1895) *The Importance of Being Ernest*, London, Methuen.
YOUNG, M.F.D. (1971) *Knowledge and Control*, London, Collier Macmillan.
YOUNG, M.F.D., and SCHOFIELD, R. (1976) 'The social responsibility of the physicist', *Physics Education*, 11.7, pp. 498–503.
YOUNG, M.F.D. (1976) 'The schooling of science' in WHITTY, G., and YOUNG M., (Eds) *Explorations in the Politics of School Knowledge*, Driffield, Nafferton Books.

2 'Years of Plenty, Years of Draught' — National Developments

The Social and Political Context

Though twenty-five years is a relatively short span of time, the twenty-five from 1960 to 1985 encompassed quite dramatic and traumatic changes in the social and educational scene, and saw changes occurring at a rate, arguably, unparalleled in other periods of history. This is not the place for a social history of that period but, inevitably, such changes that occurred in the social, political and economic climate of the country were to form the climate for what was to happen in the schools and for this reason it is necessary to remind ourselves of just how far reaching those changes have been.

If the period started as an idealistic, optimistic and socially well ordered society, it was to close much more cynical, disillusioned and socially disordered. Through the social revolutions of the permissive sixties, British society had broken out of the straightjacket of dullness and conformity which had pinnioned it since the Victorian times but was to arrive in a climate where, in Marwick's view there was a 'new hedonism abroad' (Marwick, 1982, p 156). Economically, the period started in an expansive mood, it was to close with recession having introduced the cold winds of monetarist accountability. It was a period of two distinct halves, of reckless expansion followed by fiscal contraction, with the oil crisis of 1973 neatly splitting our period in half; it forced the country to come to terms with the harsh, economic realities of living in an industrially inefficient country.

Politically, though the period both started and closed under a Conservative government, the mood of the two was quite distinct (see table 1). The early years were ones of liberal, benevolent, *laissez faire* encouragement towards a humane, unified society. The latter years were ones in which a much more centralist, monetarist government was encouraging the advancement of the individual good to the detriment of a corporate wholeness, in which Swift's description of 'the ruin of the public interest

23

Of People, Policy and Power

and the advancement of a private' had become almost a national policy. It was Harold Macmillan who lead the country optimistically into the 'new age' of the sixties. Twenty-five years later he was to declare, in relation to the divisions in society highlighted by the miners strike, that 'it breaks my heart to see what has happened to this great country of ours'. Such changes of mood and perspectives were to intrude into the classroom in a way that was to make the task of teaching physics both different and much more difficult.

Table 1: Significant political, social and educational events of the period

Government	Prime Minister	Sec. of State for Ed.	Significant Events	
Conservative 1959–64	Harold Macmillan –63	David Eccles –63	1961	First manned space flight
			1961	Kennedy elected President USA
	Alec Douglas Home 63–64	Edward Boyle 63–64	1963	CSE introduced
			1963	Kennedy assassinated
Labour 64–70	Harold Wilson 64–70	Michael Stewart 64–65	1964	Schools Council set up
			1965	Churchill dies. 10/65 Paper
			1966	Nuffield O level Physics introduced
		Tony Crossland 65–67	1966	England win World Cup
			1967	Abortion Act
		Patric Gordon Walker 67–68	1968	Student protest movement
		Edward Short 69–70	1969	Divorce Reform Act
			1969	First Educational Black Paper
			1969	First man on moon
Conservative 70–74	Edward Heath 70–74	Margaret Thatcher 70–74	1971	OU opens
			1973	Rise in oil prices. Britain joins EEC
Labour 74–79	Harold Wilson 74–76	Reg Prentice 74–75	1974	RoSLA
			1974	William Tyndale affair
	James Callaghan 76–79	Fred Mulley 75–76	1975	Direct Grant schools abolished
		Shirley Williams 76–79	1976	Callaghan opens Great Debate
			1978	Youth Opportunities scheme starts
			1979	Winter of discontent
Conservative 79–85+	Margaret Thatcher 79–85+	Mark Carlisle 79–81	1980	Assisted Places introduced
		Sir Keith Joseph 81–86	1982	Falklands War
			1982	Schools Council abolished
			1983	TVEI introduced
			1984	Miners strike

Conservatives	14 years	4 Prime Ministers	5 Secretaries of State for Education
Labour	11 years	2 Prime Ministers	7 Secretaries of State for Education

Perhaps the greatest change that occurred was the change in personal attitudes and social habits, especially among the young people and the newly emancipated, newly created, group of teenagers. The permissive sixties brought a revolution in accepted values, in the arts, in fashion, in moral values and personal lifestyles. The Beatles, flower power, the growth of the drug culture and the wider acceptance of sexual freedom all reflected the loosening of traditional constraints. Laws liberalizing a whole range of social relationships were introduced in the late sixties. The Abortion Act (1967), the National Health (Family Planning) Act (1967), the Sexual Offences Act (1967), the Divorce Reform Act (1969), all gave public recognition to a new set of social norms. While these undoubtedly gave personal liberty to many previously restrained individuals, they also led to license of a less constructive nature. Liberal permissiveness, while liberating the individual, especially the role of women, also loosened many of the conventional bonds holding families together. The period was also to see a growth of divorce, of illegitimacy, of single parent families, of children growing up in the context of broken homes, and of crimes against both property and persons. A national survey undertaken in 1980 by the magazine *19* among 10,000 of its readers found that 26 per cent of girls under 21 claimed to have had their first sexual experience before the age of 16. Despite the easy availability of the pill in the sixties, the more open discussion and education in sexual matters and the Abortion Act of 1967, the illegitimacy rate increased rapidly — more than doubling, from 5.8 per cent to 12.7 per cent, in the twenty years from 1961 to 1981. Family breakdown was also increasing and, in 1973, there was one million single parent children in schools. Such personal problems and priorities greatly increased the demands put upon the schools, tensions caused both by the pupils and for the teachers who were themselves 'children of their age'.

At the same time there was a substantial improvement in real disposable incomes and in material conditions. We had entered an age of consumerism. The range of opportunities opened to young people widened enormously, an increasing proportion stayed on after the minimum school leaving age, with the ability to afford buying their own radios, hi-fis, even cars. Women, particularly mothers, were more likely to be employed with the consequent increase in the number of 'latch key kids' of school age. Working people had shorter working weeks and longer, and more expensive, holidays — the number of holidays abroad had risen to nine million per year by 1978. And yet, alongside this steady growth, and public flaunting, of affluence in society at large there was to grow a contrasting poverty among the unemployed, and socially disadvantaged. Unemployment was low throughout the sixties, about half-a-million or less, but rose considerably in the Wilson government in the economic crisis following the rise in oil prices when it jumped from 571,000 in 1974 to 1,250,000 two years later. Worse was to follow in the wake of the monetarist policies of the Thatcher government, with unemployment rising from one-and-a-half million in 1980 to well over three million in 1984. This rise in unemployment centred on the old industrial cities of the north, with the demise of the heavy steel and coal industries and their associated communities, and the corporate neglect and decay of the inner cities. The public display of affluence through the media and the advertising pressure groups made the new poverty all the harder to bear.

Through the sixties and much of the seventies there had been a large political consensus, independent of which party was in power, concerning the way that the country as a whole should develop. After the oil crisis of 1973, and the increasingly extreme solutions proposed by the left and the right, the political scene became more polarised. With the Conservative government through the last seven years of our period and the strident tones of a materialistic, self-centred, Thatcherism, society became more and more divided, with the affluent south isolated from, and apparently agnostic of, the depressed, underprivileged north. The public concerns of society in general, and thence transferred upon the schools, were ones of financial and industrial prosperity. For the schools this meant a greater emphasis on tightly vocational aims, and the direct intrusion of the Department of Trade and Industry into the school curriculum in 1983 when the MSC laid its cuckoo's egg with the Technical and Vocational Education Initiative (TVEI). With rising problems in society in general, and industry in particular, schools were again to become the national scapegoat. For physics teaching, the justification had moved from being part of a liberal education to one of being the perceived salvation and rejuvenation of British industry.

The Educational Context

From 1960 to 1985 physics education was to develop in a rapidly changing educational climate. The size and organization of the school system was to increase considerably, with educational funding growing rapidly during the first half only to be severely constrained in the second, and with the type of schooling becoming slowly but surely more comprehensive. The type, scale, and aims of schooling in 1985 was barely recognizable from that of 1960. The fact that the same could not be said of physics teaching in those, quite different, schools was to cause many of the ensuing tensions.

The most obvious change was in the growth in the number of pupils in the schools and the consequent growth in the number of young, inexperienced, teachers who entered the profession through the seventies.

National Developments

The variation of the number of pupils in maintained secondary schools is shown in figure 1 (DES, 1977, p 48). Following a sharp rise in the second half of the 1950s, the secondary school population increased slowly through the next decade. This was followed by a quite dramatic increase from 1970 to 1978 when the secondary school population rose from about three to four million, an increase accompanied by a corresponding expansion in the number of new schools, new teachers and job opportunities for teachers in post. Thereafter, as the bulge moved through and out of the secondary schools, they were to suffer the converse and more painful situation of falling rolls, with all the reduced opportunity and resourcing that was to follow.

Figure 1: Number of Pupils in Maintained Nursery, Primary and Secondary Schools in England & Wales

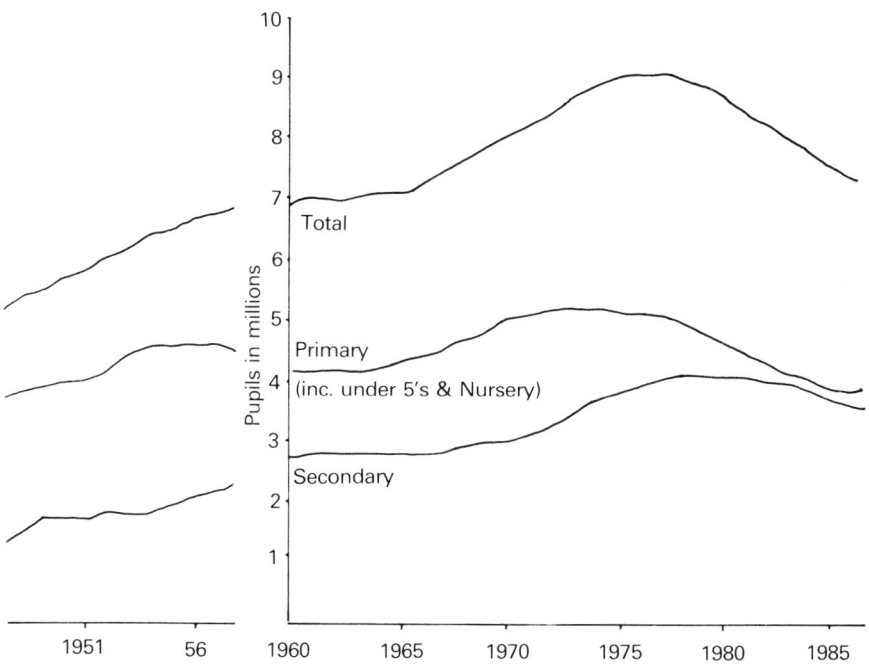

The expansion in the secondary schools was the result of both the number in the appropriate age cohort and the staying-on rate. The birth rate was to rise from 1955 to a maximum in 1965, the year which produced the population bulge that was to move through the primary schools and into the secondary schools in 1976. Subsequently, the birth rate was to decrease until in 1977 it reached a trough, two-thirds of its 1965 value. Thereafter the birth rate increased again, but only to a much smaller extent. Alongside the growing population, was a steady increase in the degree to which pupils stayed on in schools, both voluntarily and through legal obligation when the minimum school leaving was raised from 15 to 16 in 1974. This change, in itself, was to make a dramatic impact on the character and tasks of the secondary schools. Prior to 1974 the only students who had stayed on into the fifth year were those who had deliberately chosen to do so, and who had largely chosen to stay to do GCE or CSE examinations. Subsequently, many of the 15-year-olds were in the schools only because they had to and this group of, often reluctant, learners were to make considerable demands on the time, energy and imagination of the teachers to provide them with an appropriate curriculum.

As the school population grew, so too did the teaching force, and nowhere was this more true than for teachers of science. In 1960 science in general, and physics in particular, was largely restricted to the grammar and independent schools. Though the younger classes in the secondary modern schools had some basic science, there was very little science taught beyond the age of 15. As schooling went comprehensive it was expected that all pupils would receive an increased amount of science teaching, and that that teaching should be of a 'grammar school type by grammar school type teachers', ie graduate scientists. From 1960 to 1980 the total number of teachers increased by 73 per cent, the number of science graduates teaching increased by 200 per cent. This demand for, and increase in, new teachers was to have a significant influence on the way that science was taught and organized in the schools. For with a high proportion of young inexperienced teachers entering the profession through the seventies, the heads of departments, themselves often young too, needed to provide a strongly supportive structure for teachers in their hierarchically organized departments. This led to a common, standardized, form of science teaching which, in the first place at least, was to be a replication of the grammar school science, for all. In the 1960s the question that physics teachers asked was 'what type of physics is most appropriate for my, able, grammar school pupils?'. In the 1970s the preoccupation was with 'what ways are appropriate for teaching grammar school science to the whole ability range of pupils, often in mixed ability classes with inexperienced teachers?'. It was not until the 1980s that physics teachers were to start asking the more fundamental question again as to 'what type of physics or science is appropriate for the whole range in ability, age and aspirations of pupils in the comprehensive schools?'.

In the *Times Educational Supplement* of 1 January 1960, Professor Elvins is quoted as urging on the Conference of Educational Associations, in his presidential address, the need for radical changes in British education (Elvins, 1960). And the first of his radical changes was that the country should spend more money on state education. 'Who said that 3 per cent of the national income was about the right proportion for a reasonably prosperous country to spend on education?', he asked. In the subsequent twenty-five, certainly in the next fifteen, years this cry was to be answered most expansively as education was to make steadily increasing demands on both the national and the local authority budgets. Five years later educational expenditure in the UK had risen to 4.5 per cent of the Gross National Product, and by the end of the decade to 5.2 per cent, rising five years later to a peak of 6.3 per cent, in 1975/76. Subsequently the harsh realities of the oil crisis, and the changed priorities of a monetarist government, (which was to reverse the previous proportion and spend more on defence than on education), were to reduce educational spending to 5.3 per cent of the GNP by 1982/83.

Education was to become an increasingly expensive service, and the money poured into the schools through the late sixties and into the seventies was to have a fundamental impact on the teaching of physics. Money was available, especially in those expanding or new schools where new laboratories were being built, for apparatus and equipment to be bought on a lavish, and commercially manufactured scale, which enabled pupils and teachers of physics alike to indulge themselves in playing with their exciting new toys. The Nuffield projects were to develop and recommend specific experiments and kits of apparatus, and the manufacturers were only too ready to satisfy the physics teachers' scientific covetousness by providing it for them. It was not until the late seventies, when ten years of use were causing the apparatus to wear out and financial restriction were preventing the teachers from replacing them, that rethinking about simpler, self-developed, apparatus was revived. The golden age of pre-packaged, readily available, physics apparatus was to last perhaps for only the central fifteen years of our period; physics teachers had started the period poor, relying much on their own inventiveness for producing their apparatus, they were to end it facing similar constraints! It may well be that the ready availability of money for buying apparatus had the effect of determining the curriculum by apparatus, and restricting creativity and personal initiative. Lord Rutherford at the beginning of the century, when responding to the request from one of his physicists at the Cavendish Laboratories for more money for buying new apparatus, is reputed to have said 'we haven't the money so we will have to think'. Certainly the financial restrictions affecting most state schools in the 1980s were causing teachers to think of alternative sources for funding. In the event they were to find some from parental support and some from the seductive distractions of TVEI money. For those who were unable to tap either of these sources of funding, the shortage of money was to have the effect of reducing the amount of practical work being done. For some there was a reversion to cheaper ways of learning, to chalk and talk, and to more reliance on the text book. For others, however, the enforced abandonment of the ubiquitous practical stimulated the introduction of more imaginative teaching styles such as discussions, simulations and projects. It's an ill wind . . .!

The School Context

The development of the English educational system along comprehensive lines has been well documented elsewhere but it is important to remind ourselves of various aspects of relevance and importance to the development of physics education. In 1960, despite initiatives to remove the disadvantages of 11+ selection by the introduction of comprehensive schools in progressive LEAs such as Anglesey, London, Coventry and Leicestershire, the vast majority of secondary education was still organized on the tripartite lines of the 1944 Education Act. In 1960 less than 5 per cent of the pupils were attending comprehensive schools, the rest had been designated to the type of school most suited 'to their different ages, abilities and aptitudes' according to the 1944 Education Act and their performance at the 11+ examination. Twenty-four per cent had been selected to go to grammar schools, 11 per cent to go to technical, or bilateral, schools and the remaining 60 per cent went to the local secondary modern school. Though the pious hope was that the schools should be 'different but equal', with 'parity of esteem' between them, it was clear from the status, the resourcing, and the products of the different schools that there was a definite pecking order between the schools, in the social as well as the academic standing of the schools and their pupils. The 'alternative road' through the secondary technical schools was available in some areas but finding it 'most difficult to compete with well-established grammar schools' (McCulloch, Jenkins and Layton, 1985, p. 46).

But the move towards comprehensivization was steadily, and irreversibly, on its way. Pressure from educationalists, parents and politicians was mounting for the removal of the 11+ selection. Evidence from the NFER (Yates and Pidgeon, 1957) was showing that at least 10 per cent of children allocated to a particular type of school at 11 were probably wrongly placed, a questioning of the reliability of selection that was further undermined by the evident underachievement of the lower sections of the grammar school population and the academic success, against all the odds, of many secondary modern pupils. Educationalists were arguing that the very nature of children, their wide range of different attributes and skills, their varying rates of development, and the specific, limited nature of the test instrument, made the whole concept of selection into different pupil types inappropriate. Children did differ from each other, but in a wide and continuous variety of ways. Children did not naturally fall into three types, the fact that they could appear to do so after four or five years of segregated, tri-partite, schooling was the result of the system producing a self-fulfilling prophecy. Parents, wanting the best for their own children, were becoming increasingly articulate in their dissatisfaction at the prospect that they might be given only a second class education. And politicians at both the local and national level, reflecting the popular demand for an increasing degree of social equality and unity in society, were becoming increasingly supportive of comprehensivization as a political necessity; though many, including the editor of the *TES*, carried on reservations about its educational and academic efficacy.

National policy for the introduction of comprehensive education for all was introduced by the first Wilson Labour government in 1965, with the avowed aim of providing 'grammar school education for all'. Circular 10/65 obliged all local education authorities to prepare and submit plans for reorganizing secondary education in their areas along comprehensive lines. Though this was repealed when the Heath Conservative government was elected five years later (Circular 10/70 withdrew Circular 10/65 as the government felt it wrong to impose a uniform pattern of secondary education) the die had been cast. Indeed, on Labour's re-election in 1964, a new Circular was introduced, 4/74, which in its turn withdrew Circular 10/70, and reinstructed LEAs to develop fully comprehensive systems of secondary education and of ending selection at 11+, or at any other stage. Now the aim was to provide an 'appropriate education for all'. The climate was set for comprehensivization, though with ultimate power still resting with the LEAs, the rate of change was very varied in different areas, and did not always follow simple party political lines. Some Conservative councils prevaricated and strove, successfully, to maintain their selective systems; of the 155 grammar schools still in existence in 1985, Kent had twenty-eight, Lincolnshire fifteen and Buckinghamshire fourteen. Most counties, however, including most of the Conservative shires, moved steadily to a comprehensive system. It is interesting to note that the greatest rate of increase in the number of comprehensive schools took place in period of Conservative government from 1970–74, ironically when Margaret

Thatcher was Secretary of State for Education! In those four years the number of grammar schools fell from 975 to 655 (Baker, 1987).

But the actual process of changing schools from one system to another takes time, and the time for a school to become genuinely comprehensive longer still. A school which would take its first comprehensive intake in 1978, say, would not have its first comprehensive cohort for 'O' level until five years later, and would not be fully comprehensive through to the end of the sixth form until 1980. Society, which in the sixties had been promised Utopia quickly on the introduction of comprehensive schools, was not always patient when such was not immediately delivered in the seventies. Though the number of pupils in comprehensive schools increased rapidly from 1965 to 1973, from 8 per cent to 48 per cent, this gives a misleading impression as very often it reflected no more than a secondary modern school changing its name — in the same period the number of pupils in the grammar schools had only decreased from 25 per cent to 18 per cent (TES, 1975). It was not until the late seventies that the demise of the grammar schools became a reality (in 1976 there were 8 per cent of pupils still in grammar schools, in 1981 that number had fallen to 3.4 per cent) and comprehensive schools could flourish without being creamed of their more able pupils by remaining grammar schools.

The Two Halves

And so we find physics education in state schools developing in a context of two distinct halves. As the oil crisis in 1973 acted as the focal point for the change in economic climate, so the Tyndale school crisis which came to a head in 1974 could be seen as the cold front in the educational climate. The first half of our period saw schooling largely in a tripartite, segregated system of different types of school for different types of pupils with different types of aspirations; the second half saw that system becoming rapidly more comprehensive, with common schools trying to readjust to a perspective which stressed those things which pupils had in common, their individuality, their equality of opportunity, and their educational entitlement, rather than their differences. The period started expansively, with the schools enabled to cope with the problems of rising numbers because of the magnaminity of the public exchequer; it ended with the reverse problems of schools trying to cope with the problems of falling rolls in a climate of severe financial constraints. The period started with a general belief in a liberal education for all so that every individual could develop their potential; it ended with a widespread public belief that schools could concentrate on vocational issues so that industry should prosper. There had been a great expansion during the post war years, with the abolition of fees for grammar schools opening up 'good education' to all. But, with comprehensivization, the educational consensus was to collapse. In Maclure's phrase (1985) education moved from a period of 'high hopes to low spirits'. Up to say 1973, he summarized, there had been a wide measure of agreement among educators and the politicians associated with them about the next reform, the next advance. Since the mid-1970s, in the face of sharp external criticism, in a climate of declining industrial performance and growing unemployment (for which the schools were to be held to blame), there had been no such confidence. With 'a combination of severe financiual constraints, harsh external criticism and a new propensity for centralist intervention, the public education system had temporarily lost its sense of self-direction and initiative to a politically astute and ideologically rigid Secretary of State' (p. 1).

The Public Schools

In England, the existence of the public schools has had a significant influence on the educational system as a whole, far in excess of what might be expected from their size alone. Having provided the education for many of the most influential leaders of the country, and for their children, the public schools had the power to affect both the public perception of, and the curriculum in, the state schools too. They were to have an important part in shaping the physics curriculum; in the early part of the period teachers in them were instrumental in reshaping the way physics was taught through the progressive Nuffield projects, in the latter part their role was much more conservative and reactionary.

In the early 1960s, the public schools fitted naturally alongside the grammar schools in a system that accepted selection and segregation as the norm. Graduate physics teachers, often of a very high ability, would have entered them to teach the accepted academic physics to able, well motivated pupils. Few physicists would have gone into the secondary moderns; there were few comprehensives in existence. There was easy movement between the grammar and public schools, both of which catered for a similar type of pupil with similar academic aspirations. The leadership of the physics teaching community was shared between teachers from the grammar and the independent schools. They became the natural leaders for the curriculum development in the SMA and through into Nuffield, indeed the Nuffield 'O' level physics course and, to a lesser extent, the 'A' level course too, owed a lot to the quality and initiative of able physics teachers in the public schools who had the freedom and the resources to develop and trial new material. But as the sixties developed, and the popularist mood brought in comprehensivization and the demise of the grammar schools, the public schools were to find themselves increasingly detached and isolated from the main stream of educational debate. Initially the public schools felt themselves threatened, especially in periods of Labour governments, but in the event they were to survive and finished the period as strong as ever. However they were to become increasingly different and separated from the state system, who regarded them as an unwelcome competition able to seduce away many of the ablest and most motivated students whose parents were able to buy privilege for them in these private schools.

Professor Elvins second radical suggestion reported in the first TES of our period (Elvins, 1960) was that the public schools should become more fully, and genuinely, integrated into the state system of education, a theme that was to be developed by the Public Schools Commission, set up by the Wilson Labour government soon after it regained office in 1965 with the brief to 'advise on the best ways of integrating the public schools with the state system of education' (Newsom, 1968). The Commission's work was reconstituted in 1968 to specifically include consideration of the prestigious, semi-autonomous, direct grant grammar schools, and reported in 1970 under its chairman Professor Donnison. This reiterated its faith in a fully comprehensive system of education throughout the country, which avoided any segregation of pupils before the statutory school leaving age, and therefore concluded that there could be no place for fee-paying schools coming wholly into a comprehensive system, and that the existence of even a small number of direct grant schools (catering for 2·5 per cent of the secondary school population) was incompatible with the nationwide, government directed policy of comprehensivization. Clearly, the public schools, along with the direct grant schools, were feeling threatened and sought to increase their security and public esteem by the founding of ISIS (the Independent Schools Information Service) in 1972. They were offered a respite during the Heath Conservative government of 1970–74, though not reassured when in 1973 Hattersley, the shadow Secretary of State for Education and Science, revealed Labour's plans to abolish public schools. When Labour actually came to power again, in 1974, it left the public schools untouched but, in 1975, removed the direct grant status from those grammar schools that retained it. Such schools were then offered the choice of joining an increasingly non-selective state system or of going independent. The majority of the best direct grant schools took the latter choice so that they could maintain their traditional academic curriculum and so resulted in strengthening, rather than weakening the private sector in education. With the demise of the bridging grammar schools, more and more parents were faced with the stark choice of a free comprehensive education or a fee-paying academic one. When the Conservatives returned in 1979 they tried to support the second of these alternatives by introducing the Assisted Places Scheme, in 1980, designed to enable bright pupils whose parents could not afford the public schools fees to obtain scholarship places to them, assisted by grants from the state. Not surprisingly, it worked out that most of the pupils awarded these assisted places came from the middle class and that the scheme was doing little to break down social barriers or to help the working class pupil (Douse, 1985). Though the number of pupils attending public schools on Assisted Places Schemes was to be relatively small (by 1985 only 23,000 pupils were being supported by such grants, representing about 5 per cent of the total number of pupils in private schools [ISIS, 1986]) the psychological effect on teachers and parents in the two sectors was enormous. By giving official government acknowledgement that the public schools could better educate the able child, the confidence of the independent sector was restored and the morale in the state system correspondingly undermined. It also provided justification for not resourcing state education adequately, when both the rich and the poor able pupil could be said to be provided for in the, so called, public schools.

The significance of the public schools to physics education related to their status in society, especially with the universities and the examination boards, and their natural tendency to maintain a curriculum which was essentially academic and elitist, and one which reinforced the position of the high status subjects. Though the actual number of pupils in the public schools was not high compared to the overall number of pupils in full time education, the proportion of pupils involved with serious physics teaching was much more significant. The total number of pupils in 'non-maintained schools' was to remain fairly constant throughout the period. Though the total number was to drop from nearly 500,000 to rather more than 400,000 in 1985 (DES, 1970; and ISIS, 1986), the majority of that demise was to come about by disappearance of the less reputable private schools through the sixties. The number of pupils attending the major, secondary age, public schools remained remarkably constant, though the proportion of the whole school population varied inversely as the age cohort. For most of the period the proportion of all pupils attending full-time education who were in private schools was about 6 per cent. But the proportion of the pupils staying onto the sixth form, and the proportion of pupils going onto university, was significantly higher. In 1985, and typically, the overall proportion of pupils in private schools was 6 per cent, but the proportion of the 16–19 age group still in full time education who were in such schools was 21 per cent, and the proportion of boys in this age group, the group most strongly represented in physics 'A' levels, was 25 per cent. A corresponding proportion of 'A' level passes were from the public schools too, and almost half of the Oxbridge university entrants. Clearly, when so much of what happens in schools is determined from a 'top-down' perspective, with curriculum pressure feeding down from the universities, the significance of what the public schools were doing, and the way they taught physics, would continue to have an important influence on the state system too. The acceptance and credibility of an integrated science course in the comprehensive schools would continue to be undermined while other pupils could produce their high status physics qualification which was being maintained in the curriculum of the private schools. The introduction of more applied forms of practical technology in the state schools would be devalued while the public schools maintained the academic forms of pure physics. So changes in the comprehensive school curriculum were held back because of the essential conservatism of the public schools. Whether that was to be a beneficial maintenance of high standards or detrimental hindrance of desirable progress is, of course, a matter of personal, educational, and political judgment. But the power of the independent schools to exert pressure, by their very existence, on the maintenance of the educational 'status quo' was to prove highly influential in the development, or non-development, of the physics curriculum.

The Physics Pyramid

It is helpful to recognize the pattern of physics teaching in a school as a pyramid, the steepness of the pyramid depending on the type of school and the choices made by the individual pupil. Typically, all pupils in their first two years of secondary schooling will be taught physics, either as a separate subject or, as has become increasingly the dominant norm, as part of a combined science course. In the third form most pupils will maintain their contact with physics, being offered it alongside the other sciences to give preparation for the choices they have to make in their subject options in years 4 and 5. In these years about a third of the age group will opt to do physics as a separate subject, and take either the 'O' level or the CSE examination in it at the age of 16. After 'O' level, a fraction will choose to continue to physics up to 'A' level, and of this section a further fraction will continue to use their physics in higher education either as physics or, more likely, in engineering. Boys were much more likely to choose physics than girls. Figure 2 illustrates this pyramid for the year 1977. In that year about 800,000 pupils would be meeting physics from 11—14, about 240,000 from 14–16, about 40,000 in the sixth form, leading to 2000 reading physics at university, along with 10,000 engineers. A pyramid 400 pupils wide at its base would produce a single student going to read physics at university, and

Figure 2: Physics Teaching Pyramid (1977)

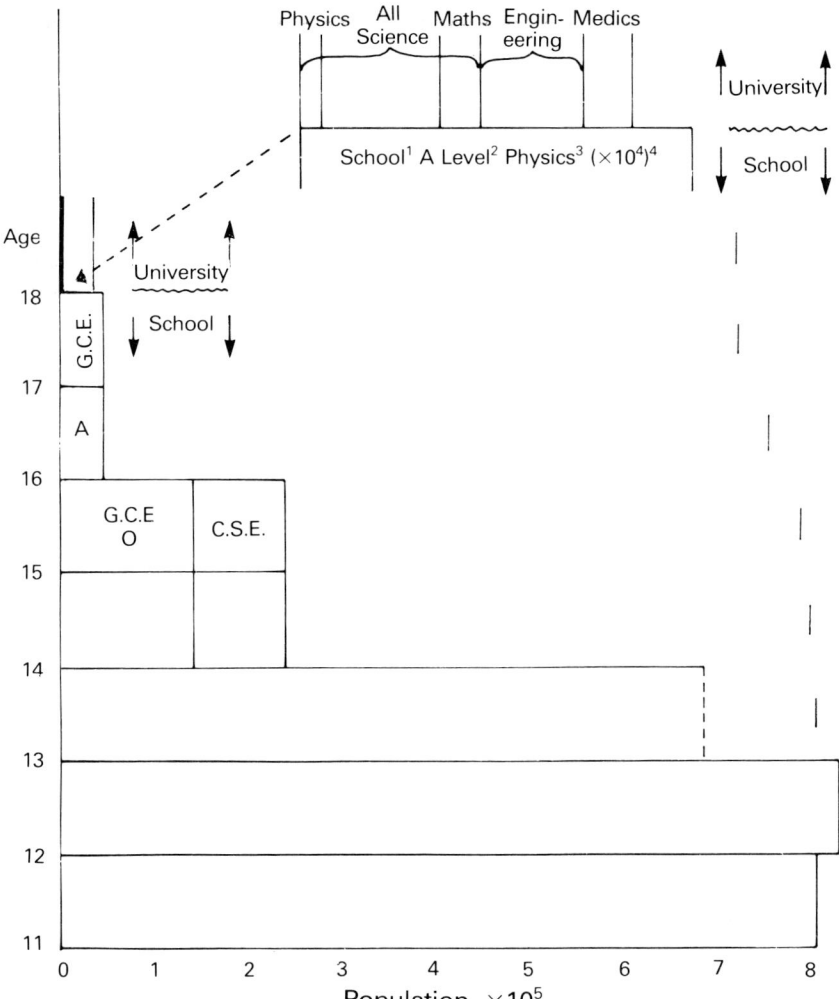

yet, throughout our period, the university physicists were to have a considerable influence on all the physics taught 'leading up to' the 'A' level climax. Many of the tensions in the secondary science curriculum arose from teachers fighting this inequitable 'top-down' dominance in favour of a 'bottom-up' approach which sought a type of physics appropriate to the 400 as well as being adequate for the one.

The pattern was, of course, different from school to school. The boys grammar and public schools, with their more academic pupil and higher rate of staying on into the sixth form would have a much less steep pyramid, possibly with all pupils maintaining physics up to 'O' level and about a third continuing physics into the sixth form. Girls schools would do less physics than boys, girls in coeducational schools less still. Secondary modern schools, and some 11–16 comprehensives in deprived areas would do little physics beyond the age of 14. The variation between the scientific education of different pupils was also considerable. A pupil coming through a grammar school could well keep up three sciences, or two sciences and maths, from the age of 11 to 18. He might then spend 15 per cent of his first three years, 30 per cent of years 4 and 5, and virtually all of his sixth form study specializing in science. At the other extreme, a pupil in a secondary modern could drop his physics, indeed all science, at the age of 14. With schools going comprehensive, and option patterns being introduced into years 4 and 5, these variations of curriculum were allowed to be carried through into the new (sic!) system. When HMI did their survey of the schools in the late seventies they found less than 10 per cent of pupils were studying the three sciences, physics, chemistry and biology, while over two thirds were studying one science, or less (see table 2). Clearing the option choice system was allowing many pupils to opt out of an adequate scientific education. The virtues of pupil choice in the comprehensive, which were so popular through the 1970s, were becoming to be seen as the cause, rather than the result, of pupil differences. Maurice Holt crystallized the situation in his inimitable way when he challenged teachers 'who were not prepared to allow pupils to choose the colour of their sweaters but did allow them to drop science at the age of 14' of perpetrating a great 'educational cop out'. As schools entered the 1980s, teachers were to become less reticent to offer advice and guidance to pupils and it became common for schools to insist that all pupils should take at least one science up to the age of 16, moving towards a position when they could introduce a balanced science for all. But through the sixties and seventies, great variations existed, some pupils were to obtain perhaps the best, certainly the fullest, scientific education of any country in the world, others were to have such a limited amount that no one could be content with it.

Physics Trends

The overall trend for physics over our period has been one of growth and development, and growth on a quite remarkable level. Professor Keohane, looking back over the period, rightly said that 'more [of the great hope and expectations of the sixties] has been realized than for which credit is commonly given' (Keohane, 1987). The period started with physics being considered the exclusive preserve of the select few in the grammar and public schools, it ended with every effort being made to teach an appropriate form of physics to all pupils. In that period, the number of 16-

Table 2: Number of science subjects studied in 4th year

Number of subjects studied	3 or more	2	1	0
Boys	10%	32%	49%	9%
Girls	5%	19%	60%	16%
Total	7.5%	25.5%	54.5%	12.5%

Source: *Aspects of Secondary Education in Schools*, DES, 1979

year-old pupils studying physics had increased five-fold (see figure 3 and table 3). The period started with a shortage of physics teachers in the schools, it finished with the same cry but whereas in 1960 the perceived need was to teach physics only to the more able 20 per cent, in 1985 the need was recognized as being to teach physics to all pupils. The period started with an unrecognized sex bias in the subject; in 1960, no-one seemed particularly concerned that very few girls considered doing physics; by the end of the period, though parity had in no way been reached, teachers had become aware of the reasons for girls rejecting physics and the consequent disadvantages to them and had moved some way to improving the situation (see table 4, and Kelly, 1981). In 1960, physics teachers taught content laden syllabuses with dull, wordy, impersonal textbooks and a limited supply of nineteenth century apparatus. By 1985, the physics syllabuses had been modernized and pupils enabled to be actively involved with their own

Table 3. Growth in number of pupils studying physics

	Number of pupils studying physics in 4th and 5th year[1]	Number of pupils studying physics in 6th form[2]
1960	69 K	33 K
1965	108 K	43 K
1970	159 K	41 K
1975	223 K	42 K
1980	304 K	49 K
1985	350 K	52 K

Source: DES Statistics 1 Measured by the combined entry of O level and CSE Physics
2 Measured by entry to A level Physics exam

Table 4. Boy to Girl ratio in entries for GCE and CSE physics

	O level	CSE	A level
1961	6:1	—	6.2:1
1968	5:1	12:1	5.4:1
1977	4:1	7:1	4.6:1
1981	3:1	4.5:1	4.2:1
1984	2.66:1	3.6:1	4.0:1

Source: DES statistics

Figure 3

Number of Pupils in Maintained Secondary Schools,
in England & Wales
4m
3m
2m
1m
0
1960
65
70
75
80
85

Number of Pupils studying Physics in 4th & 5th year,
as measured by combined entry of 'O' level & C.S.E.
350K
300K
250K
200K
150K
100K
50K
0
Physics
General Science
1960
65
70
75
80
85

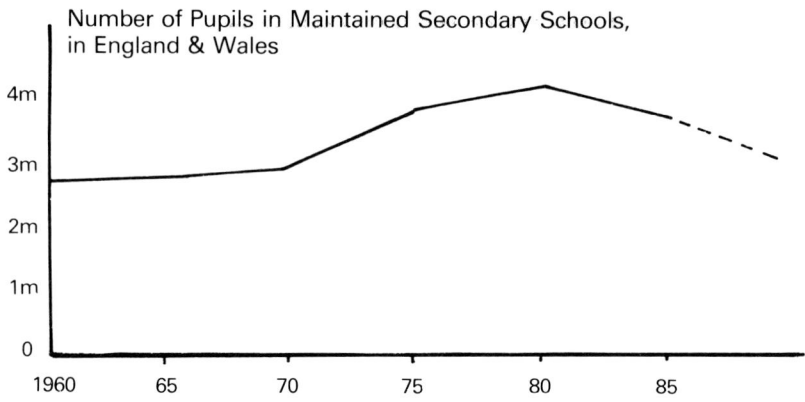

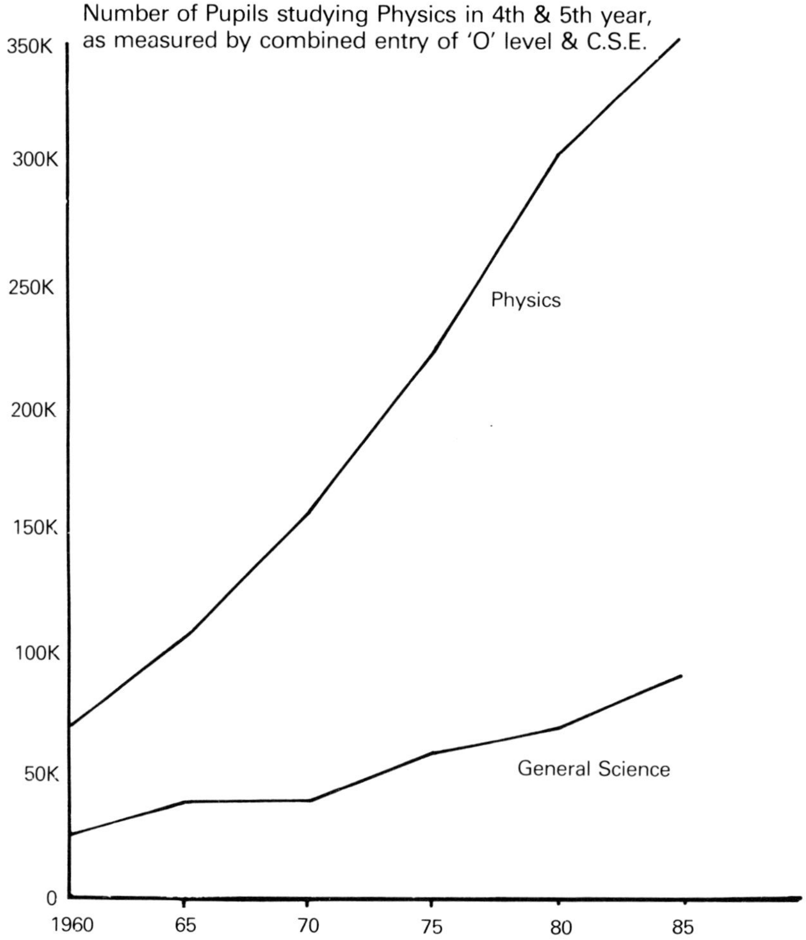

learning, using lively, colourful, humanised textbooks and a wide variety of modern equipment. The physics laboratory of 1985, (certainly the laboratory of 1980!), looked quite different and better equipped than the one of 1960. But the growth of physics, responding as it did to the mood and opportunities of society at large, was not to be steady or uneventful.

The 1960s opened on the crest of the wave from the late fifties when the government had instituted a policy to expand higher education for science and technology manpower, to meet the industrial needs of a developing economy. Great expectations were held of scientists solving the problems of the world, and this bullish climate, stimulated by the first Russian and American space flights, boosted the popularity of physics in schools. From 1960 to 1963 the 'O' level entries for physics rose dramatically, to be followed two years later by the corresponding rise in 'A' level physics entries (see figure 4). But then, from 1963 to 1966, the 'O' level entries steadied and fell, which resulted in a declining tendency for sixth formers to opt for the sciences two years later. These cohorts would have started making their subject choices in the fourth year from 1961 onwards, and were to cause considerable concern to the scientific establishment who, in 1965, set up a national committee to enquire into the flow of candidates in science and technology into higher education. Under the chairmanship of Dr Frederick Dainton, it considered the evidence about the alleged swing away from science in the schools, counter to the expansion of the science and technology departments in universities, and found that it was so (Dainton, 1968). Both the number of candidates for sixth form physics and, even more dramatically, the proportion of an expanding sixth form who were opting to study the physical sciences and mathematics was declining. Prophets of doom foretold the time when there would not be enough candidates to fill the departments in the universities to revive and expand industry. Indeed, by extrapolating the percentage of sixth formers following 'A' level science and mathematics courses, it could be shown that this would reduce to zero in 1984! Despite the general platitudes about the importance of physics for a liberal education, it was the prospect of an inability to meet the vocational goals that really stirred the scientific establishment to take an active interest in schools!

Dainton recommended certain changes that could be made to the school curriculum, but undoubtedly the fundamental reason for the problem lay outside the schools in the general social climate abroad. The swinging, permissive sixties were in full flood, with its emphasis on personal self expression, love, peace and emotional fulfillment. Such a climate was to influence the impressionable teenagers through the media, and did not match the perceived demands of the hard sciences. The arts, and the social sciences, seemed to offer more hope for the future. In the late fifties young

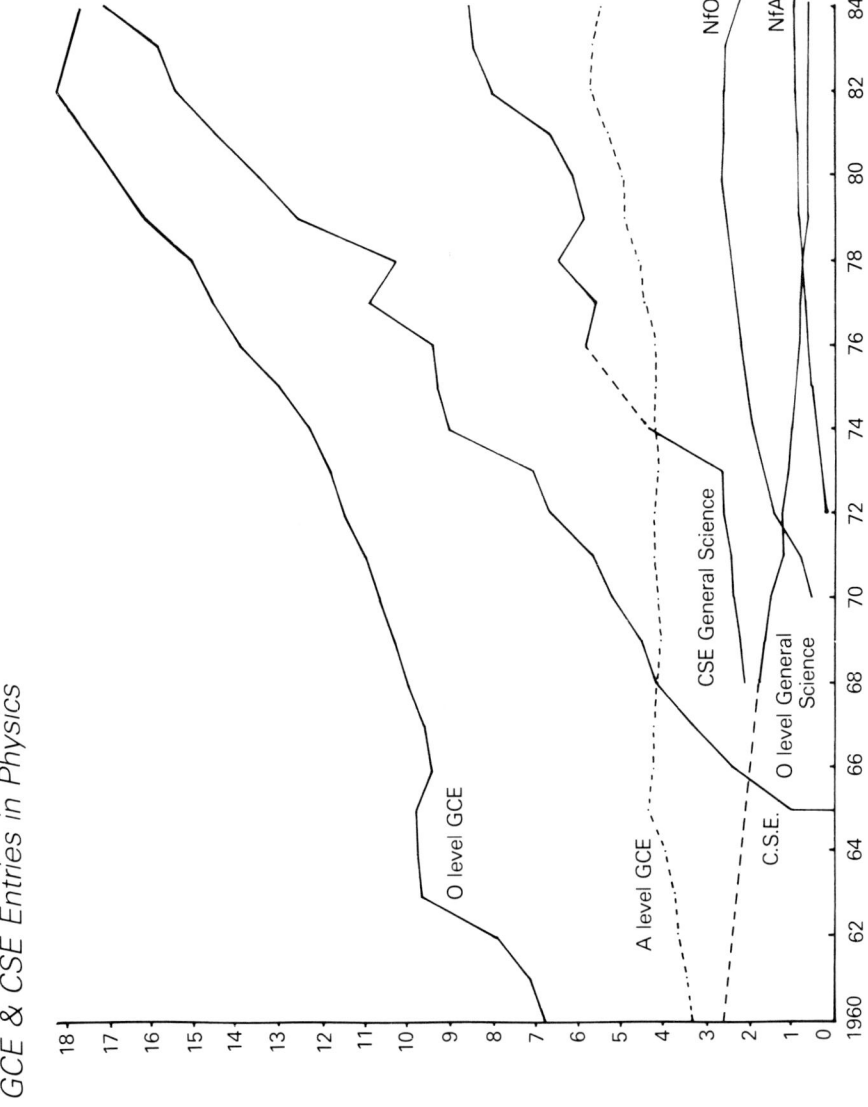

Figure 4: GCE & CSE Entries in Physics

people had seen salvation as coming through scientific progress, hence the sciences were more popular. In the sixties salvation was in individual freedom, the sciences became less promising and the arts and humanities more attractive. However, the harsh realities of life, the publication of the Dainton Report, and the early grumblings of an educational backlash with the first Black Paper in 1968 slowly reasserted themselves and by the late sixties the popularity of physics began to pick up again. Despite the persistence of the myth of a continuing 'swing away from science' in schools, (Duckworth, 1978) the reality through the seventies was quite the reverse. The growth in uptake of physics and the other separate sciences at 'O' level and for the new CSE examination was much greater than was the growth in size of the cohort or the growth in entries for exam subjects overall (Woolnough, 1976 and 1979). From 1968 through to 1976, there was a positive swing to the sciences, even the physical sciences. Biology was increasing in popularity at an even faster rate, along with its appeal, especially to girls, and its status as a serious science (that might solve the ecological and medical problems that the physical scientists had caused with their atomic bombs and chemical pollution!). From 1978 to 1983, physics continued to grow in popularity, as pupils and parents appreciated its usefulness as a job ticket in an increasingly technologically sophisticated world where unemployment was growing in an hostile economic climate. Though there were signs of a drop in uptake for physics in the last year or so of our period, the expansion of physics in that time had been considerable, especially considering the continuous shortage of good physics teachers. Figure 3 shows how the numbers studying physics up to the 16+ exams has grown steadily from 70,000 to 350,000 in twenty-five years. Despite the shortage of good teachers of physics; despite the perceived and real intrinsic difficulty of the subject; despite pupils negative attitudes to the subject and its irrelevance and impersonality; and despite the seductions and the hard sells for alternative forms of integrated science and technology, the numbers opting for physics still continued to grow in response to pupil and parent demand.

At 'A' level, the rise in numbers was less dramatic (see figure 4 and table 3). Rising from 33,000 in 1960 to 43,000 five years later, it settled at around 42,000 for the rest of the sixties and until 1976 from when it rose to 57,000 in 1982, before falling back slightly. The size of the pupil pool able to benefit from the demanding 'A' level physics courses did not appear to grow with the number studying the subject up to the age of 16, and in practice few physics teachers did much to persuade some of the less able students to continue with it into the sixth form. Physics was consistently the third most popular 'A' level subject, after English and maths. In the sixties the majority of sixth form physicists were doing physics along with chemistry and mathematics. Physics was usually their first subject and their aim was to study one of the pure sciences at university or, if they were not good enough for that, one of the applied sciences. With the growth in popularity of biology in the seventies, physics became increasingly a second or service subject for biologists. Towards the end of the seventies, however, and into the eighties, the situation had swung back in favour of the physical sciences, but now the best candidates were going onto higher education to study the applied, more obviously vocational courses or, if they were not good enough for that, physics or one of other pure sciences.

University entrance requirements were to swing around in the changed climate from educational to vocational imperatives. Where as in the sixties students found it competitive to get a physics place but easy to get a place to read engineering, (the Robbins expansion having gone faster than the student supply could appropriately fill), by the eighties it was the physics departments that were having difficulty filling these places and the engineering departments that were becoming increasingly competitive. Throughout the period, the university physicists had often looked askance at the schools, blaming them for not providing them with enough good students but, with a pool of 40,000 'A' level physicists to fill approximately 2000 university physics places, there should have been enough to go around.

Biology and Chemistry

The development of the other main sciences, as measured by their uptake in schools, followed a similar pattern to physics. The other physical science, chemistry, was most similar shadowing the growth of physics at a slightly lower level. At CSE, 'O' and 'A' level, entry for chemistry was, typically, about 80 per cent of the number for physics. Though the nature of the subject changed significantly through this period, from the bucket chemistry of 'preps and props' to the conceptual patterns of 'moles and energetics', the popularity of the subject remained. Considering that this change of emphasis, from a concrete to a formal type of chemistry, was completely at variance with the trend in the target audience, from the selective grammar school to the broader ability range of the comprehensive school, and that the subject matter in chemistry did not have the natural relevance to the pupils world that physics and biology did, the growth in uptake of chemistry might be considered surprising. This, however, is not the subject of our discussion. But it does suggest that those reasons for curriculum dissemination given in terms of the intrinsic appropriateness of the curriculum to the pupil may not be valid, and that we need to look more to the extrinsic factors of subject status, societal currency and teacher expertise and enthusiasm.

Biology, was more popular than physics below the age of 16, though its gender distribution was in the opposite direction; many more girls continued with biology than boys. At 'O' level, biology was continually more popular than physics, and grew at a not dissimilar rate. Its rate of uptake through the late sixties and the seventies was higher, however, as the popular appeal of the biological sciences to solve both environmental and medical problems matched the growing social consciences of the young. At CSE level, starting from a lower base, it overtook physics in 1970 and quickly grew to about 25 per cent more than physics. By 1985, the total number of pupils taking either 'O' level or CSE biology had risen to 65 per cent of the age group, compared with 52 per cent in physics, 40 per cent in chemistry, and 13 per cent in general science (DES 1985). At the sixth form level, however, the uptake of biology for 'A' level was far smaller, though again it grew greatly in popularity from 1969 to 1974. In 1960, biology had only just become recognized as a respectable academic subject for boys to study, and there were less than 6000 entries for 'A' level biology that year, though a further 7000 were to take the examination in zoology and 4000 in botany. By 1983 biology had nearly caught up with chemistry with an entry of nearly 45,000, and seemed to be levelling off around there. Zoology and botany as separate subjects had virtually disappeared. Competition for places in higher education to study the applied biological studies of medicine and veterinary science became very great and the high hopes of many an idealistic biologist were to be dashed by the toughness of the competition leading to diversion into the purer, softer, but less employable, biological sciences such as botany. There was a status and definition battle within biology itself, between those who saw it as a 'hard science' and those who preferred more 'ecology and field biology', a battle well described by Goodson and Ball (1984, p. 28). The slight uptake of Nuffield biology suggests that the 'hard scientists' were in the minority among the biology teachers.

General Science

The argument about what type of science should be taught to young people in schools, whether it should be a relevant, popular, people's science through some form of general science or an academic, cultural, professional science through the separate sciences, is not a new one. Indeed, as David Layton so perceptively illustrates in his *Science for the People*, it has been with us since the beginnings of science education in schools (Layton, 1973). Others, (especially Jenkins, 1979) have traced its development through the twentieth century to the beginning of our period and discussed its origins, nature and growing popularity. In 1951, for instance, there were more entries at 'O' level for general science than there were for physics, just. We will discuss later the development of the general science debate, through all its subtle variations of general, combined, integrated, unified, balanced and coordinated science. Here it is appropriate simply to clarify the uptake of any type of general science through our period. Despite the strong advocation for general science throughout our period, from the ASE, from different educationalists and from school and government administrators, (and the mixture of educational, political and pragmatic reasons for its introduction), general science was only to be found acceptable to the science teaching profession as a whole at the early years of secondary schooling. When pupils came to choose what type of science they would study, at the age of 14 and again at 16, they were to increasingly vote against any form of general science, or, to be more correct, were to increasingly vote for the separate sciences such as physics.

As an 'O' level qualification, any form of combined science was to become increasingly unpopular through our period, with respect to the separate sciences. Figure 4, illustrates this trend. Despite the introduction of the new SCISP course in 1973, and different other syllabuses and subject combinations through the GCE boards, the numbers entered for any form of general science at 'O' level fell steadily from 26,431 in 1960 to about 6000 in 1985. The much vaunted SCISP itself never proved widely acceptable and, after a slow growth to about 4000 entries in 1979, actually started to lose schools and candidates thereafter.

At the CSE level, (where the claims for studying separate sciences were less obvious and the reasons for accepting a more relevant science much more germane), there has been an increase in uptake of some of the different forms of general science. But even here the growth has been far less than might have been expected. By the end of our period, for instance, there were approximately twice as many pupils studying physics at CSE level than were studying any form of general science. The variation of uptake of general science for pupils of different ability is striking too. The most able pupils were very unlikely to take general science whilst the less able pupils might well take a general science course, based around relevant topics, such as LAMP (Driver, 1977) or Science at Work. In 1983, there were 13 per cent of 16-year-olds studying general science. However, less than 1 per cent of the most able (those in the group of pupils likely to obtain eight 'O' levels or more) were studying it, while for the group of least able pupils (those likely to get four CSEs or less) the proportion rose to 30 per cent (see table 5 (APU, 1985)). At the same time the situation was exactly reversed for the other way of obtaining a balanced science curriculum — by studying physics, chemistry and biology as separate subjects. Thirty per cent of

Table 5. Percentage of pupils taking different science course combination in each examination entry group

Course combination / Pupils' expected exam results	8 or more O levels	4 or fewer CSE
Biology, Chemistry and Physics	30%	1%
General Science only	<1%	30%

Source: APU 1983 Survey at age 15

the most able group were studying the three sciences at this level, compared with only 1 per cent of the least able group.

So, after twenty-five years, though the amount and the school context of science teaching had changed considerably, we find the curriculum pattern not radically different. Most pupils in the 11–14 age range were studying science, or the sciences. But after 14 the old grammar school/secondary modern school differences remained; the more able pupils were studying the separate sciences and the less able pupils either science or one of the sciences. The difference had been made in the amount of science that was taught to the 'middle ability' group of children who had opted to study the separate sciences in greatly increased numbers. When the government formally introduced comprehensive schooling with the 10/65 White Paper, it was stated that this was to provide 'grammar school education for all'. Though this was revised in Circular 10/70 which aimed to ensure that 'all pupils shall have full opportunities for secondary education suitable to their needs and abilities', the legacy of the grammar school curriculum was difficult to erase from the comprehensive school. General science had few influential friends inside or outside the school, there were no professional institutions or university departments of general science to press its case. In a system in which the curriculum was so influenced by 'top-down' factors, this was to prove a serious deficiency. As a school subject, it had never acquired a status which, in a new form of schooling so conscious of its need to gain popular acceptance, could compete with the well established and recognized physics, chemistry or biology. Furthermore, as Sally Brown (1977) and Paul Black (1986) so clearly illustrated, it never acquired a convincing rationale or a seriously worked out curriculum content. Lacking a coherent philosophy and an established subject base in higher education to define its boundaries, general or integrated science courses inevitably finished up as a miscellaneous collection of topics, a rag-bag of items selected at the personal whims or educational perspective of the course originator. Consequently they failed to carry conviction either for the science teachers themselves or the world outside.

Furthermore, the science teaching force itself was to consist largely of scientists trained in a single subject discipline. In the English higher education system, with its well established tradition of single subject specialism, the most able students were attracted to the honours degrees in the separate disciplines and those who did graduate with more general, combined, science degrees were not only less numerous but often less able than their colleagues whose degree training had been in a single science. For many teachers, often the most lively and creative ones, were to maintain their enthusiasm for 'their own subject' and were reluctant both to loose that and to teach other sciences for which they had little subject enthusiasm, or expertise. This was to be especially true for teachers of physics and biology who often maintained their love and belief in their own subject as being appropriate to all pupils. Many chemists, on the other hand, seemed to find the relevance of their subject to the comprehensive school more difficult to justify and more readily supported the move to some form of general science; it is interesting to note that the majority of those most strongly advocating integrated science had started with a background in chemistry.

And so throughout our twenty-five years the pattern has been maintained that, in easy times the liberal arguments for a relevant general science carry conviction, but when the going gets tough and students are fighting for jobs and scientists and politicians are looking to schools to build a science based economy, the credibility and status of physics and the other separate sciences will get more widespread support. Whereas teachers and employers were quite happy for the sciences to be studied as one in the early years of secondary schooling, and teachers were readily convinced of the personal and administrative advantages of that, in the last two years of secondary schooling the separate sciences were to reestablish themselves. The battle for a people's science, genuinely appropriate to the needs of all pupils, had not been won by 1985, though there were indications that it would make considerably more headway in the next twenty-five years.

Technology

Arguments about the relative merits of pure and applied sciences were developing throughout the period, with battles to introduce technology as a subject into the school curriculum. In the early sixties, vocational arguments were often voiced in terms of 'science and technology' being needed to provide the necessary underpinning for an expanding industrial society. It was an unspoken assumption, however, that schools would translate this into practice by teaching the academic sciences, especially physics. The grammar schools gave little regard to technology or the practical skills of the workshop, after all the technical schools were intended to cater for those technically inclined (Hudson, 1986, p. 4), and the secondary moderns for those with a practical bent who would become the future technicians.

But the engineers were getting increasingly concerned that their subject had such a low status (Hutchins, 1962; Page, 1965), and that the most able sixth formers were heading towards the pure sciences at university. Such concerns were to lead to the setting up in 1966 of the Schools Council Project Technology and the creation of the Schools Science and Technology Committee (SSTC). This led to a consequent spawning of a range of examination courses in different types of technology. The argument was that if pupils were to make a career in, or study in higher education, one of the applied sciences, they would need to have met and studied that subject at school. It was a popular argument but one not always supported by facts. In 1977, for instance, nine of the eleven most popular university subjects, measured by applications per place available, were for subjects not studied in school — this group included civil, mechanical, and electrical engineering. In the same year, seven of the nine least popular subjects for university places were in subjects which were studied at school — this group included physics and chemistry! A parallel argument was that the attitudes and hidden messages that pupils received from their teachers at school, as distinct from those of society at large, were dissuading them away from technological careers. However this too was shown to be a myth by the British Association for the Advancement of Science (BAAS) who, when investigating the factors why students were not responding positively to manufacturing industry found 'no evidence to suggest that the schools are generally and actively hostile towards engineering and industry' (BAAS, 1977, p. 12).

There was, however, evidence that pupils in schools reflected the generally low esteem that society at large had for the engineer, a symptom of the pervasive frame of mind so hostile to industry which was deeply embedded in the English culture (Weiner, 1981). In 1961 and again in 1976, Donald Hutchins carried out a survey of the attitudes of senior school students regarding the salary, status and intelligence associated with different professions. He found a largely unchanged perception over this period, at both times the students rated the engineering and technologist professions low in regard to salary, status and intelligence required, lower than the pure scientist and the academic, much lower than the doctor and the solicitor (Hutchins, 1963 and 1977). Nevertheless the mid-seventies saw the introduction of 'A' level courses in engineering science, of 'O' level courses in technology, control technology, and various applied sciences and a wide range of technical courses at CSE level, under the new, more fashionable, grouping of craft, design and technology. Though in some cases CDT developments were no more than cosmetic, (woodwork became timber technology!), in many cases genuine elements of design and problem solving made the courses distinctly technological.

The introduction of good courses was, however, no guarantee of student uptake. With the direct competition from well established and higher status subjects like physics, with the lack of clear rationale about the nature of technology, with no single subject or emphasis being given preference, and with the lack of resources in teachers, curriculum, text books, and equipment, it was always going to be an uphill battle. It was clear in the mid-seventies that a new subject like technology would make little entry into an already overcrowded curriculum, as there was no space for it (Woolnough, 1975). At 'A' level, such courses as the JMB engineering science had to compete with 'A' level physics, and teachers as well as pupils preferred the latter, which kept more of the students' options open. Most significantly the engineering and design courses failed to gain the confidence of the one group that could have given them status and currency, the university engineers, who continued to prefer physics, and maths, as the prime entrance requirements for degree courses in engineering. Engineering science never gained more than 500 candidates per year throughout the country, despite being an excellent applied physics course, and one recognized by many as providing a thoroughly adequate basis for further physics studies as well as for engineering.

In the 14–16 range, the technology courses were perceived initially as being a suitable option for the less able pupil, who could not cope with physics, and this perpetuated the low status accorded to the subject. Even at CSE level the uptake of the subject was slight. With an entry rising slowly to less than 30,000 in the 1980s it never really threatened even the more traditional technical drawing or craft courses, which were to maintain their entries in excess of 80,000 and, in the case of metal work, 50,000 respectively. At 'O' level, the subject began to gain a little ground when it was marketed as being only available to pupils alongside physics, and so its status was raised. But now the problem had changed from should it be done instead of physics, to should it be done as well as physics, and chemistry, and biology, and maths and computer studies ... providing a very unbalanced curriculum. So, through to the end of our period, technology as a separate subject had made little inroads into the curriculum of the able pupils, less than 10,000 entries at 'O' level were made from all the technological offerings. Overall by 1983 less than 2 per cent of all pupils were to take any form of technology or engineering science at the age of 15, a percentage consisting almost exclusively of boys (APU, 1985).

However, there were other ways apart from as a distinct subject, that technology could appear in the school curriculum. In the early sixties, the Institute of Mechanical Engineers set up an enquiry to consider how pupils might encounter engineering in schools, and reported in the Page Report a considerable variety of technical, project, workshop and industry related activities in a wide range of schools. Good practice did exist, but it was thinly and widely spread with individual teachers pursuing different, individualistic, paths independent of each other. When Project Technology was set up to encourage technological activites among all pupils (Harrison, 1984), it disseminated information about technological activity in schools through its magazine *School Technology*. This again revealed that there was an enormous range of diverse technological activity in virtually all subjects and at all ages of the curriculum (Marshall, 1974). Ranging from making soap to making hovercraft, from studying the environmental implications of a new motorway to the industrial archaeology of bridges and tin mining, from competitions to find ways of helping the handicapped to making balloon powered egg-mobiles, from constructing electronic devices for testing dampness in babies' nappies to marking exam papers, from constructing wind tunnels and engine test beds to studying milk splashes, the range of activity was enormous, but thinly spread and dependent almost entirely on the idiosyncratic interests and energies of individual teachers. A nationwide survey carried out by HMI showed that by 1982 teachers, though indulging in many different types of 'technology in schools', were no clearer about what form technology should take, or whether it should be a separate subject or a cross-disciplinary activity (HMI, 1982). They identified different types of examination courses, (modular courses, control technology, electronics, applied science, and design based courses) as well as courses in technological awareness and other extra-curricular activities such as hobbies clubs and technological competitions. Others have studied the way that a pupil encounters technology across the curriculum (Myers, 1984; HMI, 1985), and found that this may happen in the geography, history or English lesson, as much as in science, design or home economics.

Many of the problems concerning technology in schools have centred around this disparity of interpretation of the meaning of the word, with no single definition of technology, nor a single established discipline from which a concensus can emerge. This lack of focus in introducing technology into schools, coupled with the uncertainty as to whether it should be for vocational or educational reasons, was to prove a fatal weakness. Though many courses formally accepted one of the definitions offered by Schools Council Project Technology, 'technology is the purposeful use of man's knowledge of materials, sources of energy and natural phenomena' or 'a disciplined process using scientific, material and human resources to achieve human purpose' that still allowed a wide and uncertain area for implementation. Most courses would stress the problem solving, design process as being at the heart of technology, but this could be interpreted quite differently in a craft or a physics lesson. The artefacts of technology played an important role in some courses while others stressed the social implications of technology in society. Many physics teachers were to be involved in this area through the close relationships that such technology had to the processes and content of their own subject as well as through their technical skills and inclinations in areas such as electronics, computing and engineering.

Between 1966 and 1972 the Schools Council spent £270,000 on encouraging technology in schools through Project Technology (Walker, 1980). Much exhortation had come from industry and government along the same lines, but still the uptake of technology in schools was very slight. So concerned was the DES at this lack of impact that in 1980 it funded a research project to 'consider the factors affecting the uptake of technology in schools' (Nash et al., 1985). This case study work in one county recognized two fundamental areas hindering the dissemination of technology; curricular issues and resource issues. The lack of a clear, coordinated curriculum policy throughout a school, in which individual subjects had to fight their own power struggles, was presenting a real barrier to the introduction of new subjects. While that subject was so ill-defined, yet traditionally associated with low status work, the problem for technology was increased. Furthermore, the lack of curriculum definition or rationale undermined any credibility it might have gained outside the school with parents, employers and higher education. Within the school, the differing traditions and sub-culture of the CDT and the science teachers brought with them quite different, and ultimately divisive, approaches to the subject. In the resources area, the lack of suitable course material, of equipment and working areas, of time and ancilliary help, and most important of all, of suitably qualified teachers, were all to present considerable barriers to the introduction and dissemination of technology in schools. The fact that so much excellent technological activities was going on at all was the result of individual teachers, often with previous experience in industry or the forces, bringing to their teaching a vision, commitment and creative energy 'over and above the call of duty', and to an extent that no centrally imposed policy could, or had the right to, expect. Often the technology in a school was dependent on the expertise and commitment of an individual teacher and was consequently vulnerable in the event of his (and it almost exclusively was a he!) leaving. In the event, with no charismatic people propagating technology at the national level, no coordinated policy for its nature or place in the curriculum, and no political, or educational power to combat the established high status subjects such as physics, it is not surprising that technology made such little effect on the secondary school curriculum. By the time the results of this research had come through, the political imperative concerning the nature of a technological education had changed, the initiative for introducing it had moved from the DES to the MSC of the Department of Trade and Industry, and the TVEI bandwagon was set rolling, loaded with all its tempting, technological gadgetry, and tempting many schools and physics teachers to avail themselves of these useful and gratuitous resources.

Ironically, computer studies, which in the late seventies was to be introduced into the curriculum much later than technology, and which had no better rationale and even less educational justification than technology, was to increase in acceptability at a much greater rate at both 'O' and CSE level. By 1984, computer studies had rocketed in popularity with 55,625 entries at 'O' level, 48,820 entries at CSE and even 8152 at 'A' level. There were various factors contributing to this rapid growth of computer studies; the immediate glamour and status of computing, the strong governmental encouragement and resource incentive to introduce computing (the Department of Industry introduced the Micros in Schools scheme in 1981 and provided 50 per cent funding to any school who wished to purchase a BBC or a 80Z computer), the PTAs readily acknowledging the appropriateness of spending PTA funds on additional computers, the enormous expansion of cheap, home computers boosted largely on their games appeal, and the ease and convenience with which many maths and physics teachers found they could teach computing (especially when supported by the lavishly funded MEP teacher training programme [the £9 million, four-year project was launched in 1980] and the BBC TV Computer Literacy project launched two years later). With such rich encouragement, it was found that a subject could be accepted into the curriculum even without a coherent rationale. When the political will was there, and that will supported strongly by generous resourcing for the schools and training for the teachers, when the climate was favourable to the introduction of such a subject with its own status and glamorous appeal as well as its apparent currency in the job market, then a subject would find a ready, if premature, growth. There were, however, signs by the end of 1985 that teachers were becoming more critical of computer studies as a separate and distinct subject, seeing the value of computer awareness coming through the integration of computers throughout the whole range of school subjects and activities (Kahn, 1985; and Wellington, 1985). It may well be that the rapid growth of computer studies may yet wither away with roots in shallow ground, but time alone will tell.

The Impact of New Courses

The sixties and the seventies were spectacular in their generation of new curriculum packages for all areas of schools work, and physics and the sciences were not to be excluded. The Nuffield Foundation and the Schools Council between them were to produce over twenty different courses covering every aspect of school science teaching (see Ingle and Jennings, 1981, pp. 21–57). Reading the educational press around the middle of our period one could have been persuaded that everyone was doing the new courses; reading it at the end of our period that no-one was! In reality, both were far from the truth; the new courses were to have a significant effect on physics teaching, though the extent of that influence is not easy to quantify. For, though some teachers took a new course and taught it fully, in line with the developers' intentions, and other teachers studiously rejected any such new-fangled ideas, many others, perhaps the majority, took some aspects of the new courses and incorporated them into their own courses to suit their own needs and perceptions. In 1970 it was sensible to talk of Nuffield and non-Nuffield schools, but by the end of the seventies there had been so much infiltration of all courses with Nuffield ideas and experiments that it was difficult to tell whether a physics department was or was not working for a Nuffield exam solely by seeing what was going on in their laboratories. It is possible, however, to get some measure of the influence of the Nuffield, and other new courses by considering the examination entries for the different exams and different surveys of the schools through the period.

In 1960, the pattern of teaching science in the first two years of secondary schooling, age 11–13, depended on the type of school; the grammar schools would usually teach the three sciences separately with three different teachers while in the secondary modern schools it was more common for a single teacher to teach science as a single subject. As comprehensivization came in it became increasingly common for the secondary modern pattern to predominate, as science teachers acknowledged the pastoral and administrative value of a single teacher working with a class for all of their science lessons and, in line with the comprehensive principle, of keeping all pupils working on a common curriculum at least up to the age of 13. By 1980, 70 per cent of all schools taught their 11–13 science with a single teacher, 11 per cent had three separate teachers for the three sciences and 15 per cent had two teachers with a physical science/biological science split (Beatty and Woolnough, 1982). The difference within different types of school still remained, however, with 78 per cent of comprehensive schools teaching their sciences as one, while for grammar and independent schools that figure was 36 per cent and 26 per cent respectively.

During the sixties there was no one common course at this level, most courses were built around the teachers' interests or particular textbooks. In 1966, the first two years of the Nuffield 'O' level physics course became available for this group and found a ready welcome from many physics teachers, for its overall philosophy, its experimental approach and the accompanying new apparatus. The course had been designed for the more able child in the selective schools, and was none too easy for those! It became obvious that it would not be immediately suitable for transferring to the whole ability range, who were studying science in the comprehensive school. Consequently, a combined science course was produced from the appropriate sections of the Nuffield physics, chemistry and biology courses, with this wider range of ability in mind. The resulting Nuffield Combined Science course was available from 1970 onwards. This course, or derivatives from it, was to become the standard menu for the majority of 11–13 science courses by the beginning of the 1980s. HMI surveyed the schools in 1973 to find how many were 'doing' or 'using' the new course materials. For the first two years of the Nuffield physics course they found 6 per cent doing and a further 8 per cent using parts of it, for the Nuffield Combined Science course, still only a year or two after its publication, the corresponding figures were 30 per cent doing and 23 per cent using the curriculum material (Booth, 1975). By 1980, a survey for the Schools Council 'impact and uptake project' found that 80 per cent of the schools were using the Nuffield combined science material, to some extent (Steadman et al., 1980), a figure very much in keeping with the ubiquity of the material found in most schools.

It is, perhaps, remarkable that such a course, so cheaply and pragmatically produced, should become such common practice in a school system in which there is so much teacher autonomy, and at a stage where the constraints of the external exam system need not dictate the syllabus. Clearly, the practically-based, content-led course with its accompanying sets of pupil apparatus matched well both the need to keep the pupils occupied with practical work and the teachers' perception concerning the nature of science teaching; that it should be directed at helping pupils to discover the right scientific knowledge. It was not until the 1980s that serious doubt began to be expressed at the suitability of such an essentially academic course, however practically disguised, for the majority of 11–13-year-olds.

The Nuffield combined science course spawned a variety of derivative work-sheet dominated courses in the mid seventies when individualized learning was in fashion, and work sheets seen as the answer to getting all pupils through experimental work, irrespective of whether they comprehended it or not! Of particular note is the Insight to Science course developed, very professionally and attractively packaged, for the London schools in the late seventies (ILEA, 1979). This, though being very highly directive of what the pupil had to do, gained a wide popularity in other areas too. An alternative to the Nuffield course, and one well favoured in certain areas, was the Scottish integrated science course, Science for the 70s.

At the same time as these essentially academic, content-led courses were being developed, another, more process approach was being developed out of the child centred primary school context. The Schools Council Science 5 to 13 course was published from 1972 to 1974 and offered a more open, investigative, approach to science teaching for the 11–13 age range. Unfortunately most heads of science were unaware of this approach, or if they were aware of it would have dismissed it as 'not being proper science' and preferred to stick with their high-status, tightly structured combined science courses. Towards the end of our period, however, there were increasing signs that this 'primary school approach' was not only acceptable but increasingly recognized as 'better science' than the top-down, content dominated, science of the grammar school. Ironically, the well structured Nuffield courses which were so much appreciated by science teachers as giving them a recognized support for their lessons, were to be perceived as less of a support and more of a constraint from which they needed to be released before rethinking an appropriate approach to teaching science in the comprehensive schools.

For most pupils the serious start to physics teaching began when they opted to study it for an examination course in the fourth and fifth form, and at this stage we can get some indication of the influence of the Nuffield physics through the number of pupils entering for that exam. If we consider figure 4 we will see how entries for the Nuffield 'O' level GCE examination rose steadily after the pilot phase, from 1968 to 1972 and then increased at a slower rate until reaching a peak around 1980 with 26,200 entries. Thereafter, the number declined, quite steeply from 1983. This pattern, as Tebbutt has shown, demonstrates a very similar characteristic for all the new Nuffield 'O' and 'A' level courses, and for SMP maths (Tebbutt, 1978). Each show an exponential growth during the early years of the curriculum diffusion, followed by a slower rate of growth up to a maximum. Figure 5 illustrates this rather surprising similarity and suggests that the spread of the different courses may depend on other factors than those intrinsic to the merits of the new course itself, or even the particular method introduced for disseminating a particular course, which were quite different for the different courses. It suggests that the degree of diffusion depends on two factors; first the dissemination mechanism when the proliferation of centres produces an exponential growth followed by those factors in the schools which determine how well matched the new course is to the needs of the school, what Tebbutt called a 'kind of pent-up demand'. This second factor,

National Developments

Figure 5.1

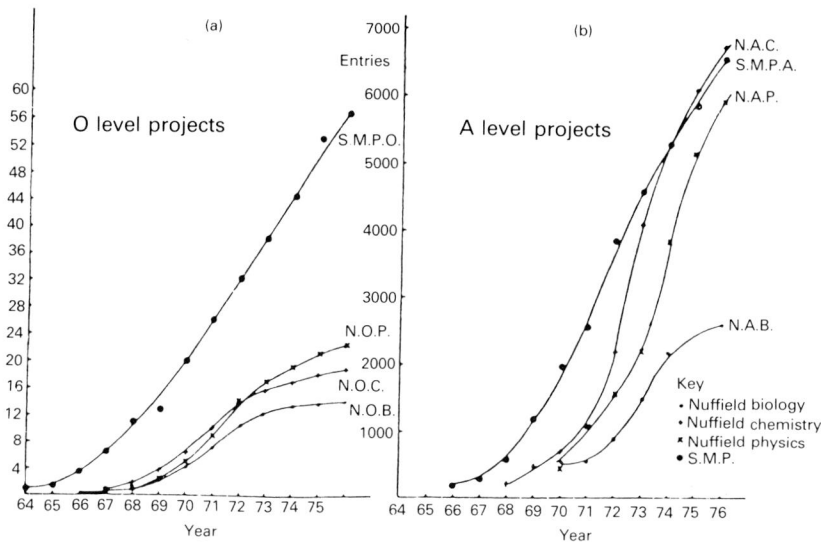

Figure 5.2

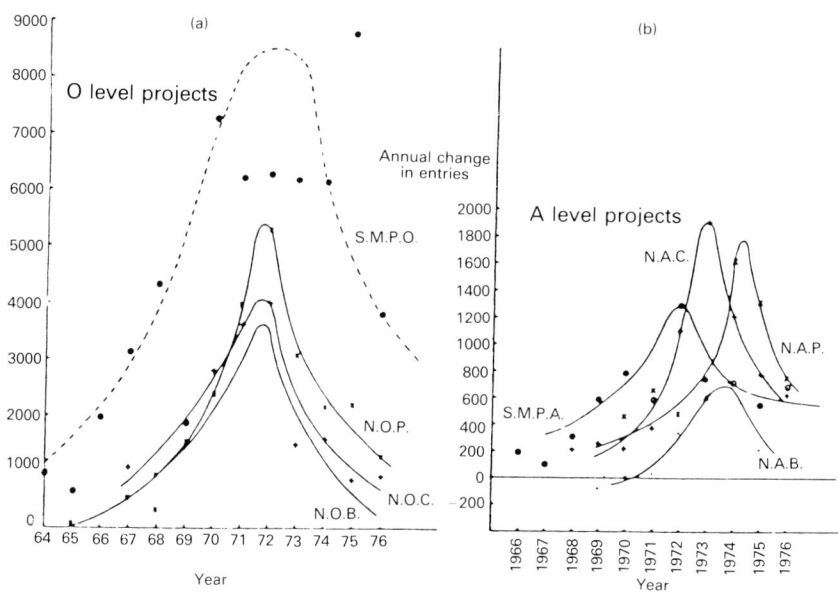

57

which will be determined both by the intrinsic merits of the course itself and the 'readiness for change' of the teachers, will determine what proportion of the market the new course will ultimately capture.

For Nuffield 'O' level Physics this represented just 14 per cent of all 'O' level entries in the year that it reached its peak, compared with 15·5 per cent and 7 per cent for the 'O' level courses in Nuffield Chemistry and Biology, respectively (see table 6). So, although the Nuffield course was an important and influential development both in its own right and in the way it changed other physics courses and examinations, it clearly did not suit the perceived needs of the majority of the physics teaching in the schools. These continued to teach for a traditional exam, though with an increasing dependence on the 'Nuffield apparatus'. The figures for the uptake of the Nuffield 'A' level exams are very similar, 17 per cent of the physics entries, 21 per cent of the chemists with the biology being again least popular with 8 per cent. It is likely that the majority of these courses are taught by the same teachers, Nuffield teachers who have chosen the Nuffield course at both 'O' and 'A' level. It is also true that there were proportionately more Nuffield physics teachers in the independent schools than in the state schools, though there they may be offering both traditional and Nuffield physics, keeping the former to satisfy the needs of the Oxbridge entrance examination.

The examination entries do not, of course, give the whole story. Indeed it was the original intention of Nuffield that their examination should be merely a short-term expediency, needed only until other examinations and courses had been modified appropriately. The 14 per cent figure for physics teachers 'doing Nuffield' in the fourth and fifth form is both too high, and too low. When Professor Egglestone instituted a study in the early seventies to investigate the influence that Nuffield 'O' level courses had had on the teaching of physics, and the other sciences, he found that the classroom practice of many so-called Nuffield teachers was very far from what the initiators of the Nuffield courses had hoped and anticipated. He found that their teaching style was determined more by their personality and individual preferences than by the particular course they were teaching (Egglestone, 1976). Some Nuffield teachers were teaching their physics in a very traditional, didactic way. On the other hand, many 'traditional' teachers

Table 6. Peak uptakes of Nuffield courses

	O level				A level			
	Peak year	Nuffield entry	Total entry	%	Peak year	Nuffield entry	Total entry	%
PHYS	1980	26,200	191,611	14	1982	9,485	55,728	17
CHEM	1980	20,749	134,139	15.5	1983	10,183	47,792	21
BIOL	1977	14,800	221,183	7	1978	3,030	39,841	8

were teaching their physics in line with the Nuffield aims, and using their apparatus. The HMI survey of 1973 found 13 per cent of physics teachers 'doing' Nuffield in years 3, 4, and 5, but a further 34 per cent saying that they were 'using' material from the course (Booth, 1975). This corresponds well with Steadman's (1978) 47 per cent who said that their school made extensive use of Nuffield 'O' level physics. By the end of the seventies, the ideas, approaches, and experiments of Nuffield 'O' level physics had, in Tall's phrase, 'taken root in the schools' (Tall, 1981, p. 17). It was certainly difficult to find a school which did not have in its laboratories much apparatus developed specifically for the Nuffield course. It was not difficult, however, to find a school where the 'spirit' of Nuffield was sorely lacking and where the teaching, especially in the fourth and fifth form, was very didactic, aimed at giving the pupils the knowledge they required for physics exams which were to remain heavily content dependent to the end of our period.

Though the Nuffield 'O' level Physics course was the most obvious new initiative to affect physics teaching in the fourth and fifth forms, there were other developments of significance too. Nuffield physics was introduced at the CSE level too, but this was even less popular than its GCE equivalent because of the essentially conceptual nature of a Nuffield course.

More appropriate for this ability range was the Nuffield Secondary Science material, with its emphasis on topic bases, relevant work and student investigations. Secondary Science, however, launched in 1971, was not a course, but a resource for the teachers. It consisted of a large amount of splendid material from which teachers needed to develop their own courses, which could then be submitted for a Mode 3 CSE examination. In certain areas teachers combined together to produce a joint syllabus but, although a large proportion of teachers claimed to be using the materials, 34 per cent in 1973 and 67 per cent in 1978, it was not taken up in any great numbers. The lure and status of the separate subject physics, at a time when comprehensive schools were seeking to provide a 'grammar school education for all', was too great. The intrinsic worth of the secondary science course did not elicit the extra work required to put together a Mode 3 course for it, except by the ambitious teacher who was able to use that initiative and demonstration of competence to gain promotion and move away to another school!

Another new course to hit the fourth and fifth form science scene was the much heralded SCISP, Schools Council Integrated Science Project, aimed at the more (most!) able pupils. This was launched in 1974/75 and superficially met many of the administrative and educational demands of the schools. In a double subject block it could provide a balanced science course, obviating the needs to choose between the three separate sciences while still maintaining an overall balance in the curriculum. The details of the course will be discussed later, suffice to say here that it never gained a significant foothold in the curriculum, never attracting more than about 4000 candidates. It did not meet a perceived need among the majority of science teachers, who found the whole tone of the course foreign to their traditional views of teaching their own subject at this level. Whereas Nuffield Secondary Science was competing for the market among the less academic pupils, and lost because they were trying to up-grade the status of their own qualifications, SCISP was competing for the most able pupils and lost because they needed their separate sciences for entry to higher education. The place of physics was not seriously threatened. Though both courses contained much novel, innovative, and worthy material, the political realities of the subject war were stacked against them. Neither had a charismatic leader to fight its cause, nor a school or central policy to enforce their introduction. It was left to the Nuffield Foundation to pick up the pieces, to take the two courses and make a modular amalgam from them in the shape of the Nuffield 13–16 course, and wait for central government policy to decree that all pupils should have a balanced science course of 20 per cent of the curriculum time, as it did in the last year of our period (DES, 1985). No doubt the new climate would make teachers more receptive to the many good things developed prematurely in SCISP and Nuffield Secondary Science. Perhaps!

Other new initiatives were to make a significant impact on the fourth and fifth form physics teaching which was directed at the lowest ability, or the lowest attainers, in the school. Most of the Nuffield and Schools Council courses had been developed on the centre-periphery model. It was clear that this had not met the needs of many teachers in the schools who were trying to cope with science classes who were responding negatively to the essentially academic courses of GCE and CSE. With the raising of the school leaving age in 1974 this problem was accentuated as teachers had to cope with pupils who were reluctant even to being in school. So, from the mid-seventies science teachers got together at the local level and developed courses, or course units, especially for these 'less academically motivated pupils' (LAMP). ASE groups produced the LAMP modules, commercial manufacturers harnessed the expertise of local teachers to produce courses for them such as modular Science (1978), Open Science (1979), and most successfully of all Science at Work (1979). Soon Mode 3 CSE syllabuses were built around these courses for the less able ('they won't take the courses seriously unless we prove they are worth taking an exam in it'!), and meeting such a real need in the schools they gained widespread acceptance. For teachers of such groups, status was less important than survival! As GCSE appeared on the horizon in 1985, teachers and science advisers were already trying to build up GCSE courses from the science at work material, material which had proved to be so much more acceptable to the previously underachieving student than CSE physics.

References

APU (1985), *Science at Age 15*, Hatfield, ASE.
BRITISH ASSOCIATION FOR THE ADVANCEMENT OF SCIENCE, (1977), *Education, Engineers and Manufacturing Industry*, Aston, BAAS.
BAKER, K. (1987), written answer to House of Commons of 19 January, reported in *The Independent*, 20 January.
BEATTY, J.W. and WOOLNOUGH, B.E. (1982), 'Practical work in 11–13 science', *British Educational Research Journal*, 8.1, pp. 23–30.
BLACK, P. (1986), 'Integrated or co-ordinated science?', *School Science Review*, 241, pp. 669–81.
BOOTH, N. (1975), 'The impact of science teaching projects on secondary education', *Trends in Education*, pp. 25–32.
BROWN, S. (1977), 'A review of the meaning of, and arguments for, integrated science', *Studies in Science Education*, 4, pp. 31–62.
DAINTON, F. (1968), *Report of the Committee of Enquiry into the Flow of Candidates in Science and Technology into Higher Education*, (The Dainton Report), London, HMSO.
DES (1970), *Statistics of Education*, London, HMSO.
DES (1977), *Education in Schools: A Consultative Document*, London, HMSO.
DES (1985 a), *Statistics of Education*, London, HMSO.
DES (1985 b), *Science 5–16, A Statement of Policy*, London, HMSO.
DONNISON, D. (1970), *Second Report of the Public Schools Commission, Vol 1; Report on Independent Day Schools and Direct Grant Grammar Schools*, London, HMSO.
DOUSE, M. (1985), 'The background of assisted places scheme students', *Educational Studies*, 11.3, pp. 211–7.
DRIVER, R. (1977), *LAMP Projects)*, (15 topic briefs and 2 teachers guides), Hatfield, ASE.
DUCKWORTH, D. (1978), *The Continuing Swing?* Windsor, NFER.
EGGLESTONE, J. (1986), Personal communication about unpublished evaluation of APU.
ELVINS, H.L. (1960), 'Report on presidential address at conference of education officers', *Times Educational Supplement*, 1 January, pp. 13 and 14.
GOODSON, I. and BALL, S. (1984), *Defining the Curriculum; Histories and Ethnographies of School Subjects*, (especially, 'Subjects for study; towards a social history of curriculum' pp. 25–44), Lewes, Falmer Press.
HMI (1977), *Aspects of Secondary Education in England*, London, HMSO.
HMI (1982), *Technology in Schools*, London, HMSO.
HMI (1985), *Technology and School Science, an HMI Enquiry*, London, HMSO.
HARRISON, G.B. (1984), 'Technology in schools' in LAYTON, D. (Ed.), *The Alternative Road*, Leeds, University of Leeds (pp. 75–87).
HUDSON, J. (1986), 'Whatever happened to technical schools?' *Times Educational Supplement*, 3 October.

HUTCHINS, D.W. (1962), *Technology and the Sixth Form Boy*, Oxford, Oxford University Department of Educational Studies.
HUTCHINS, D.W. and HEYWORTH, P. (1963), *Technology and the Sixth Form Boy*, Oxford Department of Educational Studies.
HUTCHINS, D.W. (1977), *Mechanical Engineering as a Career*, Department of Mechanical and Production Engineering, Loughborough Technical College.
ILEA (1978), *Insight to Science*, London, Addison-Wesley.
INGLE, R. and JENNINGS, A. (1981), *Science in Schools, Which Way Now?*, Windsor, NFER.
ISIS (1986), *Annual Census*, London, ISIS.
JENKINS, E. (1979), *From Nuffield to Armstrong*, London, John Murray.
KAHN, B. (1985), *Computers in Science*, Cambridge, Cambridge University Press.
KELLY, A. (1981), *The Missing Half: Girls and Science Education*, Manchester, Manchester University Press.
KEOHANE, K. (1987), 'Physics education — 21 years on', *Physics Education*, 22.3.
LAYTON, D. (1973), *Science for the People*, London, George Allen and Unwin.
MCCULLOCH, G., JENKINS, E., and LAYTON, D. (1985), *Technological Revolution?*, Lewes, Falmer Press.
MACLURE, S. (1985), '75 years of the TES', *Times Educational Supplement*, September, pp. 1–56.
MARSHALL, A.R. (1974), *School Technology in Action*, London, English University Press.
MARWICK, A. (1982), *British Society since 1945*, Harmondsworth, Penguin Books.
MYERS, F.C. (1984), 'How technology is encountered in the curriculum', unpublished SDES dissertation, Oxford University, Department of Educational Studies.
NASH, M., ALLSOP, R.T., and WOOLNOUGH, B.E. (1985), *Factors Affecting the Uptake of Technology in Schools*, Oxford, Oxford University Department of Educational Studies.
NEWSOM, J. (1968), *First Report of the Public Schools Commission*, London, HMSO.
PAGE, G.T. (1965), *Engineering Among the Schools*, London, Institute of Mechanical Engineers.
STEADMAN, S.D., PARSONS, C., and SALTER, B.G. (1980), *Impact and Take-up Project*, London, Schools Council.
TALL, G. (1981), 'British science curriculum projects — how have they taken root in schools', *European Journal of Science Education*, 3.1, pp. 17–38.
TEBBUTT, M.J. (1978), 'The growth and eventual impact of curriculum development projects in science and maths', *Curriculum Studies*, 10.1, pp. 61–73.
WALKER, R. (1980), 'Project technology' in STENHOUSE, L. (Ed.), *Curriculum Research and Development in Action*, London, HEB, pp. 115–34.
WEINER, M. (1981), *English Culture and the Decline of the Industrial Spirit*, Cambridge, Cambridge University Press.
WELLINGTON, J.J. (1985), 'The message of the medium; Computer simulations in science education', *School Science Review*, 238, pp. 139–42.
WOOLNOUGH, B.E. (1975), 'The place of technology in schools', *School Science Review*, 196, pp. 443–8.
WOOLNOUGH, B.E. (1976), 'A fresh look at some current myths', *Education in Science*, 66, pp. 18–20.

WOOLNOUGH, B.E. (1979), 'A further look at some old myths', *Education in Science*, 81, pp. 21–4.
YATES, A. and PIDGEON, D.A. (1957), *Admission to Grammar Schools*, Windsor, NFER.

3 'More precious than rubies' — The Teachers

The Supply of Physics Teachers

Of central importance to the teaching of physics in schools was the role of the teachers themselves, who they were, how well their supply matched the demand, and how they were trained. These were the people who, in the last resort, mediated the physics to the pupils. On the quality and quantity of them did the quality of physics teaching depend. We will first consider the supply of physics teachers, and then their initial training and the people and traditions responsible for that training.

A shortage of physics teachers has, like the poor, always been with us. It has been a perennial concern throughout our twenty-five years and showed no sign of relenting by 1985; indeed the poverty and insolvency of the situation in the schools appeared at the end of our period more intractable than at the beginning. Since the beginning of the century there has been a sequence of reports, from government sub-committees, from the Royal Society, from the British Association for the Advancement of Science, from the Institute of Physics and from the Association for Science Education considering the current situation and recommending remedies to ameliorate the situation. Hooper (1980) has summarized the work done by government committees leading to the Thomson Report (1918), the Morris Report (1953), the Dainton Report (1968) and the Swann Report (1968). All stress the vital need for high quality maths and science teaching (especially in physics) as a prerequisite for providing sufficient manpower for the scientific and technological welfare of the nation. All point to the inadequacy of the existing stock of such teachers and recommend, among other things, better resourcing and better pay for science teachers. Each report has been motivated by a vocational need and perceived the prime function of physics teaching to be the provision of future physicists for higher education and thence into industry or research. Few of these, or other such reports, have stressed the need for physicists to provide an appropriate science education for all.

Setting the scene for the sixties was a conference organized by the British Association for the Advancement of Science in 1958 which brought together authorities from universities, government and schools. They were convinced that, as a matter of urgency, more attention should be focused on the conditions of science teaching in schools but were concerned, in the words of their President Sir Alexander Fleck, FRS, not only 'from the vocational view to produce more men and women who are trained to play their part in complex technological processes', but that science education should be a unifying rather than a divisive influence carrying 'traditional humanism into a new industrial setting' (Perkins, 1958, ppv-vi). It was a time when the unusually high birth rate of the 1940s was finding its way into the secondary schools, a time of great expansion from two million in 1950 to 2.9 million in 1961, and a time when there was a great demand for increasing the science base of the nation. The aim, as summarized by Dr Barton, was to 'double the annual output of science graduates every ten years, whose training begins (sic!) in the sixth forms of our schools' (Perkins, 1958, p. 52). The report that he gave to the conference about the supply of science teachers has a depressingly modern ring about it. His surveys had shown that in 1957 there were 103 science posts unfilled, and 148 new posts needed for larger sixth forms, 222 posts unsatisfactorily filled and 614 posts held by non-graduates ('about 1100 posts, out of 7000, were either unfilled or unsatisfactorily filled'). If we think that was bad, we should remember that he was only talking about the maintained grammar and public schools in which were virtually all the future scientists and all the graduate teachers. The situation for the majority of pupils in the secondary modern schools was far worse — they would have been very unlikely to have had any graduate scientist on their staff at all. He concluded that, 'although there had been a big increase in the salary of all teachers since 1950, the good science teacher is still underpaid and the grammar schools will go short of science teachers until this is put right' (p. 58). He also challenged the university scientists to show by their example and precept that they were interested and enthusiastic about their teaching as well as their research, 'only when the universities again take their teaching seriously will a reasonable proportion of their undergraduates feel that teaching in a school is a worthwhile and honourable career' (p. 59). Both of these conclusions have remained at the heart of the problem since, and have been accentuated as the schools have become comprehensive.

And so we enter the 1960s with the Ministry of Education reporting that despite the increases in supply of graduate teachers of maths and science 'the supply is still far from sufficient for their needs; in particular the shortage of teachers of mathematics and physics continues to cause concern' (Ministry of Education 1961, p. 19). In 1960, though a potential teacher could get a teaching certificate at a college of education, (from a course which had only that year changed from two to three years in length), or do a one-year, postgraduate certificate in education after graduating in physics, a considerable proportion of graduates went straight into teaching without any professional training. It was not until 1974 that the government made it necessary for teachers in state schools to have been professionally trained, and even then an exception was made for physics, and other science, graduates and for mathematicians because of the continuing shortage of these subjects. It was not until 1984, after continued lobbying from the teacher unions, the ASE, UCET and, eventually, the Royal Society and the Institute of Physics that this waiver was rescinded. The independent schools have, of course, never made it necessary for their staff to have received any professional training though an increasing proportion of them have done so. Many teachers are still recruited direct from university on the strength of their academic or sporting prowess, and personality. Though it is even more difficult to get precise information about the qualifications of teachers in the private than in maintained schools, it is evident that the shortage of physics teachers has not been limited to the latter.

Different people at different times have collected statistics about the number of physics teachers in training and in teaching in the schools, (the DES, the Institute of Physics, the Royal Society, the ASE and the Graduate Teacher Training Registry (GTTR) have all done so at different times), but because they have done so in different ways it is surprisingly difficult to get consistent figures for teacher supply over this period of time. However, the following discussion is, I believe, based on sufficiently accurate figures to be reliable.

The number of physics teachers who were professionally trained are shown in figure 6. The majority have been graduate physicists or, increasingly, engineers with a PGCE, probably from a university department of educational studies. The numbers coming through this route increased steadily through the sixties reaching a peak of 600 in 1972. Thereafter recruitment showed a steady decline, with upturns in 1975 and in the early eighties. The BEd route had its first intake in 1966, but had, along with the CertEd route for potential physicists, been reduced to zero by 1980. With the expansion of higher education in the universities and polytechnics during the sixties and seventies, the bright sixth form physicist would have been encouraged to get a degree first even if there was a possibility of becoming a teacher later. Consequently the colleges of education were rarely able to attract good physical science students to their CertEd courses, and when the draconian cuts in teacher training places in the colleges occurred in the mid-seventies, the corresponding staff cuts meant the virtual elimination of physics staff to teach any of the, undersubscribed, physics

Figure 6

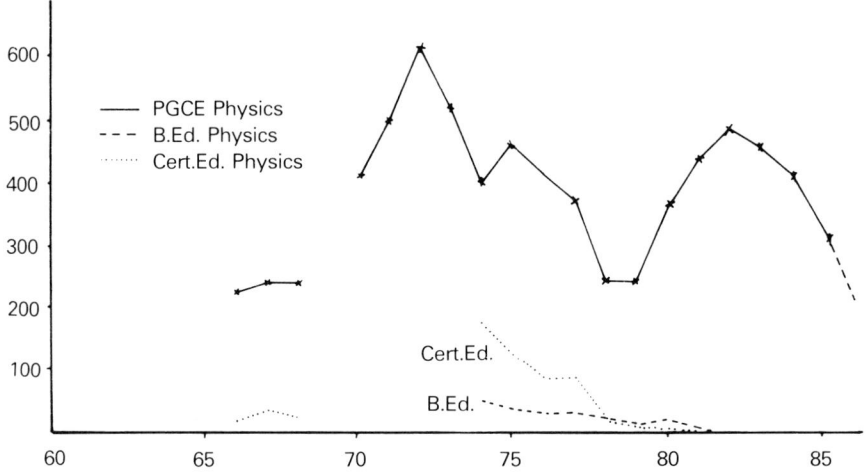

course. Thus, the BEd courses could not be staffed for physics and this route dried up too until, by the eighties, the only route available for a potential physics teacher in the secondary school system was the consecutive degree plus PGCE.

It would be instructive, if rather depressing, to consider in more detail the trends in recruitment to physics teaching through the most important route, the degree plus PGCE. Through the sixties, when it was widely believed that schools and science could make the world a better place and schools were being well supplied with resources, the supply of physics teachers was increasing. Nevertheless, this supply was not meeting the demand, which was increasing even faster. The secondary school population was increasing and the demand in an increasingly comprehensive system was that all pupils, not just the selected few, should be open to good, graduate science teaching. Moreover, the age distribution of the teaching profession which had been depleted by war and subsequent industrial expansion was such that the quantity and quality of those leaving the profession through retirement was not being replaced by succeeding cohorts. Indeed the Royal Society report in 1969, on the *Shortage of Science and Maths Teachers in Schools*, made very depressing reading. Though perhaps overstating the case by expecting the previous grammar school standard of teaching to be immediately transferred to the whole system, they spoke of 'many schools where serious instruction in science and maths has ceased' and concluded that a 'chronically deteriorating position has now become disastrous'. The 199 schools in their survey had lost 1656 science and maths teachers in period 1963–68, 49 per cent to other schools, 10 per cent to other parts of the vineyard, but, most alarmingly, 26 per cent had deserted teaching altogether for reasons other than death, retirement or marriage. Interestingly, this proportion is very similar to the 'desertion rate' found by Bryan Chapman's survey of 1977 and the Institute of Physics' survey of 1985. However, through expansion of the system and confident publicity, there were 620 on the PGCE physics courses in 1972, apart from those being trained in the colleges of education. This was to be the peak, a false dawn, from which the decline through the more educationally cynical seventies was to be far reaching.

Though figure 6 appears to indicate that the supply of physics teachers in training shows a random fluctuation of peaks and troughs, it could be interpreted as a steady decline punctuated by two abnormal upturns. In 1975 the teaching profession had a very significant pay rise as a result of the Houghton award, and this resulted in an increase in popularity the following year. In the early eighties the depression of British industry lead to the rapid rise in unemployment, from 1.2 million in 1979 to 3 million in 1983, and this affected both graduate as well as non-graduate employment. Consequently this led more physics graduates to seek jobs in school teaching, and the numbers on the physics PGCE courses increased. This inverse relationship between opportunities in industrial employment for physics graduates and the popularity of school teaching is shown clearly in figure 7, where the dips in employment prospects are matched by growth in teacher training, and vice versa (IoP, 1979, fg 28). (The disparity between the numbers in figures 6 and 7 are due to the former referring to all graduates on physics PGCE courses, whereas figure 7 refers only to physics graduates.) It appears that the only way to increase the number of physics graduates entering teaching is to introduce large pay rises, every year, and cause industry to be in a permanent state of decline! The economists tell us that these two factors can never go together, and that I suggest is at the very heart of the problem. A booming economy draws physicists into the better paid jobs there, a declining economy will not allow the reasonable salaries for teachers that would attract them into schools.

During this period the Government, and certain LEAs, have instituted various policies to try and attract more physicists into teaching each of which have had only limited success. There have been various recruitment and publicity drives, the most effective one being ILEAs who were able to

Of People, Policy and Power

Figure 7: First Destination of University Physicists – (First Degrees Only) (hundreds)

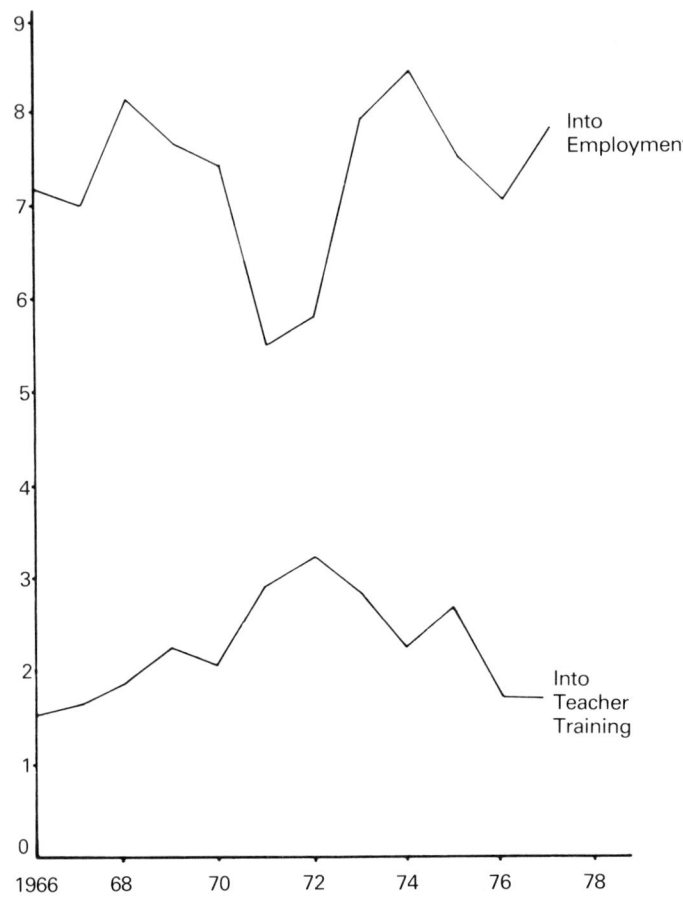

Statistics Relating to Education & Physics, Institute of Physics, 1979.

pay trainee physics teachers from industry a full teaching salary and immediately second them for teacher training. There was the enhanced grants for mature students and late entrants to training from industry through the MSC scheme of 1978–83. There was the DES scholarship scheme offering additional PGCE grants of £500 to selected high quality science and maths graduates to train in selected institutions in 1982–84. And there was, in 1985, a proposed sponsorship policy to give additional grants of £1200 to all trainee teachers of shortage subjects, including physics, in their training year. There have been various retraining schemes to enable teachers of other subjects to retrain as physics teachers. And there has been the waiver of the necessity for professional training itself for physicists from 1974–84, a policy which was to increase the entrants to physics teaching by about 12 per cent and, arguably, do more to spread the practice of bad physics teaching in schools than anything else. It also lead to a wastage rate among such, ill-prepared, recruits more than twice that of their professionally trained peers (DES, 1980, table A-C).

One policy that has never been instituted, despite the recommendation of so many interested parties, was the payment of higher salaries to teachers in shortage subjects such as physics, to attract them into teaching. In the early 1960s, physics graduates were, *de facto*, receiving higher salaries than the majority of the teaching force. They were teaching in grammar schools and in independent schools and as such had more special responsibility allowances and were placed higher on the salary scales than their non-graduate counterparts in the secondary modern and primary schools. This differentiation lead to proportionately better salaries for graduate teachers in general and physics teachers in particular, as well as placing them in higher regard in society. With the growth of comprehensivization, and its correspondingly egalitarian ethos in schools, the graduates and non-graduates were teaching alongside each other in the same school. It was argued by the teacher unions, especially by the NUT, that the commonality of all teachers work inferred that they should have a more common salary and hence that differentials should be reduced. The hope was that all teachers salaries should be brought up to the previous level of the higher paid graduate teacher, a hope even more reasonable when, in the eighties, the profession had an all-graduate entry. In the event, perhaps inevitably because of the large number of almost half a million teachers involved, the effect was to proportionately 'level down' the salaries being offered to physics graduates. It is unlikely that any policy of differential salaries for shortage subjects, even if it was to be allowed by the unions, would ever be effective in paying sufficiently attractive salaries to outbid a more affluent and voracious industry. But despite all such central policies, there were fundamental problems which could not be overlooked. Physicists are people too, with personal traits and wishes, and cannot be dragooned into jobs that do not match their tendencies. Though it is simplistic to over generalize, there are aspects which go to make a good physicist that are not necessarily compatible with teaching children. Personality studies noted different personality characteristics of scientists, particularly physical scientists, compared with their non-scientific contemporaries. They tended to be more introverted, less socially conscious, more concerned with 'things than with people'. They found success and satisfaction in ideas and abstractions, in regular patterns and cerebral activities. Such attributes did not lead naturally to a lifetime spent working with real, often irrational, children. Moreover, physicists had gone into the further study of physics because they enjoyed physics as a subject, and enjoyed doing scientific research. If they succeeded in this, and teaching would be the poorer if it attracted only unsuccessful physicists, they would want to continue with physics in their career. Though it was always possible for them to do physics research while school teaching, through individual initiative or the encouragement of such bodies as the Royal Society and the Institute of Physics, the increasing pressures within the schools have made it steadily more difficult. In the early sixties, it was not difficult for good physicists to develop their own researches in the context of school teaching; there is splendid evidence in the Nuffield physics courses of that having been done in curriculum development projects. Through the seventies physics teachers spent more of their time and effort teaching below the sixth form and with less academic pupils. Consequently, they would spend much less time discussing, and doing, real physics with able pupils and many would find less intrinsic job satisfaction. On the other hand, the governments and the professional institutions have positively encouraged good students to take up careers in research and industry which had, after all, been the *raison d'etre* for teaching physics in the first place. Universities too, at the potential physics teachers most formative stage, would often dissuade students from school teaching and into research. Though it was in 1511 that Erasmus responded to a Cambridge don who was trying to recruit an assistant master for St Pauls School with the words 'who would spend his life instructing boys if he could earn a living in any other way?', such sentiments have been similarly expressed by university physicists 460 years later (Blin-Stoyle, 1982, p 32).

And this is a fundamental puzzle, how to keep the cycle of physics teaching self-supporting. When the purpose of teaching physics is to produce physicists, how can sufficient of the best of them be diverted into school teaching to develop the seed corn for the future? There needs to be a genuine commitment in government and the professional institutions that physics is an important part of education for all. Otherwise, there will be the temptation to believe the vocational argument that sufficient physicists and engineers can be produced more cheaply through selective schooling. Hence we return to the basic question, should physics be taught as a 'good' for the education of all pupils or as a need for the training of some? When money and teachers are in short supply, it is easy to be persuaded that they should be devoted to teaching the more able and, vocationally more useful, pupils. Fortunately, many teachers throughout our period persisted in the belief that all pupils had a right to enjoy physics.

Future Supply of Physics Teachers

We have seen that there has been, throughout our period, a repeated and continual cry concerning the quantity and quality of physics teachers in the schools. Though the impressive analyses of Barton (1958), Mott (1969), Kirkham (1976), Chapman (1980), Slade (1981), and Thompson (1981) have produced quantitative discussions of the situation they have not been able to give an unambiguous analysis, nor have their figures agreed with those of the DES. On one thing they have agreed, however, that there was a need for more good physics teachers in school. There have been two pronouncements in the last decade which have prevented the seriousness of the situation being recognized, and held back any remedial action. In 1976, at the Institute of Physics Education Group annual conference, Brian Chapman was pointing out that schools might soon reach a steady state, even saturation, as far as physics teachers were concerned. This argument depended on the steadying secondary school population, the age distribution of the existing science teaching force, the wastage rate and the number of physics teachers in training. Most of the physics teachers in schools were young (65 per cent of physics teachers were under 40) and male, and the loss to the stock was only about 100–150 per year. There were currently about 400 physicists in the UDEs, and some coming through the colleges, more than enough to make good the wastage. Hence, with the school population remaining static and teachers, even those teaching physics who were unsuitably qualified, unlikely to be moved from their posts we would 'soon' be producing more physics teachers than the system could accommodate. He suggested that this would be reached by 1978, and his analysis was widely accepted; Jeff Kirkham thought the steady state would be reached in 1980, Norman Booth, the Senior HMI for Science, thought it had already been reached. In the event, the wastage rate proved to have been underestimated and the numbers in training in subsequent years overestimated so with an increasing demand for physics teaching in the schools that steady state was never reached.

In 1980, when the government was not able to provide enough money to fund mature students recruited for its own retraining scheme for teachers of shortage subjects, Dr Rhodes Boyson, then Parliamentary Under-Secretary at the DES, defended the governmental paucity with the astonishing claim that there were already 8000 qualified physics teachers in the schools who were not teaching their subject. This figure (quite remarkable when compared to the 10000 figure widely accepted as being the actual number of teachers teaching physics in school) had been mistakenly derived from a misunderstanding of the DES figures for the qualifications of teachers in schools carried out for their 1977 survey (DES, 1977, tb TQ6). The way that the qualifications were recorded meant that, on average, every teacher would be counted twice so that a physics graduate who had studied maths in the first year of his degree course would count as being qualified to teach both maths and physics. Most of the DES figures recorded science teachers as a single group and this too hid the particular dearth of physicists at a time when biologists, especially, and latterly chemists too were in surplus. It was not until the beginning of 1985 that the DES could be persuaded to recognize publicly that there was a real shortage still in physics, even though there was not one in biology or chemistry. The scholarship scheme of 1982–84 was addressed to teachers of science, the proposals for an additional training grant for trainee teachers in shortage subjects proposed in 1985 was directed only to physicists, and not the other sciences.

So by 1985, the serious shortage of physicists in school was recognized. It was being made worse by the growth of scientifically based industry recruiting expansively, by the low status, salaries and morale in the teaching profession caused by governmental and media vilification and under-resourcing and union action, by the decreasing standing of physics in the curriculum as a result of ASE and DES policy for integrated science, and by the increasing movement of physics teachers into more lucrative and rewarding subjects in the curriculum such as TVEI, electronics, computer studies and other technological areas. Other organizational factors were also exacerbating the situation. As roles and resources were falling through the eighties, more and more LEAs were seeing the economic advantages of separating the sixth forms from the lower schools to form sixth form or tertiary colleges. By 1984 there were 112 sixth form colleges and eighty tertiary colleges in existence, spread throughout half of the LEAs. Hence the remaining, beheaded, 11–16 schools were appearing even less attractive to physics graduates who had previously had the stimulation of sixth form teaching to maintain their subject interest. So the policies of LEAs towards sixth form colleges, of the DES and the ASE towards balanced science for all up to 16, of the teacher unions to reward all teachers more equitably and to prevent teacher redundancy, and of the ASE and the Royal Society towards a more appropriate, more socially aware, type of science, (all good and laudable policies in themselves) were acting together to discourage physics graduates from entering the teaching profession in 11–16 schools. At a time when governmental priorities were for manpower provision, rather than education for all, and when this provision could be supplied through the independent schools, the Assisted Places Scheme, and the sixth form colleges, there was no strong incentive to provide for specialist physics teaching in the 11–16 comprehensives. In 1981, Professor Elton was saying that as far as science teaching in the secondary schools was concerned 'we should face the fact that we shall probably never again get the kind of specialist teacher who has traditionally taught the 16–19 year olds over the last thirty or forty years' (Elton, 1982, p 41). Perhaps, as the teaching profession reconsiders the type of science that is most appropriate in the general education of all pupils, that prophecy when fulfilled will prove to be beneficial rather than detrimental to the constructive development of the part that physics should play in it; or so we must hope!

The Training of Physics Teachers

In 1970 Cawthorne, after a meeting at the Royal Society to discuss teacher training for science and mathematics graduates, wrote ' . . . if virtually all future physics teachers were to be trained, and if this training is going in any way to affect the calibre of the teaching in the schools and thus (sic!) the future recruitment to undergraduate courses, then the thirty or so physics tutors in departments of education bear a heavy responsibility' (Crawthorne 1970, p 54). In the event there have been rather more than thirty tutors in the UDEs who have been involved in the training of physics teachers since 1960, though only seventy-two in the twenty-eight departments that have been running PGCE courses in physics. These tutors have had the responsibility for providing the initial professional training of about 7000 physics teachers in England and Wales in that twenty-five years. There has been a considerable measure of continuity in this training, with 48 of the tutors having been involved for more than ten years, indeed fifteen have been responsible for the training of physics teachers in their departments for more than twenty years.

Clearly this group has had a significant influence on the teaching of physics in this time. Who were they? Typically they were men, (only four were women), who had themselves been successful physics teachers in, for obvious reasons, grammar or independent schools. In later years they would have been expected to have had comprehensive school experience. Almost without exception they were 'good honours graduates in physics', most would have gone into teaching after a one-year professional training of which they would speak with derision. Most would have had ten-fifteen years experience of teaching and running a department before entering the UDEs. They were also likely to have been involved with curriculum development, in-service training, or with the ASE and would have written articles or textbooks. These tutors have had complete autonomy as to how to organize that training, within the context of their own institutions. Though there have been individual idiosyncracies around the courses of some tutors, most have tended to show similar developments, exchanging ideas and being influenced by each other through their writings and at their annual Association for Department of Education Physics Tutors (ADEPT) conferences.

Over the twenty-five years, the role and activities of a UDE physics tutor has changed considerably. In 1960 the role was specifically, and almost exclusively, about the initial training of physics teachers, though even at that time the tutor would have seen this brief in the wider context of improving physics teaching throughout the country. The freedom inherent in the university enabled tutors to be involved in curriculum development projects, in assessment and examining, in providing in-service training courses for local and national courses for physics teachers, and in scholarship, research and writing. The tutor had to serve two constituents, the university with their expectation of scholarship and research and the schools with their expectation of initial and in-service training. Though at times the two task masters seemed to be driving in different directions, the tension created was, at its best, creative. The research and development work that the tutor was doing would be fed directly into the initial training of the new teachers, and the work that the tutor would be doing with his students and the schools would focus that research into the real problems facing teachers. There was, of course, little research being done in the early sixties, that was to develop with the professionalization of the group in the seventies.

In the sixties the tutor's model was much more that of transference of good practice, as had been exhibited by the tutor from his own teaching days and for which he had been appointed. Most in-service training was done, and much continued to be done, in short courses of meetings held over a few evenings or days, and would focus on helping the teachers to keep abreast with the new course material. Initially this focused around the Nuffield 'O' and then 'A' level physics courses, more lately around topics in the new examination syllabuses and electronics. Throughout the seventies and eighties, many tutors were involved, along with local science advisers, in putting on management courses for heads of department. Also, in the seventies, many tutors were setting up and teaching for MEd, or MSc, courses in physics or science education, which were seen both as a mechanism for intellectual stimulation and in-service training. Initially such courses were seen as providing a ticket for teacher promotion, in later years, with job opportunities being reduced, they have been brought back to their original function of improving the performance, in the deepest sense, of the physics teacher and his department. So whereas the physics tutor in 1960 would have devoted his time to teaching his own course of initial training, by the 1980s he would have been (a) planning and teaching the PGCE with local teachers; (b) teaching and supervising on MSc work with experienced teachers on secondment; (c) supervising higher degree work with research students; (d) running in-service courses for local heads of departments; and (e) researching and publishing for his own academic satisfaction. All of which has had a greatly enriching effect on the initial training, and prevented the tutor from becoming stale, merely retreading past practice inappropriate to the changing school situation. Increasingly in the mid eighties, at the behest of the Council for the Accreditation of Teacher Education (CATE), he will also have been teaching regularly in a local comprehensive school — though whether the time commitment needed for this at the expense, say, of his research will actually improve his overall, distinctive, function in improving physics teaching nationally remains to be seen.

The initial training courses themselves have changed considerably over the twenty-five years, in ways that reflect the influence that the courses had on entrants to the physics teaching profession. This may be illustrated by brief descriptions of how a typical trainee physics teacher would have experienced such a course in 1960, 1973 and 1985.

In 1960, the course was simple: a refreshing or frustrating change from the intensive, demanding, undergraduate physics course he had just completed. He would have spent one hour per week on physics method work in which the tutor gave a lecture demonstration on how to teach various topics on the 'O' level physics course; he would write a few essays on such subjects as 'the place of physics in the curriculum'; he would have attended a few lectures on the psychology, the sociology, the philosophy, the history of education (one hour on each per week); he might have attended classes on speech production, in which he would have learnt to enunciate and project his vowels, on musical appreciation or on taking games. After Christmas he would leave his university and go to a famous school in a distant town for a full term of teaching practice, and be visited twice by his tutor who knew little of the school, its pupils or its staff. He would return to the university for the summer term, attend rather less lectures but spend a lot of time discussing the problems of the world in general and of education in particular with his fellow students, would greatly enjoy and improve his cricket, tennis, or punting and then sit three three-hour exams in which he would express his opinion on matters of general educational import. Though he knew his answers were no more than superficial, he would pass and subsequently receive from the Ministry of Education notification that he was now eligible for the status of qualified teacher, along with wishes for many years of happiness in the teaching profession. He had been headhunted before Christmas for the job in which he would enter that profession, in a boys grammar school teaching physics to able boys from the first year through to the Oxbridge entrance level. Perhaps the main gain from the year, apart from what he learnt from his own experience on teaching practice, was that whereas he had started the year thinking like a physicist who was going to teach, he finished it thinking like a teacher who was going to teach physics.

In 1973, he would find a very structured and intensive course awaiting him. He would find a newly-built laboratory filled with gleaming new demonstration apparatus and sets of class apparatus developed for the Nuffield course and this lab would be the focus for him, and his group of twelve other physicists, for the year. He would spend up to two days each week here, familiarizing himself with the apparatus, trying out experiments, studying text books and course guides, developing his own resource material and lesson plans. He would spend quite a lot of time on discussions, simulations, case studies and microteaching with other physicists, often using STEP exercises and activities, to develop particular teaching skills such as lesson planning, concept development, questioning and lesson introduction and closure (Hayson and Sutton 1974). He would be forced to think through his own teaching aims and objectives, and to analyze for himself, in the department, why and how he would be teaching physics. He would be seeing teaching as a teacher centred activity, though starting to realize that not all pupils were alike, and certainly not all like he was at their age, he would be having classes on individualized work schemes, mixed ability teaching, teaching the non-academic, and preparing pupils for the CSE. Alongside his curriculum studies he would be introduced to the wider aspects of schooling through lectures, where the psychologist, the sociologist and the philosopher would seek to relate their discipline to the problems of the classroom, and in weekly seminar groups with students of other subjects. He would be writing assessed essays arising from his general educational work, as he would for his special project on theories of learning or assessment. His second term would be spent doing teaching practice in a local school well-known to his physics tutor, who would supervise him jointly with the head of department at the school. Though most of that teaching would be in physics, he would be expected to take some combined science in the first two years. He would return for the summer term feeling more like a teacher than a student, and find the programme similar but less satisfying than that of the first term. He would enjoy the summer, though find the deadlines for assignments irritating as his sights were increasingly on the reality of his first job which he had fixed up before Easter at an 11–18 mixed comprehensive. Continuous assessments having replaced a final examination, the term ended with a whimper rather than a bang.

In 1985, the course would be significantly more school-based and pupil-orientated. She, for although the majority of the physics group were still men the proportion of women had increased, would find herself in a group of ten with degrees from a wide range of science and engineering backgrounds. The heart of her work would still be her curriculum work in physics, though she would spend half of that time with other scientists working on issues common to them. Issues such as science in society, balanced science courses, science for the less able, as well as combined science for the 11–13-year-olds were all dealt with in mixed science groups. It quickly became apparent to her that the team of science tutors was aiming to prepare her for a job as a science teacher, with a specialism in physics, rather than as a physics teacher pure and simple. This she found, initially, rather unsettling — she had never felt confident in chemistry and had done no biology at school since she dropped it at the age of 14. She was attached to a local comprehensive in which she would spend one day per week in the first term, the whole of the second term and a week in the third term. Though she was pleasantly surprised at the relationships in the school, the teachers were normal people who seemed to be getting on well with classes of normal children, it was not the blackboard jungle filled with idle teachers and violent children that the media had led her to expect, she became more and more aware of the irrelevance of much of her own physics background to the needs of the pupils. Her course, which had been planned jointly with the science tutors and a group of local heads of departments, linked department-based work and school-based work together. In the department she would prepare for, and subsequently analyze, the school-based activities she would do either with small groups of pupils or with whole classes. Her science tutors would also introduce her to aspects of language development, sex discrimination and learning theory that their recent researches were revealing. She would also be initiated into the wonders of APU, GCSE, TVEI, SCDC, CLISP and all the other acronyms that made her feel that the school system was in a turmoil of new initiatives far removed from the day-to-day teaching she was observing and practicing. Her week became a hectic, but satisfying, whirl as she dashed from department to school preparing, discussing, analyzing, teaching, writing assignments and reading what books and articles she could get her hands on. Though there was opportunity in the department to try out experiments, the specific emphasis on Nuffield courses had now been replaced by introductory electronics and computer usage units. There was more emphasis on developing materials and strategies to engage the pupils minds in discussion and writing, than their hands in doing practical work; though whether this was an expediency to cope with the inadequate supply of apparatus that she found in her school or for genuine educational reasons she was not sure! Her general professional studies work was almost exclusively centred around school-based themes of the curriculum, active tutorial work, multicultural education, and discipline and these she studied through seminars with tutors and teachers who were in the department, seconded for their own professional development. She prepared assignments and case studies in these areas, and developed a scheme of work for a group of special needs pupils that she was working with in the summer term. Her teaching practice term in the second term she found difficult and emotionally draining, her pupils seemed to lack motivation and did not respond to her own love of physics in the way she expected. She was rather disillusioned too by the attitude of some of the teachers she met, some of whom tried to dissuade her from entering teaching, but after much heart searching and resisting the seductions of a girls independent school she maintained her original commitment and took a post teaching in her teaching practice school. She would 'give it a go for a year or two', at least she had friends in the locality.

It is interesting to speculate how far the physics tutors in the UDEs have been a conservative or a revolutionary influence on the teaching of physics. By their very nature and selection they were initiators, original thinkers, and good practitioners. They sought to improve their courses and consequently the practice in the schools through their students and their regular contact with the teachers on teaching practice, on course planning, on INSET and on joint research activities. Though they faced the perpetual problem of whether to prepare their students for 'schools as they are or as they should be', they were consistently bringing good practice to the attention of their students and the teachers. Through their own researches and development work they were in the van of current thinking and were able to give a wider and more perceptive overview to the teaching of physics and science in general than was possible for the typical school bound teacher. In this way they were undoubtedly an important evolutionary, if not a revolutionary, influence on physics teaching. On the other hand they were by background physicists and as such were often considered as reactionary by those wishing to move away from the teaching of separate sciences into integrated science. However, when students coming into PGCE courses had a single subject background, and when schools throughout the period were advertising for physics rather than science teachers, it was appropriate and responsible for the physics tutors to maintain such a supply as far as possible.

Throughout our period the physics tutor had been developing their courses to ensure that their physicists went into schools thinking of themselves as members of a science department, able to teach science to the 11–13s, physics throughout the school, and be part of a team working on balanced science courses. A survey carried out in 1980 (Woolnough 1980) showed that this was, in fact, what was required by the schools and the LEAs at that time. This survey was intended to find out whether what tutors in UDEs were aiming to do was in line with what the schools and LEAs thought they should be doing. Questionnaires were sent to each UDE, to all science advisers, to heads of science departments in four representative LEAs, and to probationer teachers. There was a remarkable, and encouraging, degree of agreement about both the preferred pattern for the course and what that course should be aiming to do. There was a clear majority support for a pattern of 'one main science course 11–16 plus a combined science course 11–13' from all of the groups, there was agreement from all of the groups about the most important skills that the student should acquire competence in (all agreed on the same seven, out of a possible twenty-seven, skills as being the most important), and there was agreement between both the providers and the consumers of the PGCE scientists that they should have a good appreciation of general issues like language skills and current curriculum developments rather than more erudite specialities such as the history and philosophy of science. Perhaps such agreement could be considered as showing the conservatism of physics, and other science, tutors. But as the survey was addressed to the leaders in the science teaching profession who were all trying to improve their professionalism of science teaching it could, and I believe should, be interpreted as a more positive indication that the physics tutors were being a constructive instrument of change.

Physics tutors are, and always have been, a collection of individual and individualistic people and as such have made idiosyncratic contributions. Though forming an association in 1968, ADEPT, they always prided themselves on its informality and lack of structure. It never had a constitution or membership fee, but provided the opportunity for all UDE tutors involved in physics education to meet annually, to share fellowship and experiences and to discuss matters of common concern in convivial circumstances. Though this provided a useful channel for cross-fertilization, there was never any intention of standardising practice or establishing a common policy — only once did it make a collective response to an official policy document when, in 1979 it responded, cautiously, to the DES Green Paper on *Science in Schools*. By the 1980s, however, it became clear that there were issues on which central government, as well as the ASE, was becoming more interventionist and that policy was being formed on which science educators in general were peculiarly well qualified to speak. After lobbying by the chemists of UCET, especially, and the biologists of UBET, the physicists of ADEPT were persuaded, in 1984, to join in a common association for tutors of all the sciences, ASET. It was ironic, and typically idiosyncratic, that ADEPT who had been so reluctant to merge into the one organization should provide both the first Chairman and the first Secretary of the newly-founded ASET, and insist on the continuing existence of ADEPT!

UDE physics tutors have been influential in the formation of policy and practice of many aspects of physics education. In the early sixties Henry Boulind (Cambridge) and Donald Scott (Bristol) were influential in the formation of the ASE policy statements of the time: Boulind and Wilfred Llowarch (London Institute) influential in the development of Nuffield 'O' level physics. Jon Ogborn and Paul Black (Chelsea College) along with their colleagues Bob Fairbrother and John Harris were central to the development of Nuffield 'A' level physics, with trialling, development and advisory work supported by Brian Chapman and Fred Archenhold (Leeds), Gron Jones (Cardiff) and Maurice Tebbutt (Birmingham). Fred Archenhold (Leeds) and Roy Schofield (Brunel) both held senior office in the ASE and were editors of *Physics Education*, Ros Driver (Leeds) was the Director of LAMP, on the APU team, and then Director of CLISP. Richard Hull (Nottingham) produced the ASE Studies in Decision Making for school INSET. Bill Wilkinson (Hull) was the founding editor of the *Journal for Science and Technology Education*. Many others have been involved with various committees of the Institute of Physics, the Royal Society, the examination boards and curriculum development. Others have been involved in influencing opinion through their writings. Perhaps it is also significant to note certain areas in which physics tutors have not been involved, in the ASE policy papers of the early eighties, in the development of SCISP or Nuffield Physical Science, or in the establishment of SSCR; it would be fair to say that physicists have not shown much stomach for getting involved with the integrated science movement of the seventies.

The involvement of these tutors with political decision making is allowed by their professional position, and their independence. They have had the very important role of interpreters of, and commentators on, policy. Because of their autonomy and freedom as university lecturers, they have had the opportunity of speaking and writing in a more detached and critical way on the policies and praxis in education. Undoubtedly, this has been done on a local scale in work with students, both at initial and post-experience training. There have been notable examples where they have expressed criticism publicly and through committees. It is probably true, however, that the majority of physics tutors, as of physics teachers, have been apolitical in their work and stayed apart from many of the important political power struggles that have permeated our period. As time has progressed, and central government especially has become more and more interventionist in the schooling of pupils, this unique and important freedom of the UDE physics tutors needs to be preserved and exercised.

References

BARTON, A.W. (1958), 'The supply of science teachers' in PERKINS, W.H. (Ed) *Science in Schools*, London, Butterworth, pp. 51–61.
BLIN-STOYLE, R.J. (1982), 'The role of a university science faculty' in JENNINGS, A. and INGLE, R. (eds) *Science Teachers for Tommorows Schools*, London, University of London Institute of Education, pp. 30–7.
CAWTHORNE, R.G. (1970) 'Teacher training for science and mathematics graduates', *Physics Education*, 5.1, p. 54.
CHAPMAN, B.R. (1980) 'Supply of physics teachers — into the 1980s, *Physics Education*, 15.4, pp, 136–45.
DES (1977) 'Percentage of all full time teachers with qualifications in named subject by age group, table TQ6', unpublished mimeo.
DES (1980), *Number of Maths and Science Graduates who have Entered Teaching via the Exemption from Training Rule*, DES figures on mimeoed sheets for UCET B on 9th May 1980, London, UCET.'
ELTON, L. (1982) 'Science teachers for tomorrows needs' in JENNINGS, A., and INGLE, R. (Eds) *Science Teachers for Tomorrows Schools*, London, University of London Institute of Education, pp. 38–46.
HAYSON, J.T. and SUTTON, C.R. (1974) *Science Teacher Education Project* (STEP) Maidenhead, McGraw Hill.
HOOPER, D. (1980) 'A national problem' *Physics Education*, 15, 5 pp. 217–9.
IoP, (1979), *Statistics Relating to Education and Physics*, London, Institute of Physics.
KIRKHAM, W.J. (1976) *The Supply of Science Teachers*, Hatfield, ASE.
MINISTRY OF EDUCATION (1961) *Education in 1960*, London, HMSO.
MOTT, N. (1969) *Shortage of Science and Maths Teachers in Schools*, London, Royal Society.
PERKINS, W.H. (1958) *Science in Schools*, London, Butterworth.
ROYAL SOCIETY (1969) *Swing away from Science in Schools*, London, Royal Society.
SLADE, J.A. (1981) *The Supply and Training of Science Teachers*, Hatfield, ASE.
THOMPSON, N. (1981) *Shortage of Physics Teachers*, London, Royal Society/Institute of Physics.
WOOLNOUGH, B.E. (1980) 'The training of science teachers — perceptions of providers and consumers', *Education in Science*, 90, pp. 27–30.

4   'Streams in the desert' — The New Courses

Before the Curriculum Revolution

Perhaps the most pronounced change in physics teaching over our twenty-five years has been the change brought about by the 'curriculum revolution'. In the majority of schools of 1960, the content of the physics being taught was a matter of little debate; it was what had been taught for many years. The fact that it was basically the same as that taught by their fathers, even their grandfathers, would have been considered a virtue rather than a vice. It is true that some of the more intellectual of the physics teachers would argue passionately about the finer points of physics and some of the more creative would be devising ingenious pieces of apparatus to demonstrate specific aspects of physics. It is also true that many of the physics teachers were very able men who had entered teaching during the depression of the thirties or had entered teaching after stimulating and maturing experiences during the war. But in an expanding educational system, such critical teachers were in short supply, made even shorter by the demands for physicists made by a voraciously growing electronic, industrial society. In a stable, still conservative, society the majority of teachers were content to teach the well established syllabuses from text books written by well respected authors such as Noakes, Nelkon, Nightingale and McKenzie. It was, indeed, the text books which determined the syllabuses and these in turn were matched very closely to the external GCE exams that the pupils would be taking. Ideas and innovations would be disseminated by the SMA, through their journal *SSR* and their annual conferences, and by the Ministry of Education and the Inspectorate through their courses and their periodic publications. But, stimulating though such initiatives were, they were essentially refining the trimmings with the majority of the teaching force content with the basic structure of their syllabuses. The curriculum revolution that was about to hit the educational scene would disturb such complacency for good.

Though there was an apparent sense of calm and continuity about the physics curriculum in 1960, there were three strands which had been developing through the late fifties in which the subsequent developments in the sixties had their genesis. First there was a growing sense of unease among influential people in different walks of society that all was not well with science teaching in schools. There was a growing demand from society that the country must produce scientists at a far greater rate to cope with the expanding industrial opportunities; Sir Solly Zuckerman said in 1958, for instance, that the annual output of science and engineering graduates must rise from 12,000 to 20,000 in the next ten years (Perkins, 1960, p. 11). There was also a widespread belief that schools were not providing an adequate basis for this growth. Many of these concerns were articulated in an important conference held in 1958 on Science in Schools under the auspices of the British Association for the Advancement of Science (Perkins, 1958). Similarly the Royal Society, the professional institutions, the Nuffield Foundation, as well as politicians and professional scientists in industry and the universities were sharing a growing concern with some of the more senior science teachers in the Science Masters Association and HMI. In 1955, an industrial fund had been set up to give grants for building and equipping laboratories for physics and chemistry teaching in the independent and direct grant grammar schools. By the time it finished in 1963 it had contributed over £3 million, a very significant amount and more than the entire cost of the Nuffield projects (Industrial Fund, 1963). It was hoped that the government would provide similar funding for the maintained schools, but such was not forthcoming. Sir Graham Savage, the Chief Assessor to the Industrial Fund, reminiscing in 1968 said that 'The Minister said, at the time, "you do that and we will look after the others." He never did and neither have his successors. As a result science teachers just cannot cope with the handicaps' (Schofield and Harding, 1968).

Second, there was the growing activity of the SMA and the AWST which lead to the flurry of working parties and reports reviewing the way that science and the separate sciences should be taught. And third, there were the developments in ways of teaching physics being developed in other countries; in particular in the USA who were producing the PSSC physics (started in 1956, trialled in 908 schools with 27,800 students before being published in 1960), in Germany where new ways of teaching atomic physics were being developed, and in Scotland where they were revising their science syllabuses. All of these factors were influential in the formation of that most remarkable, most radical, and in a real sense most revolutionary of curriculum initiatives; the science teaching projects set up by the Nuffield Foundation. And that is where our story starts.

Out of SMA and into Nuffield

Others (Clark, 1972) have detailed the historical development of the Nuffield Foundation, and its involvement with science education (Waring, 1979; Ingle and Jennings, 1981; and Layton, 1984). I would especially acknowledge the excellent works of David Layton and Mary Waring and my indebtedness to them. The review that follows will not seek to emulate or repeat their work (to which readers are directed for a fuller analysis) but will trace the lineage of the Nuffield 'O' level physics through those aspects of relevance to us; through the SMA committee structure and the outworkings of their policies; and through the involvement of specific people, in particular John Lewis.

Though it is an arbitrary decision as to when and where a particular story starts, there are good reasons for choosing 1956 and the UNESCO conference in Hamburg. This conference was to discuss the science curricular in primary and secondary schools, and was attended by Dr Henry Boulind in his capacity as General Secretary of the SMA. Henry Boulind was a quiet, industrious, able physicist with an appetite and capacity for committee work. He was a man of vision who had great influence on subsequent developments through persistent, behind the scenes, paper work rather than charismatic personality. He was employed as a physics tutor at the Department of Education, University of Cambridge and was doing SMA work in his 'spare time'. In 1957 he reported back to the SMA the conviction that he had gained from the Hamburg conference: that all pupils should know about atomic energy and that the thrust in teaching science in general, and physics in particular, should be education in and through science rather than merely the teaching of science. This led, in 1957, to the SMA setting up the Science Teaching Sub-committee under the chairmanship of Henry Boulind, later to be renamed the Science and Education Sub-committee, with terms of reference 'to enquire into the aims, scope and content of science teaching in grammar (sic) schools, with special reference to the part that science can play in general education' (in Layton, 1984, p. 233). In effect, as Layton says, 'their purpose was altogether more ambitious than anything the Association had attempted previously. It was nothing less than to redefine fundamentally school science education, ... and having formulated new aims and syllabuses, to secure their widespread adoption by the exercise of persuasion and influence' (*Ibid*, p. 234). At this stage the Association was putting itself forward as the body with the power and responsibility to determine the school science curriculum; a power-bid which, at the time, appeared to have no competition. This small, but highly influential, committee of seven included two other well established physicists, H.F. Broad, then Head of The Cedars School in Leighton Buzzard, and H. Tunley from Merchant Taylors School in Liverpool, as well as the chemist E.H. Coulson, then at Braintree County High School in Essex, and the biologist W.H. Dowdeswell, teaching at Winchester College. Both were subsequently to play central roles in the development of Nuffield Chemistry and Biology. The Sub-committee set up four subject panels to develop new syllabuses for use in grammar schools at both 'O' and 'A' level for the three separate sciences and general science, with the physics panel chaired by Harold Tunley. The panel was a strong one and, though predominately made up of school science teachers, was strengthened by Professor Henry Lipson, FRS, Norman Clarke of the Institute of Physics and Dr (later Professor) Lewis Elton. Also invited to join the panel was a young, 33-year-old physics teacher from Malvern College called John Lewis. The panel worked hard and harmoniously, often throughout weekends in the congenial atmosphere of Malvern, and produced the draft of their report by 1960. The panel had been able to disregard the traditional pattern of physics syllabuses, on the whole a miscellaneous collection grouped together under heat, light and sound etc, and had built up the syllabus around more general themes such as properties of solids and fluids, vibrations and waves, and — of course — atomic structure and nuclear energy. By 1960 the physics syllabus, along with that for chemistry and biology, was ready to seek the approval of the Secondary Schools Examination Council, the body which needed to approve all new GCE syllabuses, and a weekend meeting was held at Studley Court in December 1960 with the ASE, members of the subject panels, and representatives from the Ministry of Education and the Inspectorate. Though the syllabuses for chemistry and biology were found acceptable, and most of the physics syllabus, the section on modern physics was strongly attacked by the Staff Inspector for Science, Dr R.A.R. Tricker. Dr Tricker's criticism, though deeply resented by the physics panel at the time, was to prove of fundamental importance for the development of the subsequent Nuffield courses. His criticism was essentially that, as it stood, the atomic structure and nuclear energy section would, inevitably, lead to a totally didactic way of teaching. In concentrating so much on getting the content right, the physics panel had omitted to give sufficient thought to how it should be taught.

Dr Tricker was a very perceptive, far seeing, physicist who, as SI for Science, had been responsible for inspiring many young science teachers through his Ministry of Education/HMI courses. These courses, which included astronomy, geology and ecology, along with social and environmental considerations, were quite different from any others with their strongly integrated theme and heavy emphasis on science teaching in schools being done practically. To this end he used experienced science teachers to show other teachers the experimental and demonstration work that they were doing in their own schools. He had been responsible for writing the splendid HMI report of *Science in Secondary Schools* (HMI, 1960) which even twenty-five years later has a progressive ring about it. In this report he advocated that all pupils in learning science should have experience of doing their own investigational practical work, rather than just repeating the teachers exercises. He was highly critical of much current practice and advocated a strongly child-centred approach to science teaching which went even further than the Nuffield 'O' level was to do. His ideas have, however, been picked up more fully by the investigations in the Nuffield secondary science course (1971), in the 'A' level physics (1973), in the APU (1982) and even the DES policy statement of 1985. In retrospect, many of the curriculum innovators have expressed their gratitude for the rigorous, perceptive inspiration of Dr Tricker in influencing their own thinking about teaching methods, though he, as so many other of the HMI, have not got the public credit that they deserve.

However it was not just the Tricker criticism that came out of that momentous weekend at Studley Court. It was clear that many of the ideas in the physics syllabus were quite new and needed trialling, and so the Studley experiment was set up to try out the new material in thirty schools throughout the country. Though subsequent trialling of material was to be done on a much larger scale, this was at the time a radical initiative in teacher training and curriculum development. It was clear that much more work needed to be done on the different syllabuses and, shortly after the Studley conference John Lewis was invited to convene and chair a new sub-committee on the use of atomic and nuclear science in teaching physics and chemistry, soon to be renamed the Sub-committee on the Teaching of Modern Physical Science (in 1961) and the Physical Science Apparatus Committee from 1966. The group of teachers working together in this sub-committee were to play a central role in the subsequent Nuffield physics teams. It was while working together here that Henry Boulind, Jack Goodier, Martin Harrap, Wilf Llowarch, John Osborne, Sister St Joan, Ted Wenham and John Lewis built up the relationships which were to become the heart of the subsequent work for Nuffield.

Less than a year after Studley, the Science and Education Committee met again to assess progress and explore possibilities. They met for a week at the end of August 1961 at Barrow Court, a gracious manor house just outside Bristol, and invited to join them not only representatives from the separate subject panels but also members of the Inspectorate, from the Ministry of Education, and representatives from the Royal Institute of Chemistry and the Institute of Physics. In all there were thirty-three members present, with a strong preponderance of physicists and chemists from boys independent schools. This bias reflected the composition of the Planning Committee which, under the chairmanship of Henry Boulind, contained seven other physicists and five chemists. The dearth of biologists indicated the relatively weak position of the subject in schools, especially in the boys independent and grammar schools which dominated the Association at the time. It was clear that a lot of work had already been done by the committees and the panels in establishing policy and syllabus guidelines, work done in a typically English way, on a shoe string, late at night, over the weekends, on top of each contributor's normal full-time job. It was also clear that there was an enormous amount still to do and that existing resources would not suffice. Now it was evident that what was needed was a full-scale, nationwide, curriculum development and dissemination programme for science. By the end of the week it was agreed that external financial help should be sought in order to 'produce teachers guides, to provide in-service courses for teachers, and to establish a centre or research institute where apparatus could be developed and teaching techniques evaluated' (Layton, 1984, p. 241).

In the five years since Hamburg, the aims, activities and sheer professionalism of the Association had grown enormously. It was clear that the Association was now in the market to revise and direct science teaching throughout schools, and felt itself confident to do it. It had just moved into a new headquarters building in Cambridge and had appointed Bill Tapper to be its first full-time, salaried officer as General Secretary. The Association was seeing itself as the organization with the authority and the expertise to direct and control the science curriculum and, as it made this overt power bid, there appeared to be little alternative in the field. In optimistic and imperious mood it determined to find money to develop its plans. It was agreed that different exploratory approaches should be made, to the government, to charitable foundations and to industries. Henry Boulind, who had done so much to bring the developments to their present stage, was to make the initial contact with Sir Alexander Todd, Chairman of the Advisory Council on Scientific Policy. Subsequently contacts would be made to various charities which led, ultimately, to a positive response from the Nuffield Foundation. It was always assumed that if and when the money was found for the further development of the science teaching schemes, then the control of such work would naturally revert to the Association who had done so much preliminary development work through its various committees. It came as a considerable shock, and one which caused no little long-term bitterness, when the Nuffield Foundation having decided to provide the money for such a science teaching project, also decided to keep direct control of the project (ASE, 1966, pp. 11–12).

So we have seen how by 1961 the SMA had put forward firm proposals for curriculum review. Through conferences, committees, and sub-committees, through many hours of formal and informal debate and through many draft papers, policy statements and reports, an enormous amount of progress had been made in a short time. But alongside this organizational growth there had been another development, in the thinking of many physicists (and chemists) teaching in the strong independent and grammar schools and in the formation of networks of people who were enjoying the stimulation of working together. Nowhere is this better illustrated than through John Lewis, and it is to his involvement with the physics scene that we will look now.

John Lewis

Mention of John Lewis' contribution to the development of the Nuffield 'O' level physics course merits telling both for its own sake, for his contribution both to this initiative and many subsequent ones was fundamental and unique, and also because he exemplifies the type of physics teacher which was so influential in developing physics teaching through the sixties. He was the archetypal Nuffield physicist!

John Lewis was, above all, an enthusiast with a love for physics, for doing physics and for teaching physics, which was infectious. Born in 1923 he grew up in a happy, stable, prosperous, middle-class family. He enjoyed his schooling, which from the age of 8 was spent in prep and public boarding schools culminating at Malvern College, from which he gained a love of maths and physics and an open scholarship to Pembroke College, Cambridge. When Malvern College was evacuated to Blenheim Palace during the Second World War, he was also able to absorb something of the atmosphere and traditions of the Duke of Marlborough as he lived in such grand and gracious surroundings. His time at Cambridge was split into two phases, from 1942–44 and from 1947–49, with two years in between spent at the Tank Armament Research at Porton. He was appointed as a physics master at his old school, Malvern College, in 1946, whence he became Senior Science Master in 1955 and a Housemaster in 1961. Malvern was able to give him considerable freedom and support to pursue his interests as he played his full part in the life of the College. This support released him to complete his studies at Cambridge and subsequently to spend time working on the Nuffield project. It also enabled him to use Malvern as the base for entertaining individuals, working parties and conferences in a style that was persuasively congenial in eliciting reciprocal dedication and commitment from others.

His early years of teaching at Malvern were characterized by two elements. On the one hand sound, successful, traditional teaching of physics to students who wished to pass 'O', 'A' and university entrance exams and on the other hand a personal involvement with his own scientific interests, astronomy and radioactivity. During the period 1955–61, he was carrying out his own original researches into the properties of α, β, and γ radiation using a phial of radium that had been in the school since, at least, the 1920s. These researches brought him into contact with other scientists and were to be influential in subsequent developments in physics syllabuses. He was one of the band of physics teachers (men like Wilfred Llowarch, John Osborne, Geoff Foxcroft and David Chaundy) who were themselves good scientists and were able to use the facilities in physics teaching to enable them to fulfil their scientific curiosity. They were subsequently to use these talents in curriculum development.

There were, however, other more personal influences developing through the fifties. Partly through contacts made at Dr Tricker's Ministry of Education training courses and partly through meeting other heads of science departments at the SMA meetings, a friendship grew up between many like-minded teachers; a personal and professional friendship strengthened by the formation in 1959 of the *'59 Club*, at which heads of science from different public schools met regularly to dine and discuss issues of common concern. In these days, when formal channels of communication were weak and individual science teachers were working in isolation in their schools, such informal links were important.

In 1957 John Lewis, still a young man, was invited to join the illustrious and experienced group of physics teachers and physicists on the SMA's new physics panel, an invitation probably effected by Sir Graham Savage who had been impressed by his work through visiting the College as Assessor for the Industrial Fund. John Lewis' main contribution at this stage was through the modern physics material, and also in hosting the panel at Malvern for their intensive weekend panel meetings. When, after the draft reports of the panel were presented at the Studley weekend in 1960, it became clear that more work needed to be done on devising experimental work necessary for the teaching of modern physical science, it was natural for the SMA to invite John Lewis to convene and direct the new Sub-committee. He had a free hand in selecting membership for this and was able to involve the Inspectorate through Dr Tricker and Dick Long, the highly experienced and inventive Wilfred Llowarch, as well as the new generation of young physicists including Ted Wenham (Worcester College of Education), John Osborne (Westminster School), Michael Smith (Kings College School, Wimbledon) and, later, David Chaundy (Malvern) and Geoffrey Foxcroft (Rugby School). This group, apart from introducing a whole range of apparatus to study radioactivity, (gold leaf electroscopes, cloud and diffusion chambers, spinthariscopes, pulse electroscopes, spark and geiger counters), was important in the activities of the Studley experiment and subsequently the Nuffield 'O' level physics itself.

Also in 1960, John Lewis was invited to speak at a Shell conference for science teachers on ways of teaching modern physics, and to demonstrate the equipment and experiments he had devised. This he did with great style and conviction, and made such a good impression on the Shell management that they agreed to pay for him to travel in the USA in the summer holiday to see how science was being taught there. That experience was to be, in his own words, 'a turning point' for him. He found that the Americans (in the PSSC) were searching for solutions to problems that he did not even know existed. Previously he had been thinking of curriculum reform solely in terms of 'content', what should be taught, and not about the methods of teaching and 'process'. Indeed such would probably have been true of all the teachers on the modern physics group, teachers who were recruited for their expertise in physics rather than in education. Having been so stimulated by the American trip, John Lewis resolved to gain experience from other countries too. He persuaded, first, Malvern College to give him leave of absence for a term and then the Goldsmiths Company to give him a travelling scholarship to visit Germany and Russia in the Easter term of 1961 to see how they taught their physics. He returned from this trip inspired by two factors, the excellence of the demonstration apparatus used in Germany that had been produced by Leybold and Phywe, and the consistent standard of the physics teaching in Russia: 'I must have sat through fifty or sixty lessons and the remarkable thing was that although I saw plenty of dull teachers I never saw a dull lesson'. He was immensely impressed with the structure and organization provided for the Russian teachers to guide and support them, and this was to influence the packaging of the Nuffield project later.

It was also the message that John Lewis enthused to Leslie Farrer-Brown, the Director of the Nuffield Foundation, when he dined with him at Nuffield Lodge soon after his return from Russia in the autumn of 1961. This meal was to prove important for future developments for, in the words of the Nuffield Foundation's biographer, 'The dinner party happened to crystalize the ideas of the trustees and of the Director. But there were other factors at work, notably the enthusiasm of John Lewis, the Senior Science Master at Malvern' (Clark, 1972, p. 171). John Lewis had known Leslie Farrer-Brown since 1953 when he had entertained the Malvern Swordsmen, (a folk dancing club formed by John Lewis and including Geoffrey Farrer-Brown the then Headboy and son of Leslie) to a farewell dinner at Nuffield Lodge before going on an international tour.

I have deliberately spelt-out the background of John Lewis to illustrate the humanity and interpersonal relationships which were so important in the development of Nuffield. In John Lewis, as for so many others in this group, we had enthusiastic, creative, immensely industrious young physicists working together to improve physics teaching because they enjoyed working together. It was, as John Lewis would say, 'great fun'. These were days when teachers were not concerned with behavioural objectives and educational theory; they were not concerned with power struggles, sociologists had barely raised such issues and to teach in a public school was never considered an elitist activity. They enjoyed their physics and they endeavoured to find ways so that their pupils, all pupils, would enjoy it too. The educational world was so much more straightforward and uncomplicated in 1960. It was a human world where friendship, idealism and fun were not incompatible with seeking to make the world a better place for all.

And so we have, in 1961, the Nuffield Foundation under the directorship of Dr Leslie Farrer-Brown, becoming seriously concerned about whether and how it could help improve school science teaching. The Foundation, founded in 1943 on the income from ten million 5s. shares, had a tradition of risk-taking, pump-priming initiatives to 'give support where government either feared or had no reason to give it' (Clark, 1972, pp. 168–73). It worked on the principle of recognizing the need, finding the right man for the job, and giving him freedom to work out the solution as he saw fit. There had been little involvement with education before, the majority of its projects had been in medicine. Through the late fifties, however, discussions with Sir Lawrence Bragg, then of the Royal Institution, with Peter Rowntree concerned about the secondary modern pupil, with Sir Nevill Mott representing the Royal Society and with Norman Clarke of the Institute of Physics, as well as with John Lewis, had made Farrer-Brown aware of the needs of secondary school science teaching. And so, when in the autumn of 1961 the ASE approached the Nuffield Foundation for funding of the proposals that had developed from the Barrow Court discussion, Farrer-Brown had already become convinced of the case. At a time when the total national expenditure on educational research and experiment was estimated at £125,000 (Clark, 1972, p. 164) it was clear that the expanding coffers of the Nuffield Foundation might be able to make a significant contribution — in the event it allocated £250,000, to be increased to £430,000 by 1965 (Lewis, 1965, p. 83). The only question remained whether it should give the money to the SMA to use through its growing committee structures, or whether it should stick to its normal practice and, while keeping overall control to itself, find 'the right man for the job' and give him his head. In the event, there was never any doubt and in December 1961 Farrer-Brown and the trustees of the Foundation set about finding the right people to head up the consultative committees and to direct the projects in each of the three sciences.

The Formation of the Nuffield 'O' Level Physics Project

So, in early 1962, the Nuffield Science Project got underway, with physics being the first to be established. After consultation with, among others, the National Committee on Physics Teaching, the Scottish Advisory Committee on Physics Teaching and the Ministry of Education, the Nuffield Foundation appointed Professor Nevill Mott, then the Cavendish Professor of Physics at Cambridge, as Chairman of the Physics Consultative Committee. Nevill Mott had already been very influential in physics education, both directly as a brilliant theoretical physicist and indirectly as he had organized the physics community to concern itself with the education of physicists in schools and universities (see chapter 5). He was to continue his involvement in physics education over the next two decades and was one of the most influential men in physics education throughout our period. He had grown up in a home where education in its widest sense was respected. Indeed his father was the Director of Education in Liverpool and the founder of the C.F. Mott College for Teacher Training there, and this had clearly determined his commitment and concern for the education of all children. Also on the Physics Consultative Committee were, representing higher education, Professor C.C. Butler from the Royal Society, Norman Clarke from the Institute of Physics and Professor R.V. Jones, and John Lewis and Sister St Joan representing the schools. This Committee was later to be reinforced by the school teachers Wilf Mace and John Osborne, and a Scottish HMI called Donald McGill who had been revising the physics syllabuses in Scotland. On the 1 May 1962, Donald McGill was appointed as organizer of the physics project, a project which all concerned were resolved should be directed at producing a 'physics for all', a 'physics for the educated citizen'. Donald McGill was another of the tradition of excellent scientists who had become involved in school physics after a successful academic career. A pupil at Tynemouth Grammar School he went on to study physics at Kings College, Newcastle, where he did research on the molecular spectrum of iodine. In 1936, at the age of 26, he left university to teach at Shipley, Yorkshire, where the effects of the depression were still in evidence. During the Second World War he worked at the Admiralty as a Senior Scientific Officer, and on leaving there took up a post as lecturer at the University of Bristol, where he worked in the H.H. Wills labs under Professor Nevill Mott — and established a friendship which was to be renewed through the Nuffield physics project. While at Bristol he became increasingly aware that the deficiencies in his students could only be remedied by an improvement of physics teaching at the school level and so, after six years at Bristol, he returned to school teaching in 1951 — first at Bradford Grammar School and then Glasgow Academy. In 1959 he joined the Scottish Education Department as an HMI, from where he was seconded to the Nuffield Foundation. In Scotland he had embarked on the task of revising the traditional, formal, physics course and replacing it with a liberal and modern, practical, course. He had introduced a way of working with groups of local teachers to pilot trial material in the schools and produced the new alternative 'O' grade syllabus which was to be introduced throughout Scotland in 1963 (Scottish Education Department, 1963). The experience gained in this scheme, both in the curriculum development and the way of working, was to prove an invaluable grounding for the Nuffield work to follow. Indeed it was vital for, by the time of Donald McGill's tragic death on 22 March 1963, less than a year after his appointment, he had laid the foundations for the whole physics programme, built up the team, engendered its splendid *esprit de corps*, and established the principle of involving practising teachers in all stages of development and evaluation. Under his wise, perceptive and sensitive guidance he had started the project on its way and laid its foundation with such surety that even some of the traumas that were to follow could not disturb. He was not a charismatic leader, but a very thoughtful, perceptive, industrious man with the gift of being able to elicit a similar dedication, commitment and trust from others. Perhaps the comments of two of his closest associates, John Lewis and Ted Wenham, sum up some of his strengths: 'he was a "good man", people liked him and worked well for him', his death was 'a grievous blow; the enterprise had lost a brilliant and most capable leader; the members of his team had lost a friend' (Wenham, 1967, p. 339).

The pattern of working of the Nuffield physics enterprise has been written up elsewhere by those most intimately involved (Lewis, 1965; Maddox, 1966; Wenham, 1967; and Lewis and Foxcroft, 1978). The enterprise could build on the experience of the Scots and the invaluable work of the SMA's Teaching of Modern Physical Science Committee, and in many ways was a natural development of these two initiatives. Nine regional teams were set up, each to develop the material for a particular theme. Each team consisted of six to twelve local teachers who would develop trial material. The leaders of these teams came largely from the SMA Sub-committee and had been working together on these ideas for some time; Sister St Joan (La Retraite School, Bristol), Jack Goodier (Eton), John Osborne (Westminster School), John Lewis and David Chaundy (Malvern College), Roger Stone (Manchester Grammar School), Geoffrey Foxcroft (Rugby School), Ted Wenham (Worcester College of Education),

Maurice Elwell (Birmingham College of Education), and Bill Richie and Jim Jardine from Scotland. Henry Boulind was to head the group developing the examination work. During the autumn and winter of 1962–63 the teacher teams met frequently, and the team leaders met with the Consultative Committee to produce draft material. By February 1963 the third draft of the whole scheme had been produced. The plan was that the development should take place in three phases: 1963–64 preliminary trials of materials in schools; 1964–65 full trials of materials up to 'O' level; 1965–66 feedback, modification and writing up of teacher books. It was a scheme produced by teachers, trialled by teachers, to be used by teachers. More than fifty schools were involved in different aspects of the trials, mainly grammar schools but including some independent, some secondary modern and, even, a comprehensive school. Though more would have liked to have been involved, or even to have been kept informed of what was going on, it was decided (perhaps unwisely?) to keep the enterprise on a limited, private level to prevent too much distortion and misrepresentation of the trial material taking place before publication. It was an ambitious plan, charting untried country in England, and one made all the more difficult by the change of leadership of the project necessitated in the spring of 1963. It speaks much for the effort, enthusiasm and professionalism of all those involved that this tight schedule was kept to, even if rather frenetically at times!

Under New Leadership

On the death of Donald McGill it was necessary to appoint a new leader for the team, and hurried soundings were taken. John Lewis, himself, was still not prepared to take on the leadership because of his commitments as a Housemaster at Malvern College, though he was prepared to act as joint organizer with Eric Rogers. Professor Eric Rogers had been very much involved with the development of the PSSC scheme in America through the late fifties and had been recognized as one of the four 'major creators and selectors of material at every point' (PSSC, 1960, p. 643). He had recently had published the brilliant, monumental work *Physics for the Enquiring Mind* (Rogers, 1960), a book which had been used as briefing material for the Nuffield team, as had the PSSC material. He was well-known for his interest in, and enthusiasm for, school physics teaching. In 1962 he was in England, on sabbatical leave from his post as physics professor at Princeton University, and had visited the early meetings of the Nuffield team first by invitation and then as a consultant. Consequently he had been fully involved with the enterprise when he was sounded out about his willingness to take a more leading role in its organization. In the event, he was only willing to take a leading role if he was given sole responsibility and so he was appointed organizer of the project with John Lewis as associate organizer. Later this arrangement was reinforced with the appointment of Ted Wenham as a second associate organizer and D.W. Harding as assistant organizer.

Eric Rogers was in personality and leadership style a complete contrast to his predecessor. A highly creative, mercurial, restless man he had an unbounded enthusiasm for doing physics and a deep belief that all educated people needed some lasting understanding of physics. He had a boyish genius which was, at the same time, stimulating and frustrating to work with. He had studied physics at Cambridge in the early twenties under Professor J.J. Thomson where he obtained a first class degree (at the same time as his Cambridge contemporary Wilfred Llowarch who had been influential in the work of the SMA Modern Physical Science Committee that had led into the Nuffield Science Teaching Project). After leaving Cambridge, he taught at Clifton College, at his old school Bedales, and Charterhouse School, before going to teach in America finishing as professor of physics at Princeton University. There he had been very concerned with teaching physics as a liberal art to the non-scientists at the University, and this had produced the basis for his 780 page *magnum opus*, *Physics for the Enquiring Mind*, which contained so much innovative material that was to prove stimulating for many a future physics teacher and student. His distinction as a creative physicist carried conviction, but his idiosyncrasies and single-mindedness were to produce a certain tension throughout the team during the development and the rewriting period. However, the foundations had been firmly laid by Donald McGill and the programme continued along those guidelines. Mary Waring, writing especially in the context of the Nuffield chemistry project, spoke of the importance of 'complementarity' in the function of the different members of the leadership team; she writes that 'linking a man of ideas with a sensitive, but essentially practical, deputy may be crucial to success' (Waring, 1979, p. 92). Nowhere was this more true or necessary than in the case of the physics project for (while in no way denying that they were also 'men of ideas') it was the sensitivity and practicality of Ted Wenham and John Lewis that enabled the individualism of Eric Rogers to be utilized constructively.

And so in 1966, after four years of intensive development, trialling, evaluating and rewriting of curriculum material on a scale never previously contemplated in England (and which had already cost the Nuffield Foundation £430,000), the three 'O' level projects were launched; first, chemistry and biology, soon to be followed by physics, which had been delayed because of its own peculiar problems.

The product of these years of work were disseminated through three main channels: publications, apparatus and intensive in-service training by LEAs and charismatic proponents. The physics scheme was written up in three ways, each producing a book for each year. There were five teachers guides, five guides to experiments, and five question books (Rogers, 1966). Apart from the books of questions there were to be no books for the pupils, it was believed that 'a text book in the conventional sense is not really compatible with the suggested methods, which encourage the pupils to find out for themselves. A conventional textbook gives away the answers beforehand' (Lewis, 1965, p. 92). The main thrust of the course was written out in the teachers guides, and it was here that Eric Rogers sought to talk directly to the teachers. They contained important passages on teaching physics for understanding, and on the role of examinations, and gave explicit suggestions as to how the different experiments might be taught. They continually suggested that it was the approach, rather than the content that was important, and that the topics and experiments suggested did not constitute a syllabus but were merely suggestions. It was very unfortunate that these guides came out in such a wordy, repetitive and at times patronizing style. The component parts, developed by the different groups, had clearly been put together in a great hurry (it was said that Eric Rogers wrote them all in a concentrated six-week spell), and the final products made very heavy, rather unstructured, reading. It demanded a great deal of commitment and perseverence for teachers to read them all through, in the event the vast majority of teachers did not, but resorted to the much more tightly structured guides to experiments which busy teachers found much more easy to manage. Writing before the books had been published in their final form Duff worried that teachers would use the 'excellent in every respect' experiment guides rather than the 'woolly, obscure, too long' teachers guides. The former being used without the latter having been digested would produce teaching in which much of the essential approach would be lost' (Duff, 1966, p. 13).

Unfortunately, this prediction was to prove true for many teachers who saw Nuffield physics merely in terms of a series of experiments and demonstrations to be done, without sharing the philosophy and rationale of the authors. For some, the guides to experiment became the new Nuffield Bible, one book for each year, whose authority was never to be questioned, saving the teachers the task of thinking and rethinking their own best ways of teaching. The series of question books, developed by Henry Boulind and his Cambridge group was an important and innovative venture forcing, as they did, both pupils and teachers to engage personally with problems in physics. They provided a stimulating challenge, to teachers as well as pupils as the ensuing debates in many a science prep room about 'the right answer' demonstrated. They went a long way to loosening the stereotype of questioning and examining in which only the 'right answer', rather than valid reasoning, was recognized. These books make a fitting memorial to Henry Boulind who, after many years of dedicated and faithful service to the science teaching profession, died in 1970 soon after their publication.

Alongside the books for teachers went a vast range of new pieces of apparatus for demonstration and pupil experiment, even kits of apparatus produced for whole class work. The apparatus manufacturers, especially Philip Harris, had played a very important role in supporting, developing, and manufacturing prototypes of equipment to the often demanding specifications of the physics teams. Their commitment to the project proved invaluable and the investment that they had put in, in faith, through the early sixties was appropriately rewarded by enormous sales to the schools in the following decade. Physics teachers, always susceptible to the temptation of playing with new 'toys' were readily persuaded to buy vast amounts of new Nuffield apparatus as it was excitingly advertised through the journals and the annual, entertaining 'Lewis/Wenham/Foxcroft' roadshow at the ASE conferences. In a real sense we had curriculum dissemination through apparatus.

Dissemination of the new project was effected through ASE meetings at local and national levels, through the initial training of teachers, and through LEA and DES-sponsored INSET. John Lewis, Ted Wenham, Geoffrey Foxcroft and other members of the development gave countless talks and demonstrations throughout the country and by their enthusiasm and personal conviction persuaded many physics teachers of the value of the experiments and the validity of the Nuffield philosophy. The significance of the personal charisma, commitment and energy of these evangelists from the Nuffield team in selling the new scheme to the profession cannot be over-emphasized.

The Impact of Nuffield

I have discussed the development of Nuffield 'O' level physics in some depth because of its considerable, innovative importance. Even after twenty-five years, it is difficult to realize quite how radical, how far-reaching, was the effect of this first, unique project in large-scale curriculum development. Never before in this country had anything been attempted on this scale; there were no guidelines or precedents to follow, and those involved were very much 'flying by the seats of their pants'. The Nuffield Foundation had appointed leaders in whom they had confidence and had given them their heads with almost a blank cheque. They developed their own frame work as they progressed. Though they did have a Consultative

Committee behind them they were, in the words of Professor Mott, the Chairman of the Committee, 'not very directive, . . . but very much in the hands of the school physics teachers' who decided what they would do and what was likely to be acceptable to the pupils.

In hindsight, it is easy to point out the limitations of the Nuffield 'O' level scheme, and after a honeymoon period of about twelve years in which it was considered heresy to publicly criticize Nuffield physics it became equally fashionable, in the next decade to attack it. But the project did produce a sea-change both in physics teaching and in curriculum development, in both areas things would never be the same again. There were those in the ASE, soured by not being given responsibility for directing the project and suspicious of the secrecy surrounding the development of the trial material, who greeted the launch of Nuffield with hostility. The editor of *Education in Science*, the house journal of the ASE, writing a very cool appraisal of the situation in April 1966, wondered 'if there is anything in Nuffield at all'. He asserted that 'there seems to be no statement anywhere as to what the whole scheme is about', and warned of the dangers of 'jumping on the bandwagon' before being prepared in resources and shared ideals for the introduction of such a radical approach (ASE, 1966, p. 11). But for most the bandwagon was rolling fast, and few would, or perhaps should, question the purple prose of John Maddox, then Director of the Nuffield Foundation, when he wrote 'It is also a model of how a self-conscious and deliberate innovation can be carried out within the curriculum; of how apparently outrageous and daring ideas can be made into a workable programme of teaching in the ordinary classroom; of how examinations at 'O' level can be matched accurately to a new teaching programme; and of how the process of change can be made so intimately to involve working teachers that in some real sense the curriculum becomes the possession of the schools and not some treadmill upon which they must struggle for survival' (Maddox, 1966, p. 3).

In the same article, John Maddox spoke of the 'small band of men' (sic!) responsible for the development of the scheme, and it is to these people that the success, and limitations, of Nuffield physics must be ascribed. Though they spoke with pride of their being school teachers, often 'mere schoolteachers', they were in fact a very remarkable and outstanding group of scientists who were, fortuitously, in school physics teaching at that time, or had only recently left it. They were men and women of unusual ability and creativity who committed an enormous amount of their time and effort to turning their physics into a teaching scheme for others. Some had entered teaching in the depression of the thirties, others after having gained formative experience of research or active service during the war years. History had combined to produce a high quality cadre of physics teachers, first rate

101

scientists in their own right, who were in their prime and teaching in the grammar and public schools of the early sixties ready for new challenges. It is unlikely that school teaching would be able again to collect together a team of such intrinsic quality as was found in the Nuffield teams of McGill, Rogers, Lewis, Wenham, Foxcroft, Osborne, Sister St Joan, Long, Llowarch, Goodier, Boulind, Layton, Jardine, Elwell, Chaundy, Stone, Harrison, Archenhold, Chapman, Mace, etc. They were innovators in an age of innocence. They were all grounded in the grammar and public school system, (indeed there were very few graduate physics teachers and very little academic physics taught in the secondary modern schools of the time), and consequently they naturally thought of physics teaching in terms of the more able pupils. No-one, at the time, would have suggested otherwise nor suggested that such direction had any political significance. Sociologists barely existed and had certainly not started marking out the school curriculum as an area for political battle.

But, unconsciously, the Nuffield project gave legitimization and reinforcement to academic, knowledge centred, grammar school physics as being what physics teaching should be about; initially for the more able 20 per cent but later, through its association with high-status learning, across the whole ability range. It reflected a view of learning physics which was essentially cultural, what every educated 16-year-old should know about physics and the way that physicists work. It reflected the mood of a general, liberal, education for all. Norman Clarke, writing on behalf of the Institute of Physics and the OEEC working party on the teaching of physics in schools (Clarke, 1960, p. 217) expressed this view most convincingly when he spoke of their 'strong belief that physics ... is a vital part of modern culture ... it provides a new process of thought, and new criteria of credibility and of acceptability of evidence ... it is a highly imaginative intellectual structure of concepts that gives a meaningful and creative picture or model of such of man's experience of the world in which he lives as it has yet been possible to integrate into a consistent whole.' They specifically refuted the belief that equated science with technology or that it would lead to increased material well-being, rather emphasized that science is one of the humanities, which was the concern of every pupil. This spirit, though never so clearly articulated, underlay the philosophy behind Nuffield physics. It was the day in which the educated amateur was held in highest esteem, and it was in this spirit that Nuffield grew.

The Influence of Nuffield

When Donald McGill was establishing the structure for the Nuffield 'O' level physics, he wrote

The theme is to be 'Physics for All', meeting primarily the needs of the non-science specialist whose sole experience of physics teaching this would probably be; but the treatment of the theme is meant to cultivate the interests and meet many of the needs of the future science specialist also. A modern statement of physics is called for, with a modern viewpoint built into the course throughout and not tailing the course as an addendum. It is intended that the fullest possible experimental substantiation be given to this modern viewpoint, but understanding based on direct experience is to be made the criterion, rather than completely substantiated logical development. (Wenham, 1967, pp. 337–8)

His aim was that it should be a modern, experimentally-based physics course appropriate for all pupils. In the event, of course, he was not to see the completion of the project, but others who took up his baton were to share his ideals. We can now look back and see how far these hopes were to be fulfilled by the products of the course, and will find many important strands which were to be the forerunners of much later educational thought. What was developed, however, was largely on the basis of the 'good practice' available to the team of experienced physics teachers, with a few insights from educational theory. Though Ted Wenham made reference to the researches of Piaget (*ibid*, p. 338) and Shayer spoke of the parallel ordering of the scheme to Piagetian thinking (Shayer, 1972; Shayer and Adey, 1981) the team as a whole would not claim that they were influenced by his writings. Educational theory was at a very rudimentary stage as far as science education was concerned.

There are, however, six important themes developed through Nuffield which have had a very significant influence on subsequent physics teaching, and indeed on wider aspects of school education. The first theme relates to the content, and the structuring, of the course. Though it was continually stressed that the essence of Nuffield was in the approach and not the content, and the teachers' guides when listing the topics to be included in any particular year repeatedly prefaced it with 'Note, this is not a syllabus. It would be misleading to take it as one' (for example, Rogers, 1966, TGI, p. 56), the content of the course was significant and made an important advance in providing a modern, integrated course. So many existing courses had provided a collection of isolated topics, perhaps grouped under heat, light and sound, electricity and magnetism, which held no underlying rationale or unifying themes. Most of the content would have been familiar to a pupil studying physics in the schools of 1890. Following the lead given by PSSC, by the SMA reports, and the Scottish experience, Nuffield sought for unifying themes and found them in the properties of matter, waves and oscillations, energy and fields, and the modern quantum phenomena. Such reorganization of topics was to prove intellectually more satisfying to subsequent physics teachers and text-book writers. Modern physics (ie up to about 1932!) was included and, thanks to the provocation of Dr Tricker and the ingenuity of the team members, methods found to teach it in both a logical and experimental way. Thus the course could be built up from first principles, and would reflect physics as a unified way of looking at the world.

The second theme of teaching physics for understanding, not learning, was to play a dominant and long-lasting effect. The message was spelt out in each of the teachers' guides, in Eric Rogers essay on *Teaching Physics for Understanding* (Rogers, 1966, TGI, pp. 64–78) and was reiterated throughout the course in the text and by the disseminators. It was reinforced by Henry Boulind's pupils' question books accompanying the course, and by the institution of a special Nuffield examination for the GCE. It was argued, again by Eric Rogers in another essay in the teachers guides, (*ibid*, pp. 79–99) that the teaching of a course for understanding would be quickly destroyed if it was terminated by an examination which tested only the 'cheap recall' of knowledge. It was originally hoped and intended that such special Nuffield exams would soon become superfluous as other examinations learnt from the Nuffield example and changed their style of examining to satisfactorily meet the Nuffield objectives. Although other GCE and CSE examination boards have undoubtedly moved a long way towards assessing pupils' understanding, the Nuffield special examination, at both GCE and CSE level, were still in operation in 1985. But the emphasis on understanding had been indelibly implanted, at least in the teacher's rhetoric!

A third theme running through Nuffield 'O' level physics was the emphasis on practical work, that the pupil would be learning through doing and that the pupil must be active in his own learning. 'The important thing is to DO some physics' (Lewis and Foxcroft, 1978, p. 171), and this was followed throughout the course with the pupil at every stage doing practical work wherever possible. The apocryphal Chinese saying 'I hear and I forget, I see and I remember, I do and I understand' was frequently used to justify this increased emphasis on doing practical work, and was rarely challenged or probed. Along each state of the 'hear-show-do' axis, apparatus was moved one step to the right; effects and experiments that previously had been only spoken of were now to be shown via demonstration apparatus or films, and experiments which had previously been demonstrated were now to be made class experiments for all pupils. And so John Lewis was able to harness the experience and ingenuity of the team, and resources that he had seen in the USA, in Germany and Russia, to persuade the English manufacturers to produce new and modified apparatus appropriate for the schools. Once more the hospitality that Malvern could provide facilitated the work of the apparatus group and produced class and demonstration apparatus of a very high quality. Scalors, ratemeters, Geiger Counters, cloud chambers, even pulse-electroscopes were used to demonstrate modern physics; linear air tracks were used to verify that momentum was conserved in a collision; vacuum pumps and bromine capsules were used to demonstrate the rate of diffusion of a gas. Class sets of ticker-timers and dynamics trolleys were available to enable pupils to discover Newton's laws of motion; sets of Worcester circuit boards to clarify the principles of circuit electricity and to distinguish current from voltage; sets of ripple tanks to find out about the behaviour of water waves, and sets of magnets and wire in the Westminster electromagnetic kits to make electric motors that worked and to generate electricity. The seductiveness of such apparatus was irresistible and soon the school labs were filled to overflowing with apparatus and pupils and teachers playing with them, to the sound of science advisers encouragements and the manufacturers cash registers! Such equipment found its way into most physics labs in the next decade or so, irrespective of whether the school was or was not doing Nuffield, and it was the apparatus more than the philosophy of the course that was to prove so ubiquitous in producing a commonality about much of the physics teaching throughout the country.

It could be said that more thought was given to the production of the apparatus than to the way it was to be used in practical work, indeed the teachers' guides are surprisingly silent concerning an overt rationale for practical work. There was, however, an unspoken philosophy; that the practical work should be used to support and, preferably, discover the underlying theory. The practical was seen as subservient to the theory, the theory to be developed came first and the apparatus was then provided to support that theory. It was believed that doing carefully designed experimental work would elucidate the underlying principles. 'There is a belief that through the doing of science that a true understanding of physical principles is obtained and this is the philosophy of the Nuffield projects.' (Lewis and Foxcroft, 1978, p. 162) It was not held that the pupils would discover all the laws of physics for themselves and though to some extent Nuffield was heuristic; 'it would be better to call it "directed heurism" as it is a stage-managed process of discovery, but the emphasis does not lie in the discovery process. The aim is the *understanding* of certain basic concepts'. (*ibid*) It is in this aspect that a fundamental flaw lay in the Nuffield project, on the one hand the goal was a clear understanding of basic concepts and principles, ie the right answers, while on the other it was hoped that pupils would be 'scientists-for-the-day', that they would be 'doing physics' and 'promote a spirit of enquiry' (*ibid*, p. 171). It was not recognized that there was a fundamental tension between an experiment so structured as to ensure that the 'right answer' was discovered and pupils experimenting for themselves in an open-ended way to make their own discoveries. The 'logical conflict between learning and discovering' (Stevens, 1978) was not confronted. Nor were the Nuffield team aware of the vital importance for the pupil's learning process of the information and perceptions that is brought to the learning process; researches in, and insights from, this area had not yet become available. Consequently, the team concentrated on producing a logical and lucid teaching scheme on the assumption that the pupils doing experiments in such a context would gain the required knowledge with understanding which would be implanted into the pupil's previously empty mind. So the message that came through the course materials most strongly was that the prime aim of the course was to gain an explicit understanding of the fundamental physics, an aim still thoroughly in line with the grammar/public school tradition of academic learning. There was, however, some trace of a looser, less explicit form of knowing, with much of the earlier experimental work being kept at the qualitative level to provide a range of experience on which concrete base a more formal knowledge would be built later. Indeed there was even a trace of Polanyi's tacit knowledge in the encouragement that 'pupils should begin by handling materials — and in the process gain something like an *instinctive feeling* for the meaning of density.' (Maddox, 1966, p. 5). But of course, this tacit knowledge was not seen as important in its own right, (being much too common and useful a form of knowledge!) but only as a necessary stage in attaining explicit, academic knowledge.

A fifth theme which ran through the Nuffield physics related to the use of language in learning, and preceded much of the later work on language that was to be developed by Barnes, Britton and Rosen in the early seventies (Barnes, Britton and Rosen, 1971). The pupils were to make their own notes, preferably in a diary form, so that they would learn the importance of relying on their own words. The language should be personal, expressive, and not formal so that there should be an engagement with, and commitment to, the writing. For many teachers, with an historical dependence on the formal notes, this was heresy, made all the more so by the absence of any pupil text-book in which they could find the 'right answer'. But it was the beginning for many teachers in their discovery that pupils could 'write themselves into understanding'. From this beginning it was easier for teachers to start getting genuine, rather than parrot-fashion feedback from the pupils and thus real learning, and insights into the learning process, was encouraged.

The final theme from the Nuffield course was one which no-one intended, and which all of the development team would have fought against. For many teachers, the Nuffield course became a highly prescribed, immutable series of experiments and demonstrations, the order of which was set down in the Nuffield bible, the teachers' guides — or, more likely, the guides to experiments. These gave all the experimental details which could be followed unthinkingly, the courses were supplemented by apparatus lists from the manufacturers which could be purchased off the shelf, and for those who wanted further support for themselves or their pupils, there was Tom Duncan's splendid series of books *Exploring Physics*, (Duncan, 1968–70), which matched the Nuffield course year by year, experiment by experiment. The course developers had put the spirit of enquiry at the heart of the project, but the teachers had too often taken the letter. The Nuffield team had never intended that the course should be set in stone, quite the opposite, it was merely an example. It was always intended that the course would be revised, though it was a pity that the formal Nuffield revision was lead by Eric Rogers who had been responsible for so much of the original course, both its strengths and its idosyncrasies. But the teachers took the course *in toto*, never before having had such helpful course material on which they could rely, and what was intended as an exciting exploration often became a routine journey through familiar territory, eliminating from the teacher the need to think for himself where or why he was going. And as this journey became increasingly imposed upon pupils for whom it was never designed and was quite unsuitable, the average and below average ability, the journey to be completed had to become ever more prescribed, and ever more detailed worksheets produced to get the pupils through it. The fun and the excitement of the early Nuffield teaching, with bright pupils and innovative teachers, was to become emasculated by pupils who could not enjoy the abstractions and teachers who were under-resourced, overstretched and lacking in vision.

Other Courses

When the Nuffield Foundation set up its science project it was natural that the first courses should be in the separate sciences of physics, chemistry and biology, because of the academic background of the people involved reflecting the strength and status of the specialist subjects in their grammar and public school traditions. In fact, this Nuffield 'O' level physics course was to be the only nationwide curriculum development in physics for the 11–16 age range throughout our twenty-five years. Though text books and examinations in physics were to change and to influence the teaching of that subject, and the vast majority of pupils studying science in the 13–16 age range were to do so through the separate sciences, all subsequent curriculum development projects in England, up to the school leaving age of 16, have been in science. We have had courses developed in secondary science, combined science, integrated science, and various forms of modular science but no one has again attempted to produce another physics course. But these science courses have interacted with the teaching of physics, and influenced the pupil's choices and perception of physics, and its position in the curriculum. We will consider each of them briefly, to see how and why they were developed and to what extent they have been successful in altering the traditional dominance of the high status, academic, physics.

Nuffield Secondary Science

There had been discussion at the Nuffield Foundation about the state of science teaching in the secondary modern schools in the late fifties when Peter Rowntree had alerted Farrer-Brown of the needs of the 75 per cent of the school population attending them (Clark, 1972, p. 168). However, the claims of the academic pupil, who might become the future physicists required for the expanding nuclear physics and electronics industries, gave greater priority to the reform of the syllabus in the separate sciences for the grammar schools. It was not until the mid-sixties, when the schemes for 'O' levels in physics, chemistry and biology were well under way, that the Nuffield Foundation allocated money to develop a secondary science for those not catered for by the 'O' level courses. The Ministry of Education, and their Inspectorate, had laid good foundations for the work through their reports on *Science in Secondary Schools* (HMI, 1960), *Half Our Future* (Newsom, 1963) and, most influentially of all, *Science for the Young School Leaver* (Schools Council, 1965) — the first working paper to be produced by the newly-formed Schools Council. HMI L.G. Smith, who had been central in the Schools Council working party, recommended that Mrs Hilda Misselbrook should lead the new project and, after a 'disguised interview' with John Maddox, she was appointed as organizer by the Nuffield Foundation.

It was an inspired choice, thoroughly appropriate for the work she had to do. As John Lewis was the ideal type for the academic, high status physics, so Hilda Misslebrook was the ideal for developing a relevant, common science for the people. She was, at the time of her appointment, Deputy Headteacher and Head of Science at Mayfield Comprehensive School in Putney and had, in her time at the school, seen it change from a grammar school to one of London's first and largest comprehensives. She was totally committed to the concept of a liberal education, including science, for all pupils and equally committed to involving teachers at all stages in the development of the course. She had great faith in the potential of all children and the ability of all teachers as the best arbiters of their science courses. She was the key figure in setting the style and tone of the project, 'a tireless worker and traveller she expected all who worked with her to be as committed as she was' (Walker, 1980).

The development of the course matched the status of secondary modern science at the time, with a much lower profile and budget than the separate 'O' level sciences and most of the team working on the project part-time. The project team consisted of sixteen people who were continuing their normal work as LEA advisers or college of education tutors. Each led a development team involving local teachers to ensure that it was a course 'for teachers by teachers'. After feasibility trials of two short sections early in 1966 the project involved more and more schools in intensive development and trialling over the next three years, from 1967–70. By the time it was published in 1971 it had been tried with over 10,000 students in 285 mainly secondary modern schools. Clearly the development and trialling itself had, as was intended, been a splendid form of in-service training for the many science teachers involved, many of whom had had little formal scientific background themselves. The philosophy of the course was that it should present a relevant, topic-based, investigational approach to science teaching. It started where the child was and developed the scientific approach through topics and practical investigations that were relevant to them. The children were encouraged to investigate their own environment, themselves and the way that science interacted with society. They were doing science in a social context. Though there was much excellent physics within many of the topics, this would arise out of the topic that was being investigated, (whether it was photography, extending the senses, or man and machines), rather than be the academic starting point for the study.

The product of the development work was a set of teachers' guides, one outlining the scheme as a whole, suggesting ways through it, discussing teaching methods and ways of assessing the course, and eight unit guides each containing teaching material for a particular topic (Misslebrook, 1971). The teachers' guides did not provide a course, but a resource, from which teachers could, indeed had to, develop their own route through to produce their own course. It certainly avoided the danger that the separate subject Nuffield projects had fallen into, of being perceived as providing a definitive, prescribed course, but it meant that teachers had to do a lot more work for themselves before they could produce their own CSE course. The course was strong on physics and biology, both of which had developed naturally out of the pupils' interests, but rather thin on chemistry — early drafts were so weak in chemistry that a special unit on materials had to be developed to satisfy the chemistry teachers! It fell firmly into the 'science for the people' model, and contained much excellent material which developed ways of using investigations and introducing science in society ideas that were to be built on, and to receive more recognition, in later courses. It contained, arguably, much of the best physics teaching material, certainly the most radical, of any of the Nuffield science projects.

And yet, despite the excellence of the material and the thoroughness of its development, it failed to capture much of the science teaching market. The form in which the material was provided, as a resource rather than a course, is often given as a reason for the smallness of its uptake, but more significantly was the status of this type of science in a school system which was increasingly going comprehensive, and the lack of influence of the secondary modern scientists in them. When the material was published in 1971, more and more secondary modern schools were going comprehensive, and the banner under which comprehensivization was flying was 'a grammar school education for all'. Nearly all the heads of science that were appointed were the graduates from the grammar schools, and the curriculum battle was dominated by the grammar school syllabuses, with the high-status 'O' level courses being the naturally accepted prize. In an upwardly mobile academic trend it was unfashionable to cling to a 'secondary modern science', and those who knew of its virtues did not have the personal or academic clout to out-gun the still powerful and charismatic subject specialists. Heads might be persuaded of the academic respectability of Nuffield 'O' level physics, but were still suspicious of the value or acceptability of new courses with such nebulous titles as 'secondary science' in which the pupils seemed to be enjoying themselves, playing around, even going outside the classroom! And so the merits of much of this material had to wait before the first round of comprehensivization had tried, unsuccessfully, to find ways of teaching inappropriate grammar school science across the whole ability range, and the second round started to ask more perceptive questions.

Nuffield Combined Science

When the Nuffield separate science courses were developed it was not uncommon in the grammar schools for the three sciences to be taught separately from the age of 11. However, it became increasingly common, especially in the new comprehensives, for all the sciences to be taught together by a single teacher; a move encouraged more on social and pastoral grounds than on any educational belief in an intrinsic integrity within science *per se*. There was not a natural matching of the three Nuffield courses in the early years as the projects had been developed quite independently of each other (indeed there were various unhappy clashes with, for instance, the oil monolayer experiment appearing in the year 1 physics course and also appearing in a different form in the year 2 chemistry!). So Brian Young, then Director of the Nuffield Foundation, set up a small group whose 'job was one of weaving this material into a composite fabric and of providing for a wider range of abilities than the previous courses' (Nuffield, 1970, p. ix). Maurice Elwell, a principal lecturer at the City of Birmingham College of Education, who had been involved with the development of the Nuffield physics course, and Charles Bingham, the Headmaster at Briar Mill Comprehensive School in Droitwich, were the joint organizers, working with Ken Wild, formerly Head of Science at Bromsgrove County High School and J.R. Lance, a senior lecturer at Coventry College of Education. It was a small team, with a tightly defined brief of combining the existing material and making it more suitable for the wider ability range. The first of these demands prevented any radical reconsideration of the needs of average 11–13-year-old pupils, but the re-packaging of the material was done in a way that many teachers found thoroughly acceptable. It quickly became established as the norm for introductory science teaching in England at this stage. In terms of uptake by schools, it would be rated as the most successful of all the Nuffield courses (Booth, 1975; and Tall 1981). Being so heavily derivative from the separate science courses, it was still essentially an academic, top-down, course within the grammar school tradition, with high reading demands made of the pupils in the attractively produced pupil material. However, the material was covered in a well structured practical way and this was to form the basis of many courses. Soon books were published and work schemes developed by groups of teachers which were based almost entirely on the Nuffield combined science course (for example, Green *et al.*, 1975), and this quickly became the self-imposed standard diet for most science courses in comprehensive and grammar school alike throughout the country. There was a considerable amount of physics in this combined science course, with practical experimentation to enable pupils to build up concrete experiences on which the abstract concepts would be later built; the section on materials enabled the atomic models to be introduced, a section on forces taught them the difference between mass and weight and allowed them to 'discover' the principle of moments, the energy conversion kits were used to enable the pupils to get a feel for different types of energy, and the Worcester circuit boards designed to give pupils a mastery of the behaviour of current in circuits. Of course we now know that many of these aspirations were not achieved and that for many of the pupils, the intellectual content of the course, with its underlying structure of abstract concepts, was still too

111

difficult (Shayer and Adey, 1981). But, because the course was arranged so much around practical activities, teachers found that they could happily occupy their pupils doing practical work for the whole of the science lesson; and this, especially with mixed ability classes, was no mean feat. If the practical was too complicated for the pupils to know what they should be doing, there was always the ubiquitous work sheet to lead them (by the nose!) so that they would be able to complete the work, even if they did not gain much insight into the basic concepts. It was the sort of science that science teachers were familiar with and, with the authority of Nuffield behind it, few stopped to question whether it was the most appropriate type. The immediate question that they were concerned with was 'how can I teach this (essentially grammar school type) science to pupils across the whole ability range?' and not 'is this the most appropriate type of science'. Though the phrases top-down and bottom-up had not yet been introduced as a way of describing curriculum design, if they had been this would undoubtedly be top-down. In hindsight it seems surprising, with the widening and lowering of the ability range away from that of bright selected pupils that the 'O' level courses were designed for, that there was not more consideration of a bottom-up approach building on good primary school practice — but then in the early seventies, despite the splendid work of the Nuffield Junior Science (Nuffield, 1967) and the Schools Council's *Science 5–13* (Ennever and Harlen, 1972), there was still very little good science teaching in the primary schools.

Schools Council Integrated Science Project

While the Nuffield secondary science course was being developed for the less academic fourth and fifth former, interest was being revived for an integrated science course for the more able too. The cause was advocated both by those who believed that integrated science was intrinsically a better science course, (and towards the end of the sixties it was fashionable to believe that anything 'integrated' had to be good, for its own sake — it was self-evidently better than being 'disintegrated'!), and those who saw the way to a better overall balance in the curriculum if all of the sciences could be squashed into a double subject slot. The Schools Council, with its *penchant* for integrated or cross-curricular projects, was the natural body to take such a speculative venture under its wing. And so, from 1969 to 1975 the Schools Council Integrated Science Project, (SCISP), was set up at Chelsea College under the leadership of W.C. Hall and B.S. Mowl (Hall and Mowl, 1973). They had a team of five and were guided by a consultative committee of nineteen, including Professor Allanson from Birmingham, Fred Archenhold from Leeds, Kevin Keohane from Chelsea College, and the Senior Science HMNI Norman Booth, under the chairmanship of Dr M.R. Gavin.

The course was aimed to satisfy both those for whom it was a terminal science course and also those who would want to study the sciences further in the sixth form. It was to earn a double 'O' level, and be taught in a double subject time allowance. It was aimed specifically for the more able pupils, the top 20 per cent, and aimed to integrate the three main sciences, and geology and ecology, along with social and environmental considerations. The course produced was quite different from any other science course, with its strongly integrated theme and its heavy emphasis on the applications and sociological implications of science. It had a strong liberal studies flavour to it, with an emphasis on the affective as well as the cognitive domain — both of which were to be assessed for the examination according to an assessment grid which included eight behavioural objectives relating to skills and three behavioural objectives relating to attitudes. The whole course was based around the educational theory of Gagné (Gagné, 1965) and sought hierarchical patterns through each topic included. It continually imposed the pattern of building blocks coming together to form concepts which were used in problem-solving, using the sequence 'investigation > concept > pattern > problem-solving'. After the criticism that the early Nuffield courses attracted because they did not state their objectives overtly nor take note of educational theory it may seem churlish to criticize SCISP for relying overmuch on them. But with so much stress being put on the largely unknown and unrecognized work of Gagné, it was not surprising that scientists, both inside and outside schools, should regard its foundations with suspicion. Undoubtedly, it produced some stimulating and innovative material in its course books, for both student and teacher, (Hall and Mowl, 1973) and raised the profile of 'science in society' by providing exemplar material of decision-making activities in sociological contexts. But it was never really accepted by the science teaching profession as a whole; few physics teachers in particular found much enthusiasm for it, though there has continued to be a band of committed disciples and their influence as science advisers in some counties has been strong. In practice the number of candidates entered for the SCISP exam has never exceeded 4000 per year.

The reasons for the poor uptake of SCISP were both internal and external to the schools. Few teachers felt confident or competent to teach the most intelligent pupils across all the sciences up to the age of 16, and many teachers did not find the science in SCISP as satisfying as the science specialism in which they were trained. The employers and the scientists in industry and higher education had not been convinced of the intrinsic value of the science in SCISP nor of its adequacy as a preparation for 'A' level in the separate sciences, a credibility gap which was not helped by the resignation from the SCISP examination panel of a university examiner, also on the SCISP Consultative Committee, on the grounds that he did not have confidence in the course. Clearly the power of the scientific establishment, both in the professional institutions and the universities, did much to discourage the spread of SCISP. Perhaps if the science teaching profession as a whole had had more faith in it themselves, the fight might have been more worth maintaining. But without any public champions either from the schools or the professions, and without the charisma and conviction of those in and behind the Nuffield Physics scheme, it was always unlikely that SCISP would find dissemination easy. The status and strength of physics in the schools was able to withstand any threat that this uncertain intruder might present with little difficulty. Though the Nuffield Foundation always prided itself on producing courses 'by teachers for teachers' they were always sufficiently politically sensitive to ensure that they had the backing of the scientific establishment behind their projects. The Schools Council with its unbounded faith in teacher power in the school, with its deliberate exclusion of members of the scientific institutions from some of its planning committees and with its indiscriminate proliferation of courses without adequate consideration of the implications for the whole curriculum, were politically naïve and missed the opportunity they might have had in significantly affecting the curriculum in schools.

References

ASE (1966), 'Some thoughts about Nuffield and the approach of the publication date of the O-level texts', *Education in Science*, 17, pp. 11–12.
BARNES, D., BRITTON, J.N. and ROSEN, H. (1971), *Language, the Learner, and the School*, Harmondsworth, Penguin.
BOOTH, N. (1975), 'The impact of science teaching projects on secondary education', *Education in Science*, 63, pp. 27–30.
CLARK, R.W. (1972), *A History of the Nuffield Foundation*, London, Longmans.
CLARKE, N. (1960), 'The teaching of physics in schools', *Bulletin*, (Institute of Physics), 11.9, pp. 217–25.
DUFF, A.R. (1966), '1000 lessons of Nuffield physics', *Education in Science*, 18, pp. 13–16.
DUNCAN, T. (1968, 1969 and 1970), *Exploring Physics, books 1–5*, London, John Murray.
ENNEVER, L. and HARLEN, W. (1972), *Science 5–13*, London, Macdonald.
GAGNÉ, R.M. (1965), *The Conditions of Learning*, London, Holt, Rinehart and Winston.
GREEN, G., PETFORD, S.K.C., SHORT, A.J. and WALKER, D.L. (1975), *Combined Science*, London, John Murray.

HALL, W.C. and MOWL, B.S. (1973), *Patterns; Schools Council Integrated Science Project*, London, Longman and Penguin Books.
HMI (1960), *Science in Secondary Schools*, Ministry of Education pamphlet no. 38, London, HMSO.
INDUSTRIAL FUND (1963), *The Industrial Fund for the Advancement of Scientific Education: Final Report*, London, IFASES.
INGLE, R. and JENNINGS, A. (1981), *Science in Schools: Which Way Now?*, Windsor, NFER-Nelson.
LAYTON, D. (1984), *Interpreters of Science*, London, John Murray.
LEWIS, J.L. (1965), 'The Nuffield physics project', *Physics Bulletin*, 16.3, pp. 81–94.
LEWIS, J.L. and FOXCROFT, G.E. (1978), 'The experimental approach in the Nuffield physics course', in DELACOTE, G. (Ed.), *Physics Teaching in Schools*, London, Taylor and Francis.
MADDOX, J. (1966), 'The Nuffield physics project', *Physics Education*, 1, pp. 3–7.
MISSLEBROOK, H. (1971), *Nuffield Secondary Science, Teachers Guide*, London, Longman.
NEWSOM, J. (1963), *Half Our Future*, (The Newsom Report), London, HMSO.
NUFFIELD (1967), *Nuffield Junior Science*, London, Collins.
NUFFIELD (1970), *Nuffield Combined Science*, Teachers Guide, London, Longman.
PERKINS, W.H. (1958), *Science in Schools*, London, Butterworth Scientific Publications.
PSSC (1960), *Physics*, Boston, MA, Heath and Co.
ROGERS, E.M. (1960), *Physics for the Enquiring Mind*, Oxford University Press and Princeton University Press.
ROGERS, E.M. (1966), *Nuffield 'O' Level Physics, Teachers Guides 1–5, Guides to Experiments 1–5, Question Books 1–5*, London, Longman.
ROGERS, E.M. (1977), *Revised Nuffield Physics*, London, Longman.
SCHOFIELD, R. and HARDING, D.W. (11968), 'The teaching of physics of fifty years and more,' *Physics Education*, 3.3, pp. 115–9.
SCHOOLS COUNCIL (1965), *Science for the Young School Leaver*, London, HMSO.
SCOTTISH EDUCATION DEPARTMENT (1963), *Alternative O Grade Syllabus in Physics*, Circular 49, Edinburgh, HMSO.
SHAYER, M. (1972), 'Conceptual demands in Nuffield O level physics', *School Science Review*, 186.54, pp. 26–34.
SHAYER, M. and ADEY, P. (1981), *Towards a Science of Science Teaching*, London, Heinemann Educational Books.
STEVENS, P. (1978), 'On the Nuffield philosophy of science', *Journal of Philosophy of Education*, 12, pp. 99–111.
TALL, J. (1981), 'British science curriculum projects — How have they taken roots in schools', *European Journal of Science Education*, 3.1, pp. 17–38.
WALKER, R. (1980), 'Nuffield Secondary Science', in STENHOUSE, L. *Curriculum Research and Development in Action*, London, Heinemann, pp. 79–83.
WARING, M. (1979), *Social Pressures and Curriculum Innovation*, London, Methuen.
WENHAM, E.J. (1967), 'Nuffield Foundation science teaching project 111, physics 11–16', *School Science Review*, 165, pp. 337–46.

5 'In the courts of the mighty' — Institutional Influences

The Royal Society

The Royal Society, perhaps more than any other institution, could be said to represent the scientific establishment. With a history going back to 1662, a Royal Charter establishing it ' . . . for improving natural knowledge', and a membership of about 700 eminent fellows, the Royal Society represented the elite of the scientific community. As the foremost learned society in the country, situated in most gracious buildings in Carlton House Terrace, London, its whole ethos was more one of the exclusive club than the school physics laboratory. Indeed, in 1960, it had virtually no formal contact with, or interest in schools. Yet during the subsequent twenty-five years its interest and involvement in the teaching of science in schools grew considerably, and its influence in developments there became significant.

The first involvement of the Society with schools came through the Scientific Research in Schools scheme which has supported over 400 teachers in their research projects since it was established in 1957. The aim of the scheme was to encourage scientific research in schools. Initially this meant supporting individuals who were doing research for higher degrees but over the years its emphasis changed to encourage the active involvement of pupils in this research too, and this became a necessary condition for support being given. Though inevitably the majority of that research has been in the biological field, research projects in physics have also been done. The reports to Council which the Scientific Research in Schools committee publishes each year, (RS, 1965–) record the progress of each project being supported, and illustrate amply that the Society's aim to encourage excellence in schools through genuine scientific research is, if in only a few schools, being fulfilled.

In 1961 the Council of the Royal Society agreed with the Institute of Physics, and the Physical Society, that a committee on physics education in this country should be set up (IoP, 1961 a). It was to be called the British Committee on Physics Education with Professor N.F. Mott, from the Cavendish Laboratory at the University of Cambridge as its first Chairman. Nevill Mott, FRS, who was instrumental in setting up this Committee, was to play a central and influential role in developments in school over the next two decades. His concern, along with others, led to the Committee deciding that 'physics teaching in schools would be the most urgent problem to be considered' (IoP, 1961 b): a concern which led to it supporting the initiative from John Lewis and his Modern Physics Committee and the subsequent setting up of the Nuffield Foundation physics curriculum panel. This Committee did not become an official Royal Society Committee until 1966 when, jointly with the Institute of Physics and the Physical Society, it was renamed the Physics Education Committee, with, by now, Professor Sir Nevill Mott as its Chairman. Its members were in themselves, as well as in their official capacity, influential people in these formative years: Professor K.W. Keohane (Chelsea College), Professor R. King (Royal Institution), Mr J.L. Lewis (Malvern College), Mr V.J. Long (HMI), Dr K.A.G. Mendlesohn (University of Oxford), Mr W.R. Richie (HMI, Scotland), Sister St Joan of Arc (La Retraite High School, Bristol), Mr E.W. Tapper (ASE Secretary), Mr E.J. Wenham (Worcester Training College), Mr J. Maddox (Nuffield Foundation, Assistant Director), Mr A.J. Berkin (Ministry of Education, Northern Ireland) and Dr J.A. Clegg (Institute of Physics, educational consultant). The terms of reference of the Committee were 'to promote improvement in the teaching of physics', with two main thrusts: (a) to consider methods of implementing in-service training of physics teachers; and (b) to consider university and school teaching and their interaction (IoP, 1965). In 1967 the Committee was renamed The Joint Committee for Physics Education, but was still chaired by Sir Nevill Mott who continued in the post until 1971.

Subsequently the chair was held by Professor W.E. Burchan (1972–75), Professor J.R. Holt (1976–77), Professor R.J. Blin-Stoyle (1978–83), and Professor W.F. Vinen (1984 and 1985), who were all professors of physics at Birmingham, Liverpool, Sussex and Birmingham respectively. Professor Blin-Stoyle was subsequently to become influential in the debate about the place of physics in relation to the other sciences when, in 1983, he accepted Sir Keith Joseph's invitation to become the first Chairman of the SCDC (School Curriculum Development Committee).

The reports of the Committee reflect the concerns of the time. In the late sixties the supply and training of physics teachers was, again, a matter for concern with direct implications for the supply of future scientists and engineers, and four reports on these issues were produced between 1969 and 1972, each working party being chaired by Nevill Mott (RS/IoP, 1969;

RS/CofEngI 1969; RS, 1971; RS, 1972). In the mid-seventies, when the universities were expressing concern about the variation in the amount of information known by their entrants to the undergraduate courses, the Joint Committee made a survey of the content of the various 'A' level physics syllabus and published a report under the title *Entry to Physics Courses at the Tertiary Level* (RS/IoP, 1975). The apparently wide variation shown by this survey was to be used by the Standing Conference for University Entrance (SCUE) in formulating their agreed core syllabus for 'A' level physics (SCUE, 1980). In 1982, the Committee formulated a widely-held concern about the very small number of girls studying physics beyond the age of 14 at school, with a perceptive and constructive report *Girls and Physics* (RS/IoP, 1982). Responding to the increasingly articulated concern about the excessive content load of 'O' level science courses, the Joint Committee set up a working party which reported in 1984 suggesting *A Reduced Content 16+ Syllabus in Physics* (RS/IoP, 1984); a report which did manage to reduce the content significantly while both affirming the necessity for some content and encouraging the processes of science.

It was not until 1969 that the Royal Society could bring itself to have its own standing committee 'to advise council on matters relating to education at all levels'. And even then many fellows thought it inappropriate that the Society should concern itself with science at such a lowly level as schools. But this Education Committee, first under the chairmanship of Dr C.C. Butler (1969–78), then Professor of Physics at Imperial College, London, and then Sir Harry Pitt (1979–85), the Vice-Chancellor of the University of Reading, was to have an increasingly more confident and useful role in schools. Initially the Committee concerned itself with matters at the university level and in the relatively safe area of standardizing the units for teaching science in schools. With the aid of C.B. Spurgin, the senior science master at Wolverhampton Grammar School, a series of reports was produced (RS, 1968, 1969 and 1970) on metrication at the different levels of schooling, and these were to become the basis for good practice for textbook writers and examination boards in subsequent years. No-one questioned the society's authority in speaking in these matters, nor in expressing their proper concern about the 'swing away from science' after Dainton (RS, 1969).

Through the sixties and seventies the Royal Society had naturally thought of school science teaching in terms of the traditional sciences taught independently in, largely, selective schools. Towards the end of the seventies, however, it was forced to consider, with some apprehension, the growth of comprehensivization with a decreasing number of future scientists coming through the decreasing number of selective grammar schools. Would the comprehensive schools be able to produce an adequate scientific grounding for the future manpower demands of the nation in general, and of the Royal Society in particular? Sir Nevill Mott, on a one-man enquiry, visited many schools and took advice from a wide range of involved people and produced a report in 1979 called *Science and the Organisation of Schools in England — Implications for the needs of Talented Children* (Mott, 1979). In this report, from an admittedly, and appropriately, elitist stance he came to a largely positive and reassuring conclusion. Yes, a comprehensive school could be so organized to provide an adequate scientific background, even for the most able and talented pupils, as long as the school was large enough to provide a six form entry, and consequently provide two sets of physics in the fourth and fifth forms. This conclusion came as a surprise to many fellows of the Society, and proved unwelcome to those whose political inclinations wished for a return to the days of selective grammar schooling. The report did not get the credit it deserved from teachers in the school system at large for whom the conclusion, indeed also the question, did not need stating. But, had the conclusion been different, as many had anticipated, the political consequences could have been serious and the anti-comprehensive lobby in Margaret Thatcher's newly-returned Tory government would have had a field day. It could be argued that the wisdom and perception of a single man, Nevill Mott, who had already shown a real empathy for the needs of pupils in school physics fifteen years earlier in the days of the Nuffield project, had again been decisive in shaping the development of physics education.

Two other reports from working parties of the Royal Society were to be produced in the 1980s which showed how far it had travelled in a short time to come to terms with the comprehensive system and the concept of science for all. In 1982 a report *Science Education 11–18 in England and Wales* (along with a comprehensive statistical annexe and a summary report) was published from a very high powered working group, who had thought it worth their while to look seriously at the whole school population (Pitt, 1982). Under the chairmanship of Sir Harry Pitt, Professor Blin-Stoyle, Professor Eaborn, Sir Nevill Mott (still!), Sir David Phillips, Professor Stewart, Sir Alan Wood and Professor Sugden had as their terms of reference: (a) to review the teaching and examination of science in secondary schools; (b) to consider the needs of potential employers of trained manpower; (c) to consider how best to ensure an adequate national supply of suitably trained manpower; and (d) to make recommendations. Overall, though the brief was very much concerned with manpower provision, the report was far from being a limited, utilitarian remedy. Compared with, say, the MSC who at a similar time were coming to a very vocational, instrumental, separatist conclusion with TVEI etc., the Royal Society report was essentially liberal and educational, perceiving science education as education IN science, ABOUT science and THROUGH science, and as being appropriate for all pupils up to the age of 16. They had been impressed by the discussion papers of the ASE and HMI, and were in sympathy with science being taught in terms of a correct understanding of the nature of science, its application, its power and its limitations, its applicability and its social and economic relevance. It grappled hard with the realities and the rhetoric of current debate and came up with more constructive suggestions than many of its more involved counterparts. The conundrum that everyone was struggling with at this time was how to get a balanced science, including physics, chemistry, and biology, into 20 per cent of the timetable; a goal that had become accepted wisdom by 1982. Twenty per cent of the timetable is eight periods per week, most subjects have four periods each; three into eight won't go. But said the Royal Society, nine is nearly equal to eight, and $9 = 3 \times 3$. For those who are not convinced that there is an integrated science course suitable for all, let them continue to teach the separate subjects, enthusiastically with the specialist subject teachers that the schools still have, but cut down from four to three periods a week each. It was a pragmatic solution which, by being either too much or too little, failed to satisfy most of the more polarized advocates. The report was important, however, by putting the weight of the Royal Society behind the concept of science for all, even if that science was still perceived in rather traditional forms.

The final report of the Royal Society however, published in 1985, took the concept of science for all into a far more popularist and comprehensive form. This working group, under Dr W.F. Bodmer, included Mr R.E. Artus, Sir David Attenborough, Professor Blin-Stoyle, Sir Kenneth Durham, Sir John Mason, Mr M.J. Savory, Lord Swann, Professor Dorothy Wedderburn, Dame Margaret Weston and Professor John Ziman. The report, *The Public Understanding of Science* (Bodmer, 1985), endorsed by the Council of the Royal Society, argued strongly that the type of science appropriate to pupils in schools should be directed not only towards developing the processes, the skills and the knowledge and understanding of science but should also give an understanding 'of the nature of an advanced technological society, the interaction between science and society and the contribution science has made, and can make, to the cultural heritage'. Its aim, with recommendations to the mass media, the scientific community, industry and the public services at large, as well as to schools, started with the phrase from the previous report that 'a sensible and balanced public view about science education is dependent on the development of much greater awareness and enlightenment about science and its role in society'. This report showed that the Royal Society was prepared to come out from its ivory tower and take science for the people to the people.

The Royal Society's involvement in, and influence on, school physics teaching had developed considerably through our twenty-five years as it had realized the importance of the schools both for the preparation of future scientists and for the necessity of a scientifically literate populace. In 1960 it, disdainfully, had no significant dealings with the schools. In 1970 it was concerned that the scientific elite were suitably taught. By 1980 it had accepted its responsibility towards the scientific education of all in the largely comprehensive system. By 1985 it was in some ways 'ahead of the field' and was arguing for a full scientific education for all the people, in an essentially liberal form. Through its preparedness to engage seriously with the current situation in schools, through the quality of its analysis and argument, through the status and influence of its members in the corridors of power, (corridors which had become increasingly important in latter years), the Royal Society had made a significant and welcome contribution to the teaching of physics in schools, a contribution which looked at one time essentially conservative but had become increasingly progressive.

The involvement of the Royal Society in the development of school physics teaching was determined in no small measure by the activities and commitment of two, quite different men; Donald Harlow and Nevill Mott. Sir Nevill Mott's ubiquity in physics education we have already met. He was very much the elder statesman of English physics throughout the first two decades of our period. Born in 1905, he had a brilliant career in physics, becoming an FRS by the age of 31. Being educated at Clifton College and Cambridge, he lectured first at Manchester (1929–30), then as a Fellow at Caius College, Cambridge (1930–33) before becoming Professor of Physics at the University of Bristol (1933–54). In 1954 he moved back to the Cavendish Laboratories at Cambridge as the senior professor, and stayed there until his retirement in 1971. His involvement and standing in physics education at the national and international level throughout the sixties was enormous. The Nuffield project was to use that status, as well as the wisdom, to support the new 'O' level physics course and to give it authority and credibility among the physics establishment. If the Nuffield physics courses had the senior professor of physics in the country as chairman of their consultative committees, they had to be taken seriously. Though his prime concern was always about the training of the scientific elite, he was to show a great sympathy and support for the educational needs of all children; developing the understanding and compassion which was encouraged from his own home background in which his father, C.F. Mott, was Director of Education in Liverpool (Mott, 1986).

If Nevill Mott's background was to influence the commitment that he brought to his involvement of the physics community in school physics, so did that of Don Harlow who was appointed as the first Education Officer of the Royal Society from 1969 to 1983. Don Harlow had, after the army and a one-year emergency teacher training course, taught chemistry in secondary modern and comprehensive schools in Hampshire. He had become very involved with the work of the SMA, and ASE, through its local activities, its committee structures, as Annual Meeting Secretary (1960–67) and thence on to its Council. Indeed his ASE activities were partly instrumental in his obtaining the appointment at the Royal Society, an appointment encouraged by Sir Harold Hartley, FRS, who as Chairman of the Duke of Edinburgh's Study Commission was highly influential in linking industry with school science teaching (McCulloch, Jenkins and Layton, 1985). For Harold Hartley had in his earlier days, as a chemist at the University of Oxford, organized the SMA meeting there in 1926 (at which about 240 people attended representing 90 per cent of the membership!). When thirty-six years later he wanted to contact the SMA again to see how the Duke of Edinburgh could help science teachers, it was not unnatural that he should first contact the then Annual Meeting Secretary, Don Harlow. So developed a good working relationship between Hartley and Harlow from which he was encouraged to take the Royal Society post. Thus Don Harlow was able to take into the Royal Society, an institution filled by scientists with experience and concern about only the selective schools, the knowledge that the pupils in secondary modern schools also had the potential to become good scientists, and deserved the best possible scientific education too.

Consequently, the Royal Society had Nevill Mott and Donald Harlow working together, especially in the production of the all-important 1979 'talented children' report. They brought with them the liberal traditions, the commitment and the experience which ensured that the Society increasingly gave its support to the scientific education of all pupils in the comprehensive, as well as the selective, schools.

The Institute of Physics

The Institute of Physics, constituted according to its Royal Charter to 'promote the advancement and dissemination of education in the science of physics, pure and applied', had a vested interest, perhaps **the** vested interest, in ensuring that the foundations for subsequent physics education and research were duly laid in the schools. Its roots lie with The Physical Society, founded in 1874 as 'a learned society providing means for the discussion of new knowledge in physics', and the original Institute of Physics, set up in 1918 to 'foster the work of physicists as professional men and women'. In 1960, these two organizations amalgamated, combining the activities of a learned society with that of a professional body. It represented the voice of practising physicists throughout the United Kingdom, initially for its membership of 9000, which rose to 16000 in 1970 before settling at about 15000 in 1980. The *raison d'etre* of the Institute was 'the maintenance and welfare of physics as a field of study and as a profession', which made it inevitably a conservative part of the scientific establishment. Its headquarters in Belgrade Square, London, was steeped in the very history of the subject itself with photos of past Presidents such as Kelvin, Fitzgerald, Thompson, and Thompson, Boys, Lees, Bragg, Eddington, Rayleigh, Andrade and Mott, reminding committees of the heritage they were to uphold. There was a geographical and cultural gap between the schools and the Institute, as there was with the Royal Society and the schools, and yet the Institute too was to have an important and increasing influence on the way that physics was taught in schools.

The Institute entered the 1960s with Norman Clarke well established as its Deputy Secretary after fifteen years in post. He was an energetic, influential, man who, in Nevill Mott's words, 'knew all the right people'. He was to be an important catalyst for the Nuffield 'O' level programme, introducing Nevill Mott to the Nuffield Foundation and suggesting Donald McGill as the first Director of the physics project. As the first Honorary Secretary of the new International Commission of Physics Education, from 1960–1966, as well as Secretary to many of the Institute and Royal Society committees which blossomed in the early sixties, he acted as the focus for much of the discussion and activity directed at improving school physics. When he left the Institute in 1965 to take over the Institute of Mathematics and its Applications and to immerse himself in local politics, he had been instrumental in putting the weight of the Institute's authority behind the moves which led to the reviewing of all aspects of the school physics curriculum.

Dr J.A. Clegg, from Imperial College, London, was appointed in 1965 as an Education Consultant 'with duties primarily concerned with the encouragement and improvement of inservice training of teachers' (IoP, 1965). Following the recommendation of Donald Scott's *Training of Graduate Science Teachers* report (Scott, 1963) that 'science teaching centres should be founded to give adequate accommodation for practical work for students in training, refresher courses for serving teachers, and students for higher degrees', he encouraged the setting up of physics centres around the country. The first pilot experiment was set up in 1966 in Manchester with Professor H. Lipson and local teachers, to form the North Western Physics Centre (IoP, 1966). It established the pattern that such centres should be primarily directed at physics teachers in post, and should provide room for discussion, workshop facilities and laboratory space in which they could meet regularly and informally to discuss and try out new ideas. Within a few months Dr Clegg was to have stimulated the establishment of various physics centres in universities, polytechnics and LEAs across the country, centres which were often to develop into science, and subsequently, science and technology centres and prove the forerunners of the SATRO movement of the seventies.

Subsequently the educational work of the Institute was the responsibility of Peter Flowerday, 1967–72, and, since 1973, Maurice Ebison. These education officers dealt with a multitude of queries related to careers and basic physics and were the Institute's public, and very acceptable, face to the schools. The Education Department was greatly enlarged in the eighties by the part-time appointment of a teacher, Sheila Saville (1981–84), and a full-time appointment from 1982 of a teacher educator, Brian Davies. This strengthened team was to provide an increasing supply of teaching resources to the schools. It produced careers material, video and discussion material to encourage more girls into teaching, and the delightful SNIPPETS magazine which propogated a serendipitous collection of physics applications to pupils and teachers alike. It also set up the Affiliated Schools Scheme which provided schools, at a highly subsidised rate, with copies of the educational journal *Physics Education*, and many other resources and advice. Another innovation was the introduction of a 'small grants' scheme in 1983, at the instigation of John Goddard, in which £5000 was to be made available each year to help meet the needs of classroom teachers who requested financial assistance for some development work. Through this the Institute was able to support work on such projects as the use of VELA, the improvement of a year 3 physics course, physics in industry, solar energy fact sheets, and computer control of a telescope. In the sixties, the Institute's involvement with the schools was largely second-hand, by influencing policy and curriculum development, by answering specific queries concerning careers advice or points of fundamental physics, and by providing a programme of public meetings and conferences for its members by the eighties it was also concerned with supporting individual teachers in their laboratories and daily work.

Much of the work of the Institute was developed through its committee structure, with the voluntary involvement of physicists from different branches of employment in physics. Three of these committees were involved with education in schools; the Education Committee of the Institute, the joint Royal Society/Institute of Physics Education Committee, and the Education Group Committee. The Education Committee (called the Membership and Education Committee from 1960–1971, the Education Committee from 1971–1979, and the Education and Careers Committee from 1980!) was a standing committee of the Council of the Institute and reported to it annually on matters of educational importance. Its chairmen, Dr J. Topping (1960–63), Professor M.R. Gavin (1963–66), Dr A.D.I. Nicol (1967–69), Professor C.A. Taylor (1969–75), Professor O.S. Heavens (1976–79), Dr J. Goddard (1979–83), and Mr J.L. Lewis (1983–), played an important role in deciding how far the Institute should involve itself with school physics; with Dr Topping, (who had previously been Chairman of the Education Group from 1953–56), Charles Taylor and John Lewis especially, that involvement was considerable. In 1961, as we have seen in the previous section, the influential Joint Committee, the British Committee on Physics Education was set up with Professor Mott as its first Chairman. Its first meeting could hardly have been more propitious as it was reported that already 'Professor Mott and Mr. Clarke had had discussions with the Director of one of the charitable foundations . . . and hoped that full details of proposals would be disclosed at the next meeting . . . which could develop into an extremely important project' (IoP, 1961 b). It did. It led to the Nuffield Physics Project!

Probably the most active of the committees was that responsible for the programme of the Education Group, which had been set up by the Education Committee in 1949. Its constitution, formalized in 1962, gave it two objectives; 'to hold meetings of members of the group . . . for the meeting and discussion of papers, for the delivery of lectures and for the discussion generally of subjects coming within the scope of the group, and to stimulate interest in and generally to advance the teaching pure and applied physics and matters relating to the training of physicists' (IoP, 1962). And hold meetings and stimulate interest it did! This was the level at which those actively involved in physics education worked, rather than just talked, with committed chairmen in Dr N. Thompson (1960–63), Mr F. Oldham (1963–65), Dr A.D.I. Nicol (1966–69), Mr A.W. Trotter (1969–72), Mr J.M. Ogborn (1972–73), Professor E.J. Burge (1973–76), Mr E.J. Wenham (1976–79), Professor P.J. Black (1979–82), and Mr M.J. Pipes (1982–85). Bill Trotter, John Ogborn, Ted Wenham and Paul Black were all deeply involved in the development and dissemination of the Nuffield 'A' level physics course. This Committee instituted a series of meetings for the members, an annual residential conference, and various working parties as appropriate. The meetings, typically ten a year distributed around the country, might be on educational matters, or recent developments in physics. In the latter few years of our period, an annual lecture demonstration was provided for school children and given at several different venues around the country. Cyril Isenberg lectured on earthquakes in 1983, Charles Taylor on sound in 1984, and Ken Sharples on creaks and cracks in 1985. These rapidly became embarrassingly popular and successful, providing exciting stimulation in real physics for thousands of pupils. The annual conferences concentrated on such themes as 'examining in physics' (1965 and 1977), 'the school/higher education interface' (1964, 1971 and 1986), 'the changing nature of physics education' (1968, 1975 and 1985), as well as more specific topics such as the teaching of solid state physics (1962), the new Nuffield 'A' level course (1970), project work (1974), individualized learning (1979), or concept developmentin physics (1983). Working parties produced reports on examinations in physics (Thompson, 1966), practical examinations (Scott, 1966), what earns the marks (Spurgin, 1967), relationships between maths and physics, (Goodier, 1976), statistics relating to physics and education (Thompson, 1979), and responses to various ASE and DES discussion papers. The mechanism whereby such reports were generated varied, some started in the Education Group committee, others in the Education Committee, with ad hoc groups being set up to consider the issue of the moment. All reports needed to be approved by the Council before becoming official Institute policy, and consequently the procedure tended to be slow. Undoubtedly, however, they were of high quality and, arguably, of considerable value to those forming policy.

Of lasting influence were the publications produced by the Institute. *Physics Bulletin*, the house-magazine of the Institute, had been published at approximately monthly intervals since 1950 (IoP, 1950–), and from time to time this had contained letters, articles and comments by members of direct concern to the teaching of physics in schools. From 1959–1965, for instance, 'there had been over thirty articles in the Bulletin on educational topics' (Lewis, 1965, p. 81), testifying both to be the interest of physicists in physics education and also their concern about it. The Bulletin has continued this debate among the members, especially those who are not directly involved with the schools themselves. In 1966, the Institute was to start publishing *Physics Education*, an educational journal especially directed at physics 'teachers at all levels'. It aimed 'not only to assist in establishing a sound basis to the teaching of physics and help to keep the teacher aware of the many new, important and exciting developments that are taking place but, also, help to contribute to the community spirit so urgently needed' (Keohane, 1966, p. 2). This journal was to continue publishing six editions per year throughout the rest of our period and provided a channel for teachers to share their thinking and to establish a corporate identity which was to encourage and sustain them as physics teachers. The community spirit which Keohane said was needed in the expansive, excitingly optimistic days of 1966, was to become even more important over the next two decades as the overall educational climate, and the attacks on the existence of physics as a separate subject in schools became increasingly threatening.

The influence of the Institute of Physics on the teaching of physics in schools is difficult to quantify, but important none the less. It is true that it was a common complaint from physics teacher members throughout the period that the Institute was not sufficiently involved in, or sympathetic to, the teaching of school physics. It was seen as being too readily allied to the professional physicist in industry or higher education, and too expensive and unsympathetic for the average physics teacher to feel it worth joining; the popular ASE more obviously and inevitably provided better 'value for money'. However, its existence and activities, though limited to a minority of physics teachers in schools was disproportionately significant. The meetings and conferences directly affected only a few members each year, a few score at most meetings, sixty to 100 at the annual conferences. But these were often an influential few who were at the forefront of other innovations and thus were able to refine and disseminate new developments. The working parties and policy responses were important in two respects; they enabled both physics teachers to influence the thinking of the physics profession as well as physicists influencing what went on in schools. Most educational working parties had a good representation of progressive physics teachers on them, and this helped the Institute to make an increasingly enlightened response to, for instance, DES and ASE discussion papers. The Institute sought both to advance an appropriate form of science teaching for all school pupils whilst supporting the provision of good physics teaching to maintain the future generations of physicists.

It is interesting to note the continuing involvement of different people in the Institute's activities throughout our period, especially, perhaps, Norman Thompson and John Lewis. Norman Thompson was a tough-minded, rigorous, incisive university physicist from the University of Bristol, the same physics department which also spawned Nevill Mott and Donald McGill, with a strong commitment to school physics. He started the period as Chairman of the Education Group (1960–63), and in 1962 instituted the working party looking into examinations in physics, which was to lay the foundations for much future development in the assessment of both practical and theoretical skills (Scott, 1966; Thompson, 1966, Spurgin 1967). He was active in many of the Institute's education and membership committees throughout the period, heading up working groups looking into the supply of physics teachers (RS, 1981) and the statistical situation regarding the context and trends facing different aspects of physics education (Thompson, 1979, 1984 and 1986). John Lewis, a young, dynamic, innovative physics teacher of 37 was invited in 1961 to serve on the first British Committee on Physics Education, under Professor Mott. He was to exert an important influence on that as it developed into the Physics Education Committee through the sixties, a Committee which was going to be important in giving the Institute's support to his Nuffield 'O' level physics course. He was to be influential, too, in many of the other Institute's committees, fighting hard for the cause of school physics especially in the latter years when he was both Chairman of the Education Committee and Vice-President of the Institute from 1984–87.

Perhaps more significant than the activities of the Institute was its very existence, in that it represented that branch of the scientific establishment which could speak for physics. In so far as government or the mass media sought a view from the scientific establishment about its analysis of, or expectations from, school science it turned not to a professional institute of science, such did not exist, but to the Institute of Physics (and of chemistry and of biology). In this way an interpretation of school science was perpetuated through the perceptions of the separate sciences; physics, chemistry and biology. Its presence, and function to look after the interests of physics throughout the country, made it an essentially conservative influence in maintaining the status and position of physics in schools. By its publications, especially *Physics Education*, it defined and legitimated what was acceptable in school physics. Yet for all its inherent conservatism it was to prove a significant instrument for change, giving support for the new Nuffield syllabuses at 'O' and 'A' level, keeping the needs of the physics teaching force before the public, encouraging more boys and, especially, girls to study and take a career in physics, and supporting improvements in the examination system. Whether this was the result of the physics community taking an enlightened view of school science, or whether it was the result of a few committed and politically astute physics teachers using one of the establishments levers in the corridors of power is a matter of speculation. Few, in hindsight, would not see strong evidence for the latter interpretation.

Physics Education

Physics Education started in 1966, a period which its opening editorial described optimistically as 'a most exciting time in the development of eductation in science' (Keohane, 1966, p. 1). By the end of our period, after 119 editions, 1562 articles and 620 letters to the editor, it was still going strong though the retiring editor at that time viewed the climate more pessimistically and the times 'eventful and depressing' (Deeson, 1985, p. 253). There had been five editors in that period: K.W. Keohane (1966–69), J. Goodier (1970–73), F. Archenhold (1974–76), R. Schofield (1977–80), and E. Deeson (1981–85). Kevin Keohane was another of the group who had gained experience of scientific work during the war in radar, and then research and lecturing at the University of Bristol. When he took up the editorship of the new journal he was Professor of Physics at Chelsea College and Director of the Nuffield Foundation Science Projects. He was soon to become Professor of Science Education and Director of the Centre for Science Education at Chelsea (1967–76). Jack Goodier had been involved with the SMA Teaching of Modern Physical Science Committee, the '59 club' and the early Nuffield 'O' level physics development work, leading the London group on waves and oscillations. He was currently Head of Science and Physics, at Eton College. Fred Archenhold had been a physics teacher at a northern grammar school before moving to the Education Department at the University of Leeds as physics tutor. Roy Schofield was also a physics tutor in the Department of Educational Studies at Brunel University, after previously teaching physics and running the science Department of a London comprehensive school. Eric Deeson was still teaching physics, and was Head of the Science Department in a Birmingham comprehensive throughout the period of his editorship. The background and occupations of the various editors nicely reflect the changing contexts and areas of concern facing physics education.

Physics Education (IoP, 1966–) was aimed at physics 'teachers at all levels from the upper forms in schools to the university, colleges of education, technical colleges and indeed industry' (Keohane, 1966), and more specifically at teachers of physics at the sixth form and first year university level. There were, however, often articles of interest and relevance to physics teachers in the lower years of secondary schooling too. It quickly established itself as **the** journal for those interested in physics education in schools and built up a strong and faithful readership among many sixth form teachers, in England and around the world. As these teachers were also responsible for the physics teaching throughout the schools, it was natural that the concerns of physics in the lower school should become incorporated too. Indeed, as the ASE became more and more committed to science, and less to the sciences, and reflected this commitment in its journals (in 1984 the School Science Review terminated its 'Physics Notes' section, along with the chemistry and biology section, and replaced it by 'Science Notes') *Physics Education* was to become the only journal in the UK specifically representing the interests of physics in the schools.

One of the most notable, and significant, aspects of *Physics Education* has been its consistency of style and content. Though, superficially, the journal changed in appearance and in the topics for its consideration, overall the pattern remained very similar. Publishing six editions a year, it contained commissioned and submitted articles, letters to the editor, news and comments, reviews of books, films, equipment and computer software and various other features from time to time, such as brain teasers, queries in physics and 'what's wrong with this examination question?' Editorials and invited leader articles became a regular feature since 1975. The content of *Physics Education* reflected the concerns and interests of physics teachers throughout the period, and also exerted some influence on it. For though the different editors, and their editorial boards, distinctly and directly determined the content of the journal, the articles submitted and their selection from it reflected what was perceived to be most significant and constructive at the time. Hence *Physics Education* both reflected and influenced the state of physics education in schools.

It is instructive to consider this reflection of the state of physics education by analyzing the content of the articles. Though any *post hoc* grouping is, to some extent, arbitrary and uncertain, it is possible to categorize them into four main areas of concern; articles relating to the content of physics courses (what to teach), articles relating to the methodology of physics teaching (how to teach), articles relating to the organizational perspectives (the contexts of physics teaching) and articles relating to educational perspectives (the underlying insights into physics teaching). The first two of these sections have been the main concern over the years, with about 40 per cent of the articles devoted to each. The contexts for physics teaching, (course structures, teacher supply and training, educational policy and assessment) have also been of regular, though lesser, interest. Increasingly, since the self-confident and unselfconscious days of the late sixties and early seventies, there has been an interest in the underlying educational philosophy, psychology and curriculum rationale of physics teaching. Research reports and scholarly expositions provided some 'educational navel contemplation' directed at, and produced by, an increasingly perceptive and self questioning teaching force. The articles on the content of physics teaching can themselves be subdivided into four main areas; articles on pure physics, on the applications of physics, on the history of physics and on the social implications (the STS) of physics. Table 9 and Figure 8 show how the balance of themes and articles have varied. It can be seen that the articles represented a strong interest in the subject itself, in its faithful exposition and presentation, and showed great concern for the purity of the subject in an academic, impersonal sense. This element of concern for the fine subtleties of physics has been mirrored in the letters to the editor section of the journal, the majority of which (411 of the 620 published) have been about the 'pedagogic semantics' of physics. Letters arguing about the correct, and incorrect, ways of teaching heat, or surface tension, or electromotive force, have provided a continuous source of interest for many physics teachers. The fact that such correspondence has usually been inconclusive, the editor closing the correspondence more from a sense of exhaustion than completion, probably reflects both the intrinsic difficulty of parts of the subject

Figure 8: Content of Physics Education

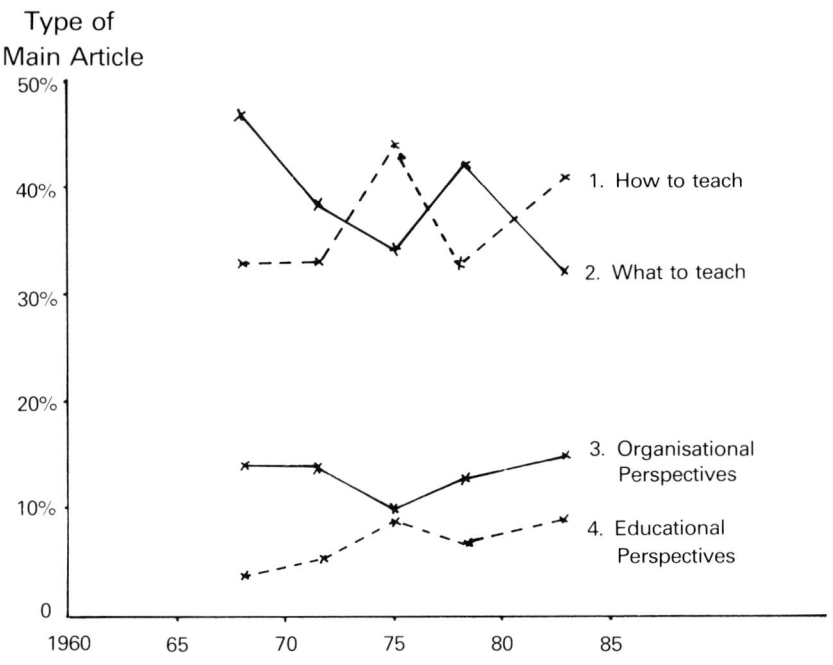

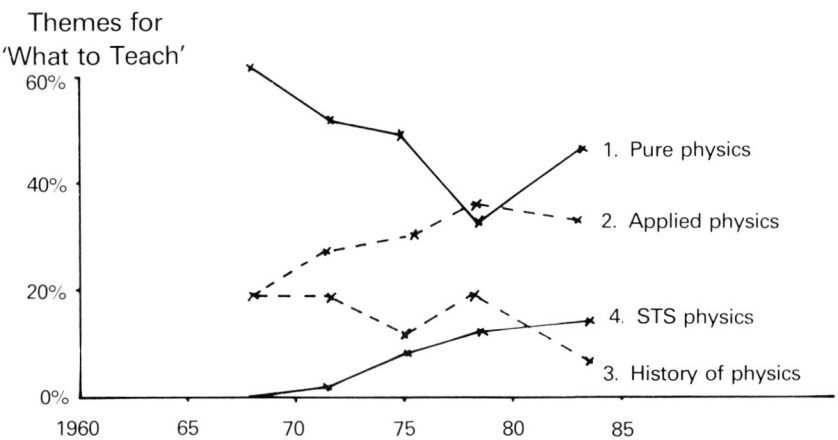

Table 7. Physics Education: Distribution of articles

EDITOR	Keohane 1966–69	Goodier 1970–73	Archenhold 1974–76	Schofield 1977–80	Deeson 1981–85	Total	
No Mains Article	255	327	270	368	342	1562	
No Letter to Editor	142	126	114	97	141	620	
What to teach	47%	38.5%	34%	42%	32%	601	39%
How to teach	33%	33%	44%	33%	41%	576	37%
Organizational perspectives	14%	14%	10%	13%	15%	210	13%
Educational perspectives	2%	5.5%	9%	7%	9%	105	7%
Others	4%	9%	3%	4%	2%	70	4%
What to teach							
Pure	62%	52%	49%	33%	46%	280	48%
Applied	19%	27%	30%	36%	33%	172	29%
History	19%	19%	12%	19%	7%	93[1]	16%
STS[2]	–	2%	8%	12%	14%	43	7%

[1] Including 13 Physics on Stamps
[2] STS (Science, Technology and Society)

(and consequently, though never admitted, its inappropriateness to normal school children!) and the pedantic and inflexible character of many physics teachers!

At the same time, other physics teachers emphasised the human aspects of their subjects through a concern with the applications of physics into real life, and in the historical and social background and development of their subject. There was a continual interest too in the pedagogical aspects of physics teaching, both in the broad methodology of teaching physics and in very specific experimental techniques. The interests of physics teachers as concerned with teaching their academic subject correctly, experimentally and, just occasionally, in its human and social context, was projected consistently through the pages of the journal.

But *Physics Education* was more than a reflection of the existing interests of physics teachers, it was also an important channel for disseminating new ideas and approaches to the profession. Curriculum developers, and other teachers and educators, used its pages to propogate their perceptions of the best way to teach the subject. The new curriculum projects, at 'O' and 'A' level, were well reported. Different approaches to practical work and to learning were advocated, and different philosophies of the subject projected by those who favoured, for instance, physics as a human activity useful in solving real life problems or physics as a rigorous academic activity existing to perpetuate the subject in higher education and research.

It is impossible to reflect the range of topics covered, perhaps a random dip into the contents of a few editions might provide something of the flavour. The first edition in 1966 contained articles on the Nuffield Physics Project, electrical resistivity, reflections on Sadi Carnot, the physics of superconducting magnets, 'A' level electrostatics, practical examinations and a simple smoke cell for Brownian motion. A 1973 edition included articles on the social responsibility of physicists, the place of physics in the secondary school curriculum, geophysical exploration of the seas, an improved Lecher wire experiment, antimatter and the employability of physics graduates. Letters to the editor concerned black body radiation, the concept of temperature, and the teaching of weight and weightlessness. A 1977 edition considered JMB physics papers 1951–76, profiles in examinations, physics curriculum work in IPN, Germany, the physics of a controversial goal in a World Cup hockey match, relativistic trajectories in homogeneous electric fields, CAL for undergraduate science teaching and physics in comprehensive schools. Letters to the editor were concerned with teaching temperature, (again!), relativity and rockets, atoms in the secondary school, and rubber elasticity. In 1984, articles considered science with handicapped pupils, nuclear weapons incorporated in a Dutch physics course, a practical approach to thermodynamics, a theoretical approach to wave mechanics, a demonstration of thermal imaging, notes on experiments to measure contact resistance and refractive indices, and a research report on pupils' preconceptions in mechanics. The letters to the editor here were concerned with the definition of units, the social responsibility of physicists and the place of electronics in the curriculum. Though most editions deliberately covered a wide range of topics, to satisfy the diverse interests of the readership, certain issues were to concentrate on specific themes and provide a more comprehensive covering. Editions concentrating on science in society (10.6), practical work (11.6), examinations (12.1), medical physics (13.2), physics in earth science (15.6), girls and physics (16.5), astronomy (17.4), and conceptions and misconceptions (20.4), typify something of the range of topics so covered.

When looking for overall trends in the distribution of articles in *Physics Education* since 1966, to see what changes in concerns have occurred, one is disappointed to find no simple pattern emerging. Possibly a decline in interests in pure physics, matched by an increase in interest in the applications of physics, a growth in educational research and philosophical questioning about the role of physics in schools, a decline in interest in the historical background to physics matched by an increase in awareness of the importance of the place of physics in contemporary society, the STS area. But these are mere 'straws in the wind', and may reflect the preferences of the editors as much as the interests of the market. What is of more significance is the changes that did not occur, the 'dogs that did not bark'. The individual articles reflected the different new courses, contemporary applications, and current educational interests. Yet, over a period when so many radical changes were happening in society as a whole and in schools in particular, when the challenges facing physics teachers were concerned with comprehensivization, with integration of the sciences, with mixed ability teaching, and with coping with decreasing resources and increasing demands from society, *Physics Education* was representing a largely unchanging image of physics teaching, continuing to support and encourage the individual physics teacher in his prime concern of teaching physics in the schools and colleges. It presented an essentially conservative influence, preserving the identity of physics education, defining and validating it in a way that conserved the natural interests of many graduate physicists in the schools. Though it was consistently humane and progressive in its editorial policy, all of the editors saw physics as a human activity as well as an academic subject and sought to encourage liberal and creative developments for the benefit of all pupils studying physics, the very medium through which they were working was the message that was conveyed. *Physics Education*, as physics education, was worth conserving and encouraging in the schools. This arm of the Institute of Physics activities played an important role in maintaining the strength, status and influence of an essentially 'grammar school' type of academic physics in all types of school. It had also done much to fulfil Keohane's other aim of contributing to, and encouraging, the 'community spirit' among those teaching physics in schools.

References

BODMER, W.F. (1985), *Public Understanding of Science*, London, Royal Society.
DEESON, E. (1985), 'Undercurrents: editorial', *Physics Education*, 20 June.
GOODIER, J. (1976), *Relationship between Mathematics and Physics, between the ages of 11 and 16*, London, Royal Society/Institute of Physics.
INSTITUTE OF PHYSICS (1950–), *Physics Bulletin*, Bristol, Institute of Physics.
INSTITUTE OF PHYSICS (1961 a), *Minutes of Membership and Education Committee*, 13 April, London, Institute of Physics.
INSTITUTE OF PHYSICS (1961 b), *Minutes of Membership and Education Committee*, 23 November, London, Institute of Physics.
INSTITUTE OF PHYSICS (1962), *Minutes of Education Group Committee*, 18 March, London, Institute of Physics.
INSTITUTE OF PHYSICS (1965), *Minutes of Physics Education Committee*, 14 December, London, Institute of Physics.
INSTITUTE OF PHYSICS (1966), *Minutes of Physics Education Committee*, 10 May, London, Institute of Physics.
INSTITUTE OF PHYSICS (1966–), *Physics Education*, Bristol, Institute of Physics.
KEOHANE, K.W. (1966), 'Editorial', *Physics Education*, 1.1, p. 1.

LEWIS, J. (1965), 'The Nuffield Physics Project', *Physics Bulletin*, 16.3. pp. 81–94.

MCCULLOCH, G., JENKINS, E., and LAYTON, D. (1985), *Technological Revolution?*, Lewes, Falmer Press.

MOTT, N. (1979), *Science and the Organisation of Schools in England — Implications for the Needs of Talented Children*, London, Royal Society.

MOTT, N. (1986), *A Life in Science*, London, Taylor and Francis.

PITT, H. (1982), *Science Education 11–18 in England and Wales*, London, Royal Society.

ROYAL SOCIETY (1965–), *Scientific Research in Schools Committee — Report to Council*, London, Royal Society.

ROYAL SOCIETY (1969), *Swing away from Science in Schools*, London, Royal Society.

ROYAL SOCIETY (1971), *Teaching Opportunities for Science, Technology and Maths Graduates*, London, Royal Society.

ROYAL SOCIETY (1972), *The Training of Teachers of Science and Mathematics*, London, Royal Society.

ROYAL SOCIETY/COUNCIL OF ENGINEERING INSTITUTES (1969), *The Shortage of Science and Maths Teachers in Schools*, London, Royal Society.

ROYAL SOCIETY/INSTITUTE OF PHYSICS (1969), *Teacher Training for Physics Graduates — A Commentary*, London, Royal Society.

ROYAL SOCIETY/INSTITUTE OF PHYSICS (1975), *Entry to Physics Courses at the Tertiary Level*, London, Royal Society.

ROYAL SOCIETY/INSTITUTE OF PHYSICS (1982), *Girls and Physics*, London, Royal Society.

ROYAL SOCIETY/INSTITUTE OF PHYSICS (1984), *A Reduced-Content 16+ Syllabus in Physics*, London, Royal Society.

SCOTT, D.W. (1963), *Training of Graduate Science Teachers' Report*, Cambridge, SMA/AWST.

SCOTT, D.W. (1966), 'Practical examinations', *Physics Education*, 1.1, pp. 52–8.

SCUE (1980), *A Minimal Core Syllabus for A Level Physics*, London, Standing Conference on University Entrance.

SPURGIN, C.B. (1967), 'What earns the marks?', *Physics Education*, 2.6, pp. 306–11.

SPURGIN, C.B. (1968), *Metrication in Schools*, London, Royal Society.

SPURGIN, C.B. (1969), *Metrication in Secondary Education*, London, Royal Society.

SPURGIN, C.B. (1970), *Metric Units in Primary Schools*, London, Royal Society.

THOMPSON, N. (1966), 'An experiment in examining at A level standard', *Physics Education*, 1.2, pp. 107–13.

THOMPSON, N. (1979, 1984 and 1986), *Statistics Relating to Education and Physics*, London, Institute of Physics.

6 'Marshalling the troops' — ASE Influences

The Association for Science Education

The ASE is the largest, most active, most influential, and most professionally organized of all the subject associations and has been involved with all the important developments in science education over the last twenty-five years. Formed in 1963 by the amalgamation of the SMA (the Science Masters Association), and the AWST, (the Association of Women Science Teachers), its roots had been the central agency for the definition and encouragement of school science since the beginning of the century (Layton, 1984). As a body it was to grow considerably, in staffing, organization and activity. In 1960 it had acquired its first permanent headquarters, in Cambridge, with its first full-time Secretary. It appointed its first General Secretary in 1962, Bill Tapper, who had previously taught physics at Dulwich College, to be succeeded in 1972 by Brian Atwood, a chemist from Great Barr Comprehensive School in Birmingham. These two men were the hub of ASE activity, and were supported as the activities increased by a growing team: in 1965 there was just one professional HQ staff, with nine clerical and ancillary; by 1973 there were three professionals with thirteen ancillaries; by 1982 it had grown to five professionals and twenty-eight ancillaries (p. 291). During the same period the annual turnover had increased from under £40,000 to over £900,000. ASE was big business!

While the Association was to prove an enormous stimulus to thousands of science teachers, its very nature and membership, as the *only* teachers organization for science teachers, was to have a significant effect on limiting the definition of science in the curriculum. In the phrase that David Layton used as the title of his defiinitive book on the history of the ASE, they set out to be the 'interpreters of science'. Representing as it did *all* science teachers it drew an enveloping boundary around the sciences and conveyed an unspoken message of the unity of science. Those things which united the membership were naturally accentuated, the distinctiveness of physics, chemistry and biology was played down. It was thus natural that such an association should move towards a united, preferably integrated, science and that the separate sciences should be discouraged. As the Association emphasized the oneness of science, it automatically drew a boundary around itself which enclosed a powerful and impregnable island state in the curriculum. The very strength of the Association made the science empire look impregnable from the outside and hindered possible negotiations with other subject areas. The existence of such a strong association as the ASE inevitably bound the sciences together in a way that was to make links with technology on the one hand, and the social sciences and mathematics on the other, less easy.

The strength and vitality of the Association always depended on the committed involvement of its lay members. In the early sixties its membership of 9000 represented almost all the graduate scientists in schools, who were teaching almost exclusively in the public and grammar schools of the day. They were a relatively homogeneous group, reflecting liberal ideas for teaching the sciences to able pupils. Through the sixties and seventies the membership grew to over 16,000, though now representing a smaller proportion of the science teaching force. By the early eighties it was reckoned to have one third of science teachers in its membership (p. 291). Furthermore, it had become not only larger but also more diverse. It increasingly drew its membership from the whole range of educational establishments, from the comprehensive as well as the public schools, from the primary schools as well as the sixth form college, and included teachers who spent their time teaching high level academic physics to the potential university students as well as those who were concerned only with teaching a more general practical science course to the less able. It was to become concerned both with education *through* science and education *in* science. As, during the seventies, the consensus among teachers concerning the aims and praxis of education broke down this reflected itself in the ASE. Inevitably, it had to contain tensions between differing groups, the conservatives against the radicals, the subject specialists against the integrationists, the idealists against the pragmatists, the elitists against the egalitarians. This variation in its membership, coupled with its constitutional position which obliged it to act democratically meant, as Layton so lucidly expounds, that it was impotent to give a single, representative lead to the science teaching profession. This left the way open for some body, or bodies, to take control of the committees and propogate a particular line. In the event, the struggles for power between the different parties ebbed and flowed but one group, one person, undoubtedly manipulated much of the ASE thinking through the seventies in a way which might not have been possible had there been less diversity. The size of the membership, and the inevitable time delay in gaining the membership's views, meant that in a time when fast responses were demanded by the media, the DES and the government, the people with influence in the inner corridors of the ASE had considerable power to present a particular view of science to the outside world which might not, which could not, represent the views of all its membership. Consequently the gap between the leadership and the membership of ASE was, at times, large.

It is ironic that in the sixties, when the ASE leadership did reasonably represent a consensus among its membership, a specific ASE view was rarely sought. When, through the seventies and into the eighties, the ASE resolved to have a greater say in articulating and defining school science, the diversity of its membership made it impossible for a single voice to be representative. It is possible, however, to see a clear development of the official policy of the ASE, a policy which became increasingly to be seen as the dominant voice of science education. It was not always a voice which found resonance among many of its members.

ASE Publications

The ASE worked at three levels: through its publications; through its local activities; and through its national committee structure which determined policy and central activities. For most of the members it was the first that has continually been most valuable in giving support and encouragement for their everyday teaching. For a very reasonable annual subscription, the members regularly received the journal *School Science Review* (SSR, 1919–), and the house magazine *Education in Science* (EiS, 1965–). *SSR* has had a most impressive history going back to 1919, and published three or four editions per year. The format of *SSR* has remained largely unchanged, containing articles on science, on science education and pedagogy, experimental notes contributed by members, book and film reviews, and letters to the editor. The continuity of the journal is recognized by browsing through old editions and finding not only the same experiments reinvented but also very similar issues being discussed as matters of topical concern. The shortage of physics teachers and the paucity of girls doing science, the sterility of current science courses and the need for more relevance, the plea for science for all and the vocational demands on teachers, were all perennial matters of debate well before 1960. Throughout our period there have only been two editors of the *SSR*, R.H. Dyball (1954–66) from the City of London School and A.A. Bishop (1966–) from Harrow School.

SSR is also the vehicle through which publishers and apparatus manufacturers advertise most freely. Most teachers found the *SSR* contained a feast of stimulating material, and it would be no disrespect to the quality of the main articles to say that these were usually read last. Most physics teachers would first skim through the new apparatus and books, then the experiments and demonstrations in the physics notes section, then the book reviews and, finally, if time and inclination was left, the main science articles that caught their interest. It was a very rare edition that did not carry something of interest and immediate utility for teaching. Like *Physics Education*, it had found a good compromise pattern and conserved that throughout the period, with only cosmetic changes in style.

As the ASE sought to play a more interventionist role, it expanded its publications as a means of communicating with, and influencing, its membership. Conceived in the prolific and increasingly influential Ed(R) Committee, a study series of publications was started in 1974 which included reports and writings on a wide range of issues of concern to science teachers. They were, by providing authoritative yet accessible, analyses of fundamental educational issues, to play an important part in the growing sophistication and professionalism of science teachers through the second half of the seventies. By 1985, the study series had published seventeen books on a wide range of topics including *Non-streamed Science, A Teachers Guide* (Sturges, 1975), *Science in the Middle Years* (Squires, 1976), *The Head of Science and the Task of Management* (Siddle, 1978), and *Language in Science* (Prestt, 1980). They were to have a wide circulation and be used individually and as the basis for discussion in many science department and ASE meetings. They were to provide important help to many heads of department faced with the new challenges of rethinking and teaching science in a rapidly changing school context.

With the raising of the school leaving age to 16, in 1974, the need to support teachers teaching science to ill-motivated 14-to-16-year olds was recognized in the books published from the ASE LAMP project (science for the Less Academically Motivated Pupil). This was also set up by the Ed(R) Committee. Under the leadership of Ros Driver, a physics tutor at the Department of Education, University of Leeds, teachers gathered together in local groups to share their ideas and the work schemes used with this increasingly populous, but low status and unresourced, type of teaching. They produced an excellent teachers' guide, outlining various approaches and stressing their rationale of using such teaching as the basis for an 'education *through* science', and a series of fifteen topic-based books centred on sets of experiment worksheets on such relevant topics as photography, flight, gardening and health (Driver 1977–78). It was the first series of books to provide help for the teacher of these 'problem' forms, and was to be the forerunner of the commercially produced material such as Open Science and Science at Work. It was an example of ASE activity at its best, with members bringing their coordinated experience together for the benefit of the profession as a whole. Though far from perfect, it established a market and provided quick, cheap support from the example of which teachers could develop their own schemes.

Similar pioneer work was later done by the ASE in stimulating the teaching of science in its wider social context. Through the sponsoring and publication of course material, first John Lewis' *Science in Society* (Lewis, 1981), then Joan Solomon's *SiSCON in Schools* (Solomon, 1983) and finally John Holman's *SATIS Project* (Holman, 1985), they both created and met a need among science teachers.

The influence of all these schemes in challenging and stimulating more arid and academic teaching was considerable. LAMP opened up the 'bottom-up' approach to science teaching and, with its emphasis on topic-based work and education through science, established a base from which such ideals could be extended upwards to, and possibly through, the average ability range too. The STS materials were targetted initially for a lower sixth form science in society course and consequently did not find a large uptake in this limited market. However their influence was far greater than their sales as, by stimulating an approach and a methodology for introducing such an approach to science teaching, they caused many teachers and textbook writers to include such material into their teaching at all other levels too.

ASE Members and Meetings

Apart from the few members who were involved with the committees of the ASE, the principal personal contact for most members was through meetings. These were held at the local, regional or branch level and at annual conferences held at different university venues around the country. The local meetings were the focus for a core of the membership and, though not actively involving more than a small proportion, proved a stimulus and source of creative debate for many. Typically meetings would be held on new curriculum initiatives, on interesting developments in science and pedagogical issues. Some would be subject specific, others concerned with science as a whole. A common type of meeting in the sixties was 'how I teach ...', with teachers sharing their latest demonstration or teaching approach with each other. In the seventies these were replaced by more general issues relating to problems of mixed ability teaching, individualized learning and language in science. Many of the meetings were led by members for members, though from time to time speakers from the scientific community in the local university or industry would bring in the latest ideas. Most regions organized social occasions and visits, many also provided lecture demonstrations for local sixth form and/or fourth form students. The local meetings also provided a mechanism, albeit a slow one, for eliciting reaction to discussion and policy statements from the ASE Executive, and a means of feeding local concerns into headquarters. As a means of mutual support and encouragement, these meetings were invaluable. As a means of communication between headquarters and its membership, of the Executive keeping in touch with the needs of the practising science teacher or of the membership getting its concerns onto the agenda of the Executive, it was less efficient. Power inevitably lay at the centre, and became more so as the scale and complexity of the operation increased. The sheer size and diversity of the local membership meant that the lay members of the central committees had to use their own experience and perspectives and trust that the membership would shout if its proceedings got too far out of line, as it periodically did!

The annual meeting of the ASE grew steadily in size and importance throughout our period. Whereas in 1960 a few hundred members attended the meeting at the University of Southampton, by 1985 the University of Keele was bursting at the seams with over 3000 members attending. With the increase in pastoral and non-scientific concerns in the schools, science teachers found refreshment by recharging their scientific batteries in the company of other committed science teachers at the annual meetings. The meetings lasted for three or four days and included a wide range of activities. Talks and seminars on scientific and science education issues were at the centre of the programme, with an increasing emphasis on the broader issues of teaching science to pupils of a wider ability range. Layton suggests that 'a turning point in the balance between science and science education components in the programme came at Leeds 1974' (Layton, 1984, p. 144). But there was always a full programme of lectures on the latest scientific developments from the host university lecturers to update the scientific knowledge of the specialist subject teachers. The annual meeting also provided a good forum for the launching and propogation of new curriculum initiatives to a wide audience.

Also popular, and influential for physics teachers, were the publishers and manufacturers exhibitions at which all the current and new books and apparatus were on display. Many teachers would take this opportunity to browse among the new books and to see and try out the new apparatus, both of which were presented with a considerable amount of professional persuasion. These exhibitions did much to disseminate a reliance on commerically produced apparatus and engendered an expectation that good physics teaching depended on the acquiring of the latest oscilloscope or ripple tank. For those with inadequate budgets it was an opportunity to make detailed notes for subsequent apparatus plagiarism back in the school workshops in the best tradition of physics teacher's industrial espionage! The increasing dependence on commercially produced apparatus was reflected in the decline in size and vitality of the members' exhibition. Through the sixties this had provided an opportunity for many of the more creative physics teachers to show off their own designs and inventions to colleagues, and this was always a lively and fertile focus for physics teachers. By the late seventies and early eighties it had become a much more peripheral exhibition with only a few demonstrations and displays from dedicated enthusiasts. This shift in emphasis was accentuated by one of the theatrical highlights of the meeting, the spectacular demonstration by John Lewis, Geoffrey Foxcroft and Jim Jardine of 'What's new in physics apparatus?'. This *tour de force* started in the early Nuffield days and was the opportunity to demonstrate the new apparatus the manufacturers had produced for the new course, it developed from this and provided the manufacturers with a public show case for their new ideas. Though the presenters showed discrimination and unbiased opinion on the value of individual items in this flood of new material, their enthusiastic and expert demonstrations inevitably conveyed the message that all physics teachers should use such equipment. The message that physics might be better taught with simpler, home made, apparatus, or none at all, could not be conveyed so visually.

Overall, however, the annual meetings provided an important encouragement to science teachers, to science education, and because of the variety of inputs, to the teaching of the separate sciences too. In effect the meeting grew so that it was a series of different conferences to different people. A specialist physics teacher could fill his time with lectures on modern physics, visits to the physics labs, and talking with other physics teachers among the exhibitions of physics apparatus and books. He would have had his perceptions of the importance and style of physics teaching reinforced. At the other extreme, certainly since 1974, a teacher committed to a common science policy for all pupils could have been occupied with seminars on mixed ability teaching and the role of language in learning, with enjoying talks on SCISP and searching for resource material from the industrial exhibitors, and talking informally over meals and drinks with other educators who were seeking to make a science curriculum fit for comprehensive education. Such a member would have come away with his, or her, perceptions of the irrelevance and terminal decline of physics, and encouraged to continue along the new path to an equalitarian utopia. There would have been very few teachers who would not have been remotivated, encouraged and returned to their, often lonely, task strengthened with new ideas, a case full of free resources, and a renewed determination to teach even better. In this way, the formal and informal inputs at the annual meetings of the ASE have provided a highly positive, if undirected, stimulus to thousands of science teachers and have done much to maintain the morale and standards of science teaching throughout the country.

ASE Policy

The formulation of policy by the ASE has inevitably been a difficult and tortuous business, and one which has not always allowed unambiguous interpretation. As it sought to establish an enlightened consensus view of the membership it necessarily produced compromise statements, but ones which reflected and encouraged good practice. In the event, the process leading up to the policy statements was more important than the product itself, and allowed groups of members to refine and articulate their own thinking which, while often 'ahead of the field', was to prove influential in the more rarified corridors of power.

There were three periods in which policy formulation was attempted, each at a time when the situation in the schools was changing significantly. In the early years of the sixties the ASE (then the SMA and AWST) produced a series of reports largely concerned with science teaching in the grammar schools. These, arising out of the Science and Education project, included the *Physics for Grammar Schools* (SMA/AWST, 1961) and *An Expansion and Teachers Guide to Physics for Grammar Schools* (ASE, 1963) which were to be so formative in modernising the physics syllabuses and seminal to the work of the Nuffield 'O' level Physics course. The overarching policy statement, *School Science and General Education*, was published in 1961 and revised four years later (ASE, 1961 and 1965). It represented, in a clearly articulated form, the traditional view of science being an important part of the 'cultural and humanistic heritage' of all pupils, and recommended that 'all pupils should follow a balanced course of science subjects up to the end of their fifth-form studies' (ASE, 1961, p. 5) as one of the core subjects in a liberal education. While the first edition was a statement mainly concerning grammar schools, (the SMA had previously reported on secondary modern science teaching [SMA, 1953 and 1957]), when the second edition was published in 1965, it was overtly claimed now to have been 'widened in scope to cater for all school pupils, not only for the minority in grammar schools'. The fact that there were so few differences between the two editions reflected the widely held belief in the ASE that 'grammar school science' was entirely appropriate for all pupils. Thus the ASE was reinforcing the status of physics, chemistry and biology, though it was perceived that in years 1 and 2 work 'would be integrated into the science of the Introductory Phase, and some time given to astronomy and geology' (ASE, 1965, p. 12), and in the Intermediate Phase from year 3–5 'efforts should be made to coordinate' the three sciences (p. 9). But the position of the sciences was strong and the policy statement was confidently able to claim that a large proportion of the whole (academic) curriculum should be devoted to science, six out of thirty-five periods in years 1 and 2,(17 per cent), and nine out of thirty-five periods in years 3, 4, and 5(25 per cent) (p. 12). The ASE policy in 1965 was for an expansion of modernized, practically-based, grammar school type, physics, chemistry and biology for all pupils.

The second phase of policy development occurred in the early 1970s when it was clear that the rapidly changing situation in the schools, in which science was increasingly being taught in mixed ability classes in comprehensive schools, demanded a fresh look at an overall policy. This resulted in three booklets, *Science and General Education* (ASE, 1971 a), *Science for the Under Thirteens* (ASE, 1971 b) and *Science for the 13–16 Age Group* (ASE, 1973 a). The first of these was a slim, bland, mouse of a document which accepted that the science courses could be '... most usefully categorized in the broad areas of interest to the biologist, chemist and physicist' (ASE, 1961 a, p. 3) and then advocated the usual truisms about needing good teachers, resources, in-service training, and curriculum development to ensure that the sciences should occupy a key position in the school curriculum. Perhaps its most (only!) contentious remark was in criticizing recent curriculum developments for the 'laboured insistence on the pupils discovering the concepts and principles of the subjects', leaving no time for applying the principles to real situations and problems in applied science and technology or to encourage creativity (ASE, 1971 a, p. 8). Clearly some of the ASE traditionalists had not accepted the Nuffield philosophy nor forgotten the perceived slight in not being given the responsibility to develop the science and education syllabuses themselves!

The other two booklets, however, were much more forward-looking. While neither espoused a clear policy, they both encouraged a fresh look at science and made clear what they considered was good practice. The 11–13 booklet (ASE, 1971 b) opened with Rousseau's quote

> Teach your scholar to observe the phenomena of nature; you will rouse his curiosity, but if you would have it grow, do not be in too great a hurry to satisfy this curiosity. Put the problems before him and let him solve them himself ... Let him not be taught science, let him discover it ... If you ever substitute authority for reason he will cease to reason; he will become a mere plaything of other people's thoughts (p. 3)

and continues to encourage a wide range of experiences on which to build the later structured thinking. It encouraged a strong emphasis on the processes of science, and of understanding the nature of science, and the pupils' personal involvement in devising, inventing and constructing to solve a problem. Suggestions were given regarding content, or appropriate 'areas of experience', and to methods of teaching with an emphasis on the child's learning rather than teacher's teaching. It was emphasizing a child-centred, relevant, stimulating science, derived from the best secondary modern practice rather than the grammar school. Whereas the experiments in *Physics for the Grammar Schools* were designed to discover the right theory, *Science for the Under Thirteens* was now talking about fieldwork, projects and pupil investigations. This approach was to be expanded in *Science in the Middle Years* (Squires, 1976), and in the *Science 5–13* material (Ennever and Harlen, 1972), but was to find slow acceptance in the subject dominated secondary schools. These were way ahead of the existing practice in most schools which still had highly structured, convergent, content-led syllabuses, in which Nuffield combined science was most popular. The policy advocated a 20 per cent time allocation to science at this stage.

Science for the 13–16 Age Group also advocated that science should have at least 20 per cent of the time available, for all pupils, and discussed in detail the essential requirements for science teaching. Most significantly it justified the place of science in the curriculum of every pupil as a balance of three different aspects, science for the inquiring mind, science in action, and science for citizenship. These three strands were to become important through many discussions over the next decade, stressing the relevant application of science and the social implications of science along with the understanding of the principles of science themselves. 'The value of this document', the introduction asserted, 'will be measured by the amount of discussion it generates amongst science teachers' (ASE, 1973a, p. 3). Unfortunately, these policy documents did not arouse the public discussion they deserved; teachers were too busy grappling with ways of teaching the grammar school science they were familiar with to too wide ability classes in their reorganized schools to worry about whether the type of science they were trying to teach was appropriate. At that time, the authority of Nuffield was convincing and child-centred, unstructured investigations did not look impressive or, indeed, feasible.

In 1976 the officers of the ASE were persuaded by the then Chairman, Jeff Kirkham, that they should have a higher profile in the public definition and pronouncements on science policy; a principle readily accepted by the succeeding chairmen, John Lewis and Dick West, and by Jeff Thompson. The Ed(R) Committee, under Dick West, was in full flow having set up the study series booklets, the LAMP project and, in 1977, a small working party to produce a forward-looking policy for the 1980s. When in 1977 the ASE had the opportunity to present its views to the House of Commons Expenditure Committee, with Shirley Williams as the sympathetic Secretary of State for Education, it did so with conviction (ASE, 1977, pp. 16–18). It repeated its belief in the three aspects of science (for enquiring minds, for action and for citizenship) as being appropriate for all pupils in a changing society which was evolving towards a more egalitarian form. It spoke, after the theme developed in LAMP, of education *through* science as being appropriate for all students, and stressed the 'clear need for the development of a core of unified science for all pupils in the 11–16 age range' (p. 16).The science which was to be an essential component of all pupils should be experimentally based with the consequent implications for adequate time, laboratory and equipment resourcing. It presented a picture which carried the support of the vast majority of the membership, amongst the teachers, the educators, the advisers and the Inspectorate. Such consensus was, perhaps, too good to last, and the setting up of the working party under Jeff Thompson in the same year was to show that beneath such superficial unity there was a radical difference of educational philosophy that could be hidden no longer.

The working party established under the auspices of the Ed(R) Committee to review the present state of science education in schools and consider 'possible strategies for action which might be adopted by the Association' (Thompson, 1978, p. 12), was to be chaired by Jeff Thompson, and contained Dick West, Kate Ellington, John Ellis, Kate Hinton, Colin Johnson and Doug Kincaid. It was clear from the start that this group, selected, *ad hominem*, for their individual contributions, were an atypical group of ASE members and unlikely to represent the membership as a whole. They were indeed a stimulating and provocative group and, after a series of lively and often confrontational meetings produced the highly contentious *Alternatives for Science Education* (ASE, 1979). This, with its highly political perspective, its sociological analysis and revolutionary alternatives caused an anguished response when sent to every member, and many public bodies in 1979.

It was the political critique, and the dismissal of the separate sciences, which caused the most dismay. Its perceptions revealed the existing structure of science in the schools as being socially, and politically divisive. Building on the work of Bernstein and Young, it exposed the retention of the separate sciences as a relic of the old grammar school system, inappropriate to the needs of the majority of the pupils and, by their very existence in the curriculum, preventing the majority of pupils from developing their potential. It challenged much of the recent curriculum development and current thinking about education in science, and postulated, redefined, science as a vehicle for general personal development. Science itself was to be replaced by science studies, which, while aiming to ensure that the pupil acquired scientific understanding, scientific skills, and the ability to function autonomously in an area of scientific studies, also aimed at giving a scientific perspective of looking at the world, at giving the youngster a sense of social meaning and identity as well as personal autonomy, and an understanding of advanced technological societies and the complex interaction between science and society. There was, consequently, much support for the inclusion of history and philosophy of science, either as a separate subject or incorporated into others. And all of this was to be taught in not more than 20 per cent of the curriculum time. Those teachers who had been teaching the three separate sciences in, perhaps, 30 per cent of the timetable time naturally felt threatened. And, indeed, that was the intention for it was believed that the new science studies would never prove acceptable, would never attain 'parity of esteem' while the high-status separate subjects remained. Twenty per cent maximum would make it impossible for the three separate sciences to be taught to anyone.

Up to the end of the second year the recommendations caused no distress, indeed they merely echoed the recommendations of the *Science for the Under Thirteens* policy statement of 1971. But the suggestions in the 13–16 age range were widely criticized. The separate sciences seemed to have disappeared, indeed in the whole of the discussion document the subject physics is mentioned only three times, compared with 197 references to science, science studies or integrated science. Integrated Science was the preferred option for years 13–16, but it was also suggested that one or two subjects could be taken from biological science, physical science, earth science, and history and philosophy of science. An alternative pattern was to take core science for 10 per cent of the time with an optional study drawn from either further science, applied science, or the history and philosophy of science. There was a third alternative, that the third year would be spent on experimental science, the fourth year on applied science and the fifth year on science and society, but few teachers or indeed working party members thought that this fragmented pattern was sufficiently well thought out to merit serious attention. Through all the proposals, many felt that undue emphasis had been given to individual study, to the history and sociology of science, and to the applications of science in society and too little emphasis to the science content itself. In emphasizing the commonality of education for all through science studies, there had been too little emphasis to the distinctive value of an in-depth study for the most able. When, in 1979, the discussion document was sent to all ASE members, and to many public bodies and institutions for 'consultation', a considerable amount of anguished debate ensued throughout the country. The political aspects of the role and type of science taught had been brought out into the open, but the majority of the membership did not recognize in it the activity of teaching physics or science in their own schools.

Traditionally ASE policy and public statements had sought to be uncontentious, representing as much of the membership as possible, and was therefore conservative. This report, though the ASE establishment hastened to state that it was not a policy document merely a discussion document, was the result of a quite different approach with the leadership seeking to lead rather than represent its membership. It represented the result of Dick West's involvement with, and determination to be progressive in policy formulation. Its line can be traced back to his 1971 paper redefining ASE's role through the Ed(R) Committee, 'to an agency for supporting the innovations found in our better schools and amongst our professional colleagues who concern themselves with defining science education' (Layton, 1984, p. 124). By his chairmanship of the Ed(R) Committee he had been able to help select those professional colleagues from 'better' schools for the working party and, as an active member of that group himself, had been instrumental in defining his view of science education and placing it to the forefront of ASE thinking. It was clear that this line did not receive complete support even from the working party. The cryptic last paragraph hints at some of the battles that went on before the report was published; while unanimously agreeing to publish the document they 'unreservedly defended their individual right to enter the public debate' that was to follow, and while recognizing that the exercise had brought the group together admitted that 'the product and the issues discussed have rightly divided us' (ASE, 1979, p. 54). If agreement could not be reached between seven handpicked members who had been working closely together on the document for nearly two years, it is not surprising that it did not elicit the support of the membership as a whole.

Indeed it caused great consternation among the ASE Council and a battle ensued between the more conservative members and the progressive 'young Turks' as to what should be done about it. A high powered policy group was set up under John Heaney's chairmanship, consisting of sixteen of the ASE's most senior members, and including Jeff Thompson and Dick West from the original working party, to produce an official ASE policy statement from the alternatives debate. In 1981, a most worthy, conciliatory, unexceptional statement was produced under the title *Education Through Science* (ASE 1981). This represented ASE's last attempt to provide 'a framework for policy decisions', which, because of the moderation of its tone, proved widely acceptable. By using the phrase that it was to 'provide a framework for policy decisions', rather than being an overt, agreed policy statement itself, it gave the leadership of the ASE a free hand to interpret a policy as seemed appropriate without further consultation of the membership. The *Education Through Science* document went a long way to present a positive statement of agreed good practice, without specifying any one particular, quantified, route. There was no reference to the contentious time allowances, no mention of 'a maximum of 20 per cent', there was bland assurances about 'a reasonable balance between the specialist and the generalist aspects of education through science' and there was even reassurance for the many subject specialists teaching in schools '... the Association remains, both here and in all its other recommendations, fully committed to the maintenance of appropriate academic standards in the basic disciplines of biology, chemistry and physics' (p. 24).

Some have accused the ASE of retreating from progress in this reactionary non-policy statement, but in fact it did contain many excellent and perceptive insights into the appropriate nature and practice of science teaching in schools — concentrating on the content rather than the labels of the science lessons taught. It discussed the current and future needs in school science and suggested broad guidelines for their development, it reaffirmed its belief in science for all up to 16, and wrote a splendid section on the pedagogic implications of such a policy; stressing the pupil-centredness rather than the subject centredness of such an approach. It spoke too of the resource implications for the science for all policy and discussed ways that the ASE might be involved in implementing it. It had backed away from the political battle, and withdrawn into the safer confines of science teaching. The ASE had made a second bid to control the curriculum, with a bold, progressive, but unrepresentative, attack led by Dick West through the Ed(R) Committee and the alternatives working party. It had not carried the day, and the headquarters command withdrew the advance guard to consolidate ground. Perhaps the ASE recognized that power for policy making would never again be open to opportunist initiatives, with central government, science advisers and HMI becoming much more powerful and interventionist in their actions.

There were signs however that, although the ASE officially withdrew from the alternatives approach, it had made a permanent mark on the battle field and left behind a few mortal wounds (or seeds of new life, if one chooses a more positive metaphor!) that would have ongoing significance. The first outcome of the 'alternatives' thinking was carried forward towards the end of 1979 when officers of the ASE met the Minister of State for Education at the DES to talk around a prepared paper (ASE, 1980, pp. 27–30). Though the early discussion of the alternatives paper had shown much opposition to it, and it had certainly not been accepted as official policy, certain central ideas from it were transmitted to the DES. The argument was set in its political context, from which it was extrapolated that separate sciences were the cause of the problem and integrated science the solution. 'It would be very dangerous if the majority of the population were to accept technological changes in an apathetic, uninterested or uncomprehending way, leaving value judgements and decisions to a cultural elite. This would be particularly dangerous if that elite were itself educated on a narrow, academic basis of pure, traditional science' (p. 27), was its assertion. 'Overspecializing in three sciences with a consequent danger that social, aesthetic and cultural development may (sic!) be neglected' dismissed the separate sciences, and this was reinforced by the statement that 'all pupils aged 14–16 should spend at least 10 per cent and not more than 20 per cent of their time studying science'. Thus, the self-imposed restriction of a 20 per cent maximum time allocation came through to the DES as the official ASE line and eventually got accepted as definitive policy in the DES policy statement *Science 5–16* (DES, 1985). Significantly, no other subject has such a prescribed time limit given to it by DES and indeed no serious policy has been established as to how the other 80 per cent of the time is to be divided up. No serious thought was given to whether technology, or electronics, should be part of that 20 per cent or additional to it, though in much of the rhetoric science and technology are inextricably joined. The 20 per cent maximum was, I believe, driven through on the political imperative of destroying the existence of the three separate sciences rather than on any precise, objective argument about balance in the curriculum as a whole.

It is interesting to note how the ASE policies have steadily reduced the time requirement for science at the 14–16 age range. In 1961 and 1965 it demanded nine periods out of thirty-five, 25 per cent for all. In 1973 it was asking for at least 20 per cent of the total time available, for all pupils. By 1980 it was asserting that 20 per cent should be a maximum, with 10 per cent being allowed for some. Whether this was due to a realistic appraisal of what a limited science teaching force could teach, a conscious belief that science teaching is worth less, or the result of reconsidering the priorities of a comprehensive rather than a grammar school education, is unclear. It undoubtedly meant that many of the more able students would be spending less time studying the sciences before the age of 16 than they, or their teachers, or many areas of industry and higher education would like. It remains to be seen whether this 20 per cent maximum policy will become a reality.

The second outcome of the alternatives working party was in the ground work it laid for the ASE/Schools Council Secondary Science Curriculum Review (SSCR) (SSCR, 1982; Ebbutt and Evatt, 1985). When Dick West was appointed Director of the new SSCR project in 1982, he took much of his alternatives thinking with him. Through that medium he was to disseminate the science studies with criteria very much in line with the rationale in alternatives. It is not easy to disentangle the influences and products in this monumental exercise in local teacher-led curriculum development, to determine how much has been the result of ASE policy, grass roots self-expression, or science adviser opportunism, but it is clear that the centrally established policy and *modus operandi* owes much to the thinking and direction of Dick West and can be traced back through the involvement in 'alternatives', the chairmanship of ASE, the chairmanship of Ed(R), the authorship of the ASE Case Studies in Curriculum Development and his earlier experiences and writing (West, 1969, 1972, 1976, and 1981). Throughout the 1970s the work and thinking of the ASE and Dick West were inextricably entwined.

Perhaps the most significant change in ASE policies, however, has concerned their view of the nature of an appropriate science education. In the early sixties, it accepted the traditional, grammar school, academic, separate subject curriculum as being the norm and appropriate for all. It was more removed from 'real life' than even some of the earlier policies, and was essentially an intellectual exercise of 'science for the enquiring mind'. Through our period, ASE has increasingly asserted that science teaching should not just be that. It should be set in its human and social context, it should relate to its applications in society and give pupils an understanding of the social implications of science in society, its strengths and its limitations. It has steadily redirected teaching away from focusing on the subject, in which the teacher is trying to find ways of getting the content of a subject that should be known into the minds of pupils, to focusing on the pupil, where the teacher is trying to find ways of helping pupils build up their own knowledge and skills in science in a way that is appropriate to their personal lives. It has tried to rethink a comprehensive school science that is genuinely appropriate to the majority of pupils from a bottom-up approach, and moved away from a grammar school science which was successful for a minority of pupils and had been dictated by a university dominated top-down approach. It has become less certain that there is one right way of teaching science to all, and less confident that the dominance of the guided discovery practical work can satisfy the other important aims such as decision making, concept formation, and social awareness that discussion, simulations, and reading can foster. It is in these fundamental, underlying concerns, rather than the more obvious but superficial changes from the sciences to science to science studies, that the ASE's policies have been most constructive and far-reaching.

Perhaps the area of policy in which the ASE had been least successful, has been in its relation to technology. The early policy statements emphasized a distinctively pure form of science, and while those of the seventies and eighties sought to put that science back into its social context, aiming to prepare pupils to play a responsible role in an increasingly technological society, its policies never really got to grips with technology. In 1973 the Association published a 'view' on school science and technology, in which they suggested a policy of technology through science (ASE, 1973 b). In this it stressed that science teaching should incorporate the applications and technological implications of science and that it should expose the pupils to decision-making activities. However, it never went further to engage with others involved in technology in school. Indeed, Geoffrey Harrison, the Director of Project Technology from 1966–72, said 'The Association was consulted time and time again but always refused to have anything to do with the project, officially anyway' (Harrison, 1980, p. 138). It was an opportunity missed. While its statements often linked science and technology, as if they were synonymous, and sought to stress the importance of science for and in a technological world, it was never clear about its relationship with the more creative and instrumental forms of technology expressed through the craft and CDT departments, through the Project Technology, the SCSST and NCST networks, or more recently through the TVEI schemes. The Association, representing and consisting of scientists, inevitably had an emphasis which lay deep in the academic, ordered, educational culture of the scientist and the science laboratories; this was out of sympathy with the more entrepreneurial, practical, opportunist, vocational culture of the craftsman and the workshop. Furthermore the emphasis that the Association gave to the integration of the sciences through the seventies turned it in upon itself and away from forming links with other subject areas. It remains to be seen whether this was a wise emphasis, or whether the scientists in contemplating their own integrated navel, were ignoring the more significant changes that were occurring in the curriculum as a whole and around technology in particular.

Where the Power Lay

If the strength of the ASE lay with its large membership, the power for determining policy resided in a much smaller group of people operating in and through the central committee structure. David Layton, in his definitive book *Interpreters of Science* (1984) has documented admirably the history of the ASE and its committee structures and has discussed the fundamental tensions within the constitution, communication and control of science education. Here, we have concentrated only on those aspects of relevance to the development of physics education in our period.

When the Trust Deed of the new ASE was set up in 1963, the objectives of the Association were defined as the promotion of education by: '(a) improving the teaching of science; (b) providing an authoritative medium through which opinion of teachers of science may be expressed on educational matters; and (c) affording means of communication among all persons and bodies of persons concerned with the teaching of science in particular and with education in general' (Layton, 1984, p. 108). Thus science, not the sciences, was to be the focus, an authoritative voice of science sought, and science perceived as a part of general education. A Governing Council was established to look after the conduct of the Association's affairs, with a smaller Executive Committee having responsibility for the management of its business. The Science and Education Committee of the SMA, which had been so influential in developing the syllabuses for grammar school physics, chemistry and biology which lead into the Nuffield projects, was to become the Education Committee of the ASE with Henry Boulind, the physics tutor at the Department of Education, University of Cambridge remaining its Chairman until 1967. By then, however, it had become clear that its work and responsibilities had become too large and diverse for one committee and, in 1968 it divided into two; the Education (Coordinating) Committee, (Ed(C)), 'responsible for the month by month coordination of and comment on matters arising in the science teaching field' and the Education (Research) Committee, (Ed(R)), designed for longer-term policy and pioneering issues. 'Just as the work of the Science and Education Committee of the SMA was said to have led to the Nuffield Projects, so, it was argued, the new committee would initiate projects of a research character . . . ' (p. 123).

Roy Schofield, the physics tutor at the Department of Education, Brunel University was the first Chairman, followed by I.D.S. Robertson from Jordanhill College of Education until 1971. In 1971 a general review of the Committee's policy was instituted, and written by the Chairman-elect, Dick West, an ex-London comprehensive school teacher then holding an educational research post at the Department of Education, University of Surrey. This was to be the platform for his meteoric rise through the ranks of both the ASE and his University department, and was to establish his powerful position of influence from which so much of the subsequent activity and policy of ASE was to spring. Dick West's vision of the role of the Ed(R) Committee was far more active and discriminating. 'If ASE is to continue to play a central part in defining science education policy and practice,' he wrote, 'and to become a think tank of creative ideas . . . and an agency for supporting the innovations found in our better schools and amongst our professional colleagues who concern themselves with defining science education' (pp. 124 and 125), then Ed(R) must change and become more consciously dirigist. No criteria were established for the value judgments inferred by 'better' schools, or how science was to be defined, or redefined, but these were to become revealed by the subsequent products of the Committee under his chairmanship, from 1972–77, especially through the Alternatives for Education discussion paper and the SSCR. When Dick West became the ASE's first, formal link with the Schools Council in 1976, as the ASE's Honorary Secretary for Schools Council Liaison, the chairmanship of the Ed(R) Committee passed to Maurice Savory (1977–82) and John Heaney (1982–85+). Though the Council had to approve any paper or statement that was published as official ASE policy it became clear that the Ed(R) Committee was the spring for much of the ASE policy and the Chairman of this Committee had considerable power to influence both the developments that were encouraged and those that were not. Dick West's own considerable role in influencing the publicly favoured definition of science in schools was evident in the development of the ASE policy statements.

Other positions of influence in the ASE were the general secretaries at headquarters, the chairmen of the Association, and the editors of the SSR. The Association was fortunate in having so much continuity and political diplomacy in the two leaders of the full-time staff, Bill Trotter (1962–72) and Brian Atwood (1972–). The Chairman of the ASE is elected annually from its membership, with a preceding year on Council as Chairman-elect and a succeeding year as immediate past Chairman. Each in their turn have had an important and distinctive influence on the ASE, though arguably Jeff Kirkham (1976), John Lewis (1977), Dick West (1978) and Jeff Thompson (1981), especially the latter pair, have been most influential in steering the ASE into a more politically active and interventionist role through the troubled and exciting last decade. In the twenty-six years from 1960 to 1985 the post of Chairman has been occupied by four women and twenty-two men, consisting of eighteen school teachers, three LEA advisers, four tutors in university departments of education, and one from the Nuffield Foundation. There had been seven physicists, fourteen chemists, four biologists and one physical scientist among the chairmen.

Interestingly, the relative involvement and influence of physicists and chemists in the ASE hierarchy has varied dramatically in the two halves, before and after 1973. From 1959 to 1973 there were six physicist chairmen and five chemists. Henry Boulind and Bill Tapper, the General Secretaries until 1972, were also physicists by training. The first Chairman of the Ed(R) Committee from 1968–70, Roy Schofield, was a physicist. From 1974 to 1986 only two of the chairmen were physicists and ten were chemists. At the same time the General Secretary and the Editor of the SSR were Brian Atwood and Andrew Bishop, who had also had their initial training in chemistry. The Chairman of the Ed(R) Committee since 1972, Dick West (1972–77), Maurice Savory (1977–82) and John Heaney (1982–85) were all chemistry teachers. Such a variation may have no significance and any speculation about a cause and effect be of little statistical validity. But the correlation between the style and activity of the ASE in these two halves, and the physics/chemist distribution does invite explanation. Were the physicists more able and more in tune with the needs of the grammar school science teaching through the sixties, were the chemists more able and more in tune to the comprehensive science needed for the last decade? Was the decline in physicists in leadership roles in the ASE a reflection of the decline in quantity and quality of physicists in schools? Were the chemists, midway between biologists and physicists, the ideal people to understand an integrated science? — certainly the vast majority of teachers advocating integrated science were chemists. Were the majority of physics teachers and biologists so contentedly occupied teaching their own subject not to want to become involved in the politics of integration? Had the chemists lost faith in their own subject as a suitable subject for a comprehensive education for all, and were searching through science for their *raison d'etre* in the comprehensive school? Did the innovative chemists lose patience with the traditional physics teacher and make him, or her, feel *persona non grata* in the heady days when integration was in fashion? Certainly in many of the debates about the wisdom of some of the more *avant garde* proposals from the ASE committees, it was the physicists who were cast in the role of the reactionary traditionalists, (Fred Archenhold, Alan Hall, Roy Schofield, Brian Chapman, and Ed James, physicists all, were well known to be on the conservative wing of the party, and often made their opposition to the evolving ASE policy public [for example, Schofield, 1974; Chapman, 1976]). Did the physicists increasingly feel more affinity with the technologies, of CDT, electronics, and computing, than with the other experimental scientists? Or was it just coincidence or a self-perpetuating dynasty?! Whatever the reason, it is unlikely that the shift in power from physicists to chemists in the ASE is unrelated to the ASEs move towards integrated science.

References

ASE (1918–), *School Science Review*, Hatfield, ASE.
ASE (1963), *An Expansion and Teachers Guide to Physics for Grammar Schools*, Hatfield, ASE.
ASE (1961 and 1965), *School Science and General Education* (Science and Education), London, John Murray.
ASE (1965–), *Education in Science*, Hatfield, ASE.
ASE (1971 a), *Science and General Education*, Hatfield, ASE.
ASE (1971 b), *Science for the Under Thirteens*, Hatfield, ASE.

ASE (1973 a), *Science for the 13–16 Group*, Hatfield, ASE.
ASE (1973 b), 'The Association view of school science and technology', *Education in Science*, November.
ASE (1977), 'A submission to the Education, Arts and Home Office Subcommittee of the House of Commons Expenditure Committee', *Education in Science*, 74, pp. 16–18.
ASE (1979), *Alternatives for Science Education: A Consultative Document*, Hatfield, ASE.
ASE (1980), 'A submission to the Minister of State and the Under-Secretary of State for Education and Science', *Education in Science*, 87, pp. 27–30.
ASE (1981), *Education Through Science: A Policy Statement*, Hatfield, ASE.
CHAPMAN, B.R. (1976), 'The integration of science or the disintegration of science education', *School Science Review*, 202. pp. 134–46.
DES (1985), *Science 5–16*, London, HMSO.
DRIVER, R. (1977), *LAMP project*, 15 topic briefs and 2 teachers guides, Hatfield, ASE.
EBBUTT, D., and EVATT, S. (1985), 'All our yesterdays, a short history of the SSCR, unpublished mimeoed draft.
ENNEVER, L., and HARLEN, W. (1972), *Science 5–13*, London, Macdonald.
HARRISON, G.B. (1980), 'Project technology — Response 2' in STENHOUSE, L. (Ed) *Curriculum Research and Development in Action*, London, HEB, pp. 137–8.
HOLMAN, J. (1985), *SATIS Project*, Hatfield, ASE.
LAYTON, D. (1984), *Interpreters of Science*, London, John Murray.
LEWIS, J.(1981), *Science in Society*, London, ASE/Heinemann.
PRESST, B. (1980), *Language in Science*, Hatfield, ASE.
SCHOFIELD, R. (1974), 'De-streaming for science in all-ability schools, a call for caution', *Education in Science*, 58, pp. 24–5.
SIDDLE, J. (1978), *The Head of Science and the Task of Management*, Hatfield, ASE.
SMA (1953 and 1957), *Secondary Modern Science Teaching, parts 1 and 2*, London, John Murray.
SMA/AWST (1961), *Physics for Grammar Schools*, London, John Murray.
SOLOMON, J. (1983), *SiSCON in Schools*, Oxford, ASE/Blackwells.
SQUIRES, A. (1976), *Science in the Middle Years*, Hatfield, ASE.
SSCR (1982), Development programme 1983–86, Science Advisers Bulletin No. 1, London, SSCR.
STURGES, L.M. (1975), *Non-streamed Science, A Teachers Guide*, Hatfield, ASE.
THOMPSON, J.J. (1978), 'Towards a policy for science education', *Education in Science*, 77, pp. 12–13.
WEST, R.W. (1969), 'Reflection on curriculum reform', *Forum*, 12. pp. 14–16.
WEST, R.W. (1972), 'Science in the general curriculum of the comprehensive school', *General Education*, 18, pp. 33–46.
WEST, R.W. (1976), 'Science education: A revolution that has ended in turmoil', *Times Higher Education Supplement*, 13 February, p. 11.
WEST, R.W. (1981), 'A case against the core', *School Science Review*, 223, pp. 226–6.

7 'Making bricks with straw' — School Influences

There are three factors which most directly affect the way that pupils receive their physics in school and which interpret the teacher's curriculum for them; the physics text books, the apparatus and the public examinations. The publishers and text-book writers, the apparatus manufacturers and the examiners have, between them, done more to shape the way that physics is taught than their self-effacing profile would suggest. Though each would claim that they would follow not influence the trends, that they would merely interpret the syllabus for the teachers, and that they were always answerable to teachers wishes, in the event they did much to change the face of physics in schools, or in certain respects, to maintain the *status quo*.

Text Books, Publishers and Writers

In 1960, the physics text book was a dull, impersonal, wordy tome which had changed little in style or content for many years. Indeed one of the most popular texts at 'O' level, and there were few enough to choose from, was McKenzie's *General Physics* which had been first published in 1948 and was to continue well into the early seventies (McKenzie, 1948). He, and Noakes (1950), had the bulk of the school market, both had started writing their text books in sectional form before the war and were still setting the tone into 1960, and beyond. The fact that McKenzie was deeply involved in GCE examining in physics in his capacity as Secretary of the Oxford and Cambridge Examination Board from 1944 to 1966, gave authority and conviction to his books. But other books too conveyed the same messages about physics; that it was a timeless, academic, impersonal body of knowledge to be passively accepted by the reader. In Jenkins' judgment, school texts in physics had followed a familiar and well worn path which had become a 'rut rather than a highway' (Jenkins, 1979, p. 298). By 1985, due both to advances in printing technology and educational initiatives, physics teachers had an enormous choice of books from a range of lively, attractive, colourful and humorously illustrated texts which set physics into a human and technological context, and often forced the reader to engage actively with the material under consideration. There was now a text book to suit almost all teaching styles and individual preferences. The schools publishing business had blossomed, to the benefit of physics teaching.

Two new books, by Jardine and by Abbott, published in the early sixties, were to be deeply influential in their effect of encouraging, or maintaining, two quite different styles of physics teaching. Jim Jardine's *Physics is Fun* series (Jardine, 1964–67) was quite revolutionary and introduced the personal, interactive style of book. Abbott's *Ordinary Level Physics* (Abbott 1963–) was to maintain the more impersonal, passive style of physics, but did so in such an excellent and rigorous way that it was to quickly establish itself as the best seller for the next twenty years.

Jim Jardine's series introduced one volume for each of the four years corresponding to the New Scottish Physics Syllabus, and was delightfully refreshing in its impact. The books introduced space, lightness and colour in their layout and were illustrated by masses of cheerful line drawings of pupils doing experiments; it was what we would now call 'consumer friendly'! The whole text was based on the idea that pupils would develop their own physics through a series of simple experiments and reflected the work that Jim Jardine, and others, were developing in Scotland and which was to be so influential in the subsequent development of Nuffield 'O' level physics. The books stated in their introductions that 'This is not a text book. It certainly gives you a lot of information but it will often demand that you, the reader, find out and work things out for yourself. The real enjoyment of physics is in the discoveries you make.' In so doing the books forced the reader also to be an experimenter, and forced the pupil to personally interact with his own learning, in a way that Nuffield was to follow and educational writers were to rationalize later. In many ways, the *Physics is Fun* books were ahead of their time and many physics teachers were not ready for them: they didn't look like physics text books! For this reason, and also because they were tied to the Scottish syllabus and in England Nuffield teachers were discouraged from using text books at all, the books never sold South of the border in the numbers they deserved. They did, however, have a profound influence on subsequent teaching and writing along this humanized, experimental, pupil-active style of physics teaching. The next writer to develop this line was Tom Duncan, who wrote an *Exploring Physics* series which exactly matched the Nuffield 'O' level course in content, order of presentation and most of the practical work. Again there was one book for each year of the course (Duncan, 1968–70) and, as with Jim Jardine's series, the books were experimentally based but well illustrated with real life applications and photos. *Exploring Physics* met a real need in the market, both from the Nuffield teachers craving some text book support and other teachers seeking a lively experimentally based course. It sold well over 10,000 copies of each volume each year, well into the late seventies when single volume texts became more financially viable. Then Tom Duncan's own *Physics for Today and Tomorrow* (Duncan, 1978) quickly became popular, establishing a market of around 50,000 per year. Subsequently, Keith Johnson's *Physics for You* books, for CSE level in 1978 and 'O' level in 1980 (Johnson, 1978 and 1980), also became a firm favourite selling about 12,000 and 35,000 copies per year respectively. This, for the first time, showed how a book could be genuinely written for the CSE market and then built up for the more able — the previous practice had been to make CSE texts by slightly watering down 'O' level texts. *Physics for You* followed the same approach in being personal, interactive and humorous, with cartoon characters pervading the text and even a Heath Robinson type device on the cover. However, it diverted from the Nuffield tradition of making the pupils find out for themselves by unashamedly printing the 'important facts or formulae in heavy type or in a box, and a summary at the end of each chapter'. Such a compromise was readily acceptable in the late seventies and the book gained a wide sale among those teachers who wanted a lively, yet confidence building, approach.

The second style of physics teaching, that involving a more traditional, didactic approach in which physics was portrayed as a corpus of knowledge to be accepted and learnt, was reinforced by Abbott's impressive tome *Ordinary Level Physics* (Abbott, 1963). Sir John Cockcroft welcomed it for its 'combination of theoretical and experimental work and for its practical outlook. The well illustrated references to the applications of physics in industry should also appeal to the more practically minded pupil (sic!)'. It was a *tour de force* and though its first edition still appeared in a traditionally heavy format when the new style of spacious, well illustrated format was produced after 1969 it swept the market both in the UK and abroad. With annual sales well over 100,000 per year it reflected the still predominant style of physics teaching in the schools. Even after Nuffield, many physics teachers still wanted their pupils to be told, and to have explained to them, the important principles and applications of physics and this Abbott did in admirable fashion. It was not until John Avison's *The World of Physics* was published in 1984, that Abbott had a serious competitor.

There were, of course, many other text books which were published throughout the period. Indeed the size and variety of the market illustrated a continued reliance on the text-book as a teaching aid, even when many teachers seemed uncertain about what they actually wanted the text book for. The ambiguity of purpose of many text books, whether they were meant to be teacher substitutes, background readers, practical guides, revision guides or sources of homework questions, was often resolved by producing a combination package that did everything, and in fact such a policy was justified by the relatively low sales of books which concentrated exclusively on one. Even the excellent series of fifteen background readers produced to accompany the Nuffield 'O' level course rarely sold more than 5000 per year over the decade or so they were in print (Lewis, 1969). The textbook continued to be a symbol of status for parents, who would bemoan the poverty of a school that could not provide every pupil with one even when the teachers deliberately preferred not to use a text book! The text book was important in defining, along with the examination syllabuses, what was acceptable knowledge in physics. It also played an important role in establishing the principle that experimental work should always be linked to the theory, that it should be used to discover it in the Jardine/Duncan tradition, or illustrate it in the Abbott tradition. Thus, of necessity, the promotion and sale of text books by the publishers encouraged physics as a content-led, standardized body of knowledge and discouraged physics as a process-led, individualized way of working.

But text books had become much more personal, more readable, more colourful and also more accurate over the period due to some public criticism of bad practice. John Warren, in his perceptive and provocative book *The Teaching of Physics* (Warren, 1965), pointed out many of the blatant examples of bad physics current in many accepted text books and he continued to be the scourge of any sloppy physics writer over the next twenty years. Educationalists in the seventies became aware of the problems of language in communicating physics, and the value of language in learning physics (for example, Lunzer and Gardner, 1979; and Prestt 1980). Barnes *et al.* (1971) and Bernstein (1971) stressed the dangers of using too much technical language and also the 'language of secondary education', which cut off those pupils still communicating in a restricted code from the mysteries of physics, hidden from them by the language of an elaborated code. This, it was argued, was another case of high status knowledge being kept from the underprivileged by the trappings of an academic, overly literate schooling. Subsequently, the language demands in physics texts, work sheets, and examination questions were deliberately reduced. Readability indices applied to existing physics texts were a popular if unfruitful source of research in the late seventies, and they consistently claimed that Abbott and even Nelkons CSE text demanded a reading age of 18 or 19! (R.K. Johnson, 1979). Authors were reminded too of the implicit sex bias transmitted through text books, with examples and illustrations almost invariably referring to boys, and male related activities. It was argued that 'the image of physics presented in physics textbooks is predominantly a masculine one' (Walford, 1980, p. 227). It was not until the 1980s, however, that publishers consciously sought to respond positively to the gender and multicultural implications of their illustrations and photographs.

Undoubtedly the physics text book had done much to make physics more attractive and accessible to the average pupil in the comprehensive. Moving from the highly literate, authoritative, impersonal, presentation of academic physics in the early sixties, to the well illustrated, interactive, humanized, form of relevant physics in the eighties, physics was portrayed as more attractive and accessible to the whole of the school population. Though Abbott still found favour among the teachers of the more able 'grammar school' physics classes, it was possible for teachers latterly to find a text book which represented an apparently 'comprehensive' appeal. Clearly the text book authors, and the publishers who found and supported such authors, have played an important role in the development of the practice and image of school physics teaching.

Apparatus and Manufacturers

As textbooks had been instrumental in defining the content of the physics courses and, increasingly, that the theory should be supported by practical experimentation, so the apparatus manufacturers have been instrumental in determining what form that experimentation should take.

By the end of the 1950s the standard and style of physics teaching in the school laboratories had changed very little since the beginning of the century. There was a lot of 'chalk and talk', encouraged by the pressure in the public schools to get their pupils through 'O' level in three, or even two, years, supplemented by the occasional demonstration and standard practical exercises. The demonstrations, of mechanics with Fletcher's trolley and Attwood's machine, of electrostatics with Whimshurst machines, electrophorouses and cats fur, of heat with Hope's apparatus and Searle's bar, represented splendid examples of Victorian ingenuity, but conveyed little of the underlying physics. The class practicals were in preparation for the practical exams and centred on the tangent galvanometer and Wheatstone bridge at 'A' level, and lagged calorimeters and optical blocks with pins at 'O' level. And if the apparatus was dated, the labs themselves were often inadequate. A national survey carried out by Henry Boulind for the SMA in 1957 had found that only one-fifth of maintained grammar schools had lab accommodation which reached the standard of provision laid down by the Ministry of Education for boys' schools; at the time lower standards were recommended for girls' and mixed schools! (Boulind, 1957, p. 67). And if the provision was bad in the grammar schools, it was worse still in the majority of secondary modern schools. There was a clear pecking order in the quality and quantity of provision from the best public and direct grant schools, through the maintained boys grammar schools to the girls grammar schools and the secondary moderns. Boulind reported that while at one extreme, an independent boys' school could spend £3 per year for each pupil taking science, and one maintained boys' school, 28s, many girls' schools spent less than 3s 6d and the average secondary modern 3s 3d. But things were changing so much that barely a decade later, John Lewis was to write, with justification, that there 'has been a ten-year revolution in the apparatus used in schools for the teaching of physics, a revolution which has profoundly affected both the kind of teaching and the content' (Lewis, 1969, p. 257).

The first impetus for improvement came through the Industrial Fund for the Advancement of Science Education in Schools, who from 1955–63 spent £3.25 m building over 200 physical science labs in direct grant and independent schools (Waring, 1979, pp. 68–70). It was hoped that the Ministry of Education would respond correspondingly for the maintained sector, but unfortunately this did not happen at this stage. It is interesting to note how the fortunes of the two sectors varied in this respect over our period. At the beginning the labs and facilities in the independent schools were much favoured by this industrial fund. Subsequently the maintained sector were able to obtain better labs, and equipment, as through the late sixties and early seventies new, lavish, laboratories were built to cope with the expanding school population; at this time the independent schools felt themselves to be the underprivileged sector. In the late seventies and early eighties, however, as the local government funding of the state schools became tighter, virtually no new building was allowed and apparatus and laboratories got worn out. It was then the independent schools that were able to demonstrate the superiority of their laboratory provision, boosted as they were by government support through the assisted places scheme, and parental support through fees and appeals.

New thinking about apparatus was to come from various directions. The American PSSC project at MIT with Eric Rogers, the Scottish curriculum development work with Donald McGill and Jim Jardine, the Ministry of Education two-week courses run by HMI Tricker, with Wilfred Llowarch and Jack Goodier, and the SMA Modern Physical Sciences Committee under John Lewis, all generated new experimentation. A whole range of creative physicists were generating and sharing ideas around a single theme, how to get pupils to learn physics by doing physics. All of these initiatives were drawn together in the Nuffield project, but they would not have made much progress without the full support of the science apparatus manufacturers.

In 1963, HMI Tricker called a meeting in his office at the Science Museum in South Kensington of all the manufacturers of science teaching apparatus along with the Modern Physical Sciences Committee. The aim was to seek the manufacturers' support and commitment to developing the new prototype apparatus that was being suggested for the new courses into a commercially available form. This was readily forthcoming, especially from Philip Harris whose representatives Dick Crook and John Pool persuaded their directors that it was in the company's interest to give them *carteblanche* support. There followed a highly stimulating and constructive period of frenetic activity with ideas and prototypes moving backwards and forwards between the school labs and the manufacturers' workshops, with ever demanding specifications and decreasing deadlines to produce the whole range of original and 'plagiarized' apparatus that the Nuffield course demanded. It was a highly speculative venture with no guarantee of the scale or potential profits in such a new curriculum initiative. But, with the perception that such a large shift of emphasis towards apparatus for pupil experiment rather than teacher demonstration would both increase the size of the market thirty-fold and also destroy the traditional market, the decision to become involved with the new Nuffield physics was not entirely altruistic! It was to be a venture which not only made big profits for the successful companies but also burnt the fingers of others, like MLI, who trying to make quick profits by undercutting their competitors with cheap versions of the equipment, cut their profit margins too finely and went 'bust'.

The range of new apparatus that was spawned from these initiatives was remarkable, encompassing every branch of physics. Not only was apparatus for modern physics developed, spark counters, geiger counters and scalers, cloud and diffusion chambers, spinthariscopes and pulse electroscopes, even school versions of Millikan's apparatus and Thompson's e/m experiment with the elegant Teltron tubes, but also class sets of apparatus to study the traditional aspects of physics. Everywhere the aim was to make apparatus so that the pupil could discover the physics for themselves. Dynamics trolleys and ticker timers were copied from PSSC and used to investigate Newtons laws of motion, ripple tanks were also copied for class experiments rather than the traditional demonstration of wave behaviour, circuit boards were developed at Worcester to allow experimentation into the properties of electricity through bulbs, batteries and microbalances, and electromagnetic kits made available small but powerful magnets, iron core, coils of wire and wooden armatures so that pupils could delight for themselves generating electricity and making an electric motor that worked!

Throughout the syllabus, every effort was made to provide an individual experiment for each part of the theory. What could not be so translated was to be shown as a demonstration, where a demonstration was not available a film would be made. This principle, while making an enormous amount of first hand experience available to each pupil from which they could build up their own insights, did have certain disadvantages. The determination that the practical should lead to the 'right result' meant that it had, sometimes, to be so structured that the individuality of the pupil's work suffered. It led to an overemphasis on convergent 'guided discovery' experiments to the detriment of more divergent, open-ended investigations. The tension between discovering and rediscovering meant that the genuine pupil investigation was distorted. The determination that every part of the syllabus should be accompanied by practical work also meant that certain important topics, arguably relativity, cosmology and nuclear fission, were omitted, as suitable practical work could not be provided for them. And the greater emphasis on pupil experiments meant that good demonstrations were underplayed. A good example of this was the Tricker Trolley, a large free running trolley on which a pupil could stand, and pull and be pulled by another. It provided a splendid demonstration of the laws of motion and enabled the pupils to feel for themselves the experience of forces, velocity, and acceleration. It was developed by HMI Tricker (HMI, 1960, p. 52–3), and incorporated into the Scottish programme. In England, however, the individual pupil's dynamics trolleys were preferred, with acceleration having to be measured by traces from ticker-timers, thus removing the direct feel of acceleration from the pupil.

But all of this is quibbling, with benefit of hindsight. The principal effect of the development of this apparatus bonanza was undoubtedly good, enormously welcomed by pupils and, most, physics teachers alike. No more need physics lesson be either dry didactic theory or equally dull practical exercises. Now all of physics could be based around experimentation, and the pupils had plenty to occupy them. In John Lewis' phrase 'nothing will ever be quite the same again' (Lewis, 1969, p. 257). With the growth of school populations in the late sixties and early seventies, and the consequent building of new laboratories and with the positive encouragement of many science advisers to equip for Nuffield, school laboratories soon became filled with exciting new apparatus and took on an altogether more stimulating image. The pace of new apparatus development was indicated by the number of editions of the Philip Harris catalogues advertising physics equipment; from 1950–59 there was only one catalogue published, from 1960–69 there were nine different editions! In the subsequent decade, as the apparatus revolution died down, Philip Harris published only five (Poole, 1975). The plethora of new apparatus became the dominant feature through the later sixties and early seventies, and this was reflected by the high profile of the manufacturers at the ASE meetings and the apparatus in the school labs. In fact, though there were to be other curriculum developments after Nuffield, none brought with them the new apparatus that Nuffield did.

The creativity of this purple period for apparatus development was never sustained. Through the seventies physics teachers were basing their teaching on commercially produced equipment and this produced an apparatus-led curriculum. The apparatus was there, the experiments could be done, the teacher's job was to organize the practical around the apparatus and they had little time to think about alternative ways of teaching physics to comprehensive school pupils in a changing world. There were no commercial manufacturers to press the virtues of the pupils doing open-ended experiments with little, or only simple, apparatus and so the high status, impressive looking apparatus held sway; until the oil ran out! And then schools were obliged to reconsider their priorities and think more about the meaning of science for the people and the best way of teaching the physics in a balanced science course. But then, in 1982, the tap was turned on again, this time by MSC under the TVEI scheme, and a new cornucopia of enticing electronic apparatus, electronic kits, computers, pneumatic systems and robot arms came on stream. A new round of apparatus-led curriculum was in vogue, and physics teachers got enticed into technology or brought electronic gadgets into their physics. It now became possible to replace messy experimentation by computer simulations. And this, in its turn, was to separate pupils from the personal, first hand experience of the physical phenomena, as hands-on experimenting became replaced by simulated experiments. Teachers were again distracted away from the creative, open-ended investigations which, not needing prescribed, expensive apparatus were unlikely to make manufacturers a profit.

Examinations

Traditionally, physics teachers have complained about the effect that the external examination system has had on their teaching, that it inhibited and restricted them and was unfair to their students. At the same time, however, they used the exam system for its structure and support and did much to maintain it. There was a strong interaction between the examining and the teaching of physics and changes in the exam system could, and did, have a significant backwash effect on the teaching. The dominance of the school leaving examinations at 16 on the English system is unusually strong and acts as a control on the preceding curriculum in a way that makes the centralized curriculum of other countries unnecessary.

Dissatisfaction with the exam system is not new, nor have its inherent faults been easy to remedy. Back in 1929, a report on the conditions of science teaching in Oxfordshire claimed that

> The evils of the examination system are many and notorious: in science the university influence has resulted in a stultified syllabus of an academic type, divorced from daily life, and obviously designed as introductory to a more advanced course. The unhappy science master is, in consequence, compelled to waste much precious time in teaching things of little or no value, for no other reason than that questions might be set on them in an examination. Practical examinations, having served their purpose in ensuring experimental methods of instruction, should be omitted at the school certificate level (age 16); they prove only too often farcical both in conduct and result. Once freed from the examination yoke, the teacher will be able to devise a syllabus, wider in scope, more closely in contact with the world at large, and better suited to the peculiar environment of his school and locality. (IAAM, 1929)

Fifty years on many would repeat this perceptive condemnation of the examination system, though would be less confident that teachers, released from the 'yoke' of exams, would readily develop improved syllabuses. Indeed many would believe, and be implementing that belief, that the examination system itself was the only way to make radical changes to the school curriculum.

More overtly political, there were arguments that the exam system was the prime instrument for stratifying society, to separate off the privileged from the underprivileged, and to be the unobtainable key that would prevent the working class from ever entering the corridors of power. Though the external examination system was originally introduced for liberal, egalitarian reasons, (as providing a fair, meritocratic means of selection in place of the existing personal advancement through social position), it clearly could not overcome all social disadvantages and some sociologists saw exams as 'an important element in the bourgeois ideology of education' (Raynor and Grant, 1972, p. 40). Consequently it became enmeshed with the whole argument about the place of physics in the comprehensive curriculum, with 'O' level exams in physics being doubly, and irreversibly, divisive compared with, say, a common, teacher-assessed examination in science.

In 1960, the examination system consisted of the GCE examination and, in the words of the Beloe report of that year, 'a growth of external exams offered outside the GCE framework by various independent examining bodies and groups . . . on an uncoordinated basis' (Beloe, 1960). Because of their worry that a continued uncontrolled proliferation of, generally sterile and unsatisfactory, exams would do 'serious harm' to the schools they recommended the introduction of another examination for 'non-grammar school pupils'. It would be taken at the end of the fifth year, be designed to suit the needs and interests of pupils in the ability range concerned (the next 40 per cent down from the top 20 per cent in grammar schools), be largely in the hands of teachers and should not be 'a replica of GCE examinations at a lower level'. Thus the CSE exam was suggested, and introduced in 1963 with the first candidates in 1965. This effectively reinforced a tripartite system in schools through the exams, pupils would now be labelled as either GCE-, CSE-, or non-examination candidates at the age of 14.

Though the Schools Council was to recommend a single system of examinations at 16+ in 1970, and to institute feasibility studies, the two systems were to remain for the next fifteen years until in 1984 Sir Keith Joseph finally agreed to replace GCE and CSE by a single examination system, the GCSE, from 1986. Most teachers wanted the single system to avoid perpetuating the unnatural splitting of pupils into GCE and CSE groups in the comprehensive school, but whether such a change would provide the opportunity to reconsider the underlying curriculum appropriate for such pupils was open to serious doubt (Macintosh, 1981, p. 4). Indeed the first draft of the national criteria for physics, prepared by the GCE and CSE boards Joint Council in 1981 (Joint Council, 1981), proved such fears well founded. This was little more than a cobbled together collection of physics topics from the 1950s grammar school syllabuses, and showed little evidence of new thinking, or even evidence of any awareness of the advance in thinking about the curriculum that had come with Nuffield. But for spirited opposition from physics educators like Paul Black, John Lewis and Ted Wenham, individually and through the Institute of Physics and the *Times Educational Supplement*, such criteria could have fossilized physics teaching into a most arid and eclectic irrelevance. Fortunately, wiser council prevailed and the final version pointed forward to a form of physics that was practically based, socially and technologically relevant, coherent in structure and with an increasing emphasis on the processes as well as the content of physics.

In fact, the development of the National Criteria for Physics (SEC, 1985 a) illustrates in microcosm the way that policy is developed in England. The Joint Council was set up in 1980 by the then Secretary of State for Education, on the advice of his DES officials with the political aim of obtaining more centralized control of the curriculum. The Joint Council consisted of representatives of the examination boards who currently had autonomy and control of their own syllabuses. Thus a working party consisting of a group of twelve examination officers, under the chairmanship of

Mr Tippett of the Southern Group, put together a draft based on their own experience as examiners, with the aim of maintaining their examination industry in as stable and financially viable form as possible. The draft was sent out for consultation to teachers, the ASE and other interested parties. The teachers, often meeting through local ASE groupings, were relatively reassured because it was recognizably the type of physics with which they were familiar. Many were willing to accept it as it satisfied their aims of teaching the way they knew and of getting their pupils through the exams. Certainly the teachers' response to the Joint Council's tightly restricted questionnaire elicited little overt criticism. The Education Group of the Institute of Physics organized a public meeting to debate the draft proposals in London on 21 November 1981, and this brought together many of the most articulate physics educators under the chairmanship of Professor Paul Black. This meeting focused and raised the level of the debate. Though Ted Wenham's wise, courteous but incisive demolition of the draft, and the almost universal antipathy to the report from the floor of the meeting, appeared to have found little resonance with Mr Pilliner (who as Secretary to the Working Party had the final word at the meeting), it was clear that the draft would not go through unchallenged. The Institute of Physics, and those present at the meeting, were primarily concerned with improving the teaching of physics in schools as well as encouraging an adequate supply of students to continue with physics into higher education and as a career. Subsequently, public and private lobbying went on among those concerned, with John Lewis involving Sir Nevill Mott and others from the Nuffield team to make a public attack in the *TES* on its old-fashioned style and 'rag bag' approach to an overfull, academic, content-dominated core (Lewis, 1981). After various further drafts, a much improved, more coherent version was submitted by a core of the original working party to the Secretary of State arguing that the physics should be set into its social, political and economic context, as part of science for action and science for citizens. It also recommended that, although practical work was desirable, it would not be realistically feasible to have it included in the new exam (Joint Council, 1981). Sir Keith Joseph was, at the time, sensitive to the abuses of political education in schools and quickly responded that no social, political or economic elements should be included in the physics syllabus (Joseph, 1983). The physics syllabus was the first of the science subjects to be submitted and it was clear that the other sciences would certainly want their subject to be set in its wider context too. Such a principle was now regarded *sine qua non* in the science education community. Vigorous, urgent, deputations went to the Secretary of State from individuals, the Institute of Physics, the ASE and, especially, HMI urging him to reconsider and, after a decent period of time, he was persuaded to 'include the social, economic and environmental implications, as long as they grew naturally out of the physics'. He also insisted that, in spite of the logistical problems, practical work should be formally assessed, and so, as this was in sympathy with the wishes of the majority of teachers and physics educators, it was to become established in the final version of the National Criteria published by the SEC in 1984, to be the basis of the new GCSE from 1986 (SEC, 1984). Thus, as an amalgam of various different vested interests and certain individuals' personal commitment to improving physics education in schools, a policy was hammered out which was not widely at variance with the aims of those who were thinking seriously about the way physics should develop. Though no-one was completely satisfied, an operational framework had been established within which different people could operate as they saw fit. There was still a long way to go before this broad policy became reality in the classroom, and still a lot more battles to be fought.

Most exam questions in the 'O' levels of the early 1960s were 'three-part' questions: define, describe, do a sum (Crellin et al., 1979). There was a predictable pattern to such questions and pupils could be well prepared by learning standard definitions and methods and practicing the few basic calculations that could be asked. Such formal repetition encouraged didactic teaching and drilling for the exams. They did little to test, or encourage, understanding of, or enthusiasm for physics. Such exams were to change significantly through the development of the CSE examination, through the thinking and example of the Nuffield physics team, and through the growing professionalism of teachers and examiners alike.

The Institute of Physics Education Group had set up a working party under Norman Thompson to consider current techniques and possibilities for assessment in physics. One of their investigations compared students' performance on American multi-choice questions with their performance on normal 'A' level questions and with their teachers' assessment (Thompson, 1966). They found a good correlation between them and thus gave the green light to the introduction of multi-choice testing, first at 'A' level and then into 'O' level and CSE. Work by the CSE examination boards developed alternative types of questions, ones which did not demand so much literary skill to disentangle the question. It also developed experience of teacher assessment, especially of practical work, and of setting questions through Mode 3 which allowed teachers to devise their own syllabus and examination. While the range of physics syllabuses and teacher assessment techniques varied considerably, (and with more than 100 different Mode 3 physics syllabuses in the West Yorkshire and Lindsey area alone, it was inevitable that not all of them could be of the highest quality!), the involvement of so many teachers in curriculum development and assessment raised the consciousness and professionalism of many physics teachers towards the goals of their teaching. More structured, short answer questions were introduced which aimed to test knowledge and understanding of physics alone. Long answer questions, comprehension and data analysis questions were also introduced to test more specific skills.

Most influential of all was the work of the Nuffield team who were determined that no traditional examination which tested 'cheap recall' would distort their course which was centred on teaching for understanding (Rogers, 1966, pp. 79–99). Consequently they introduced their own examination and set up their own team of examiners who were in sympathy with, and determined to encourage, the Nuffield aims. The original hope was that these techniques of examining would be taken up by the other examination boards and so make a separate Nuffield exam superfluous (Lewis, 1977). While other boards were undoubtedly influenced by the Nuffield questions, the degree to which they moved away from assessing content was not thought to be sufficient by the Nuffield group to replace their own function.

A greater professionalism concerning assessment was developing and examiners seeking to be more specific about what they wanted to assess. During the seventies most of the examination boards started specifying their assessment objectives after the fashion of the American Benjamin Bloom and his taxonomy of cognitive educational objectives (Bloom, 1956). SCISP even tried assessing objectives in the affective domain (Hall and Mowl, 1973, p. 50). A board would specify, for instance, that it would allocate marks in the proportion of knowledge 40 per cent, comprehension 30 per cent, application 20 per cent, evaluation and investigation 10 per cent (Lee, 1977, pp. 20–3). In practice, of course, it was never possible to be so precise or discrete. What might be knowledge for one pupil might demand understanding from another. It inevitably turned out that the papers could be answered more on knowledge than the examiners had anticipated. A survey of physics papers set in 1977 by the different boards estimated that they were awarding between 44 and 60 per cent for knowledge, between 37 and 49 per cent for comprehension, and less than 9 per cent for application and the higher skills. Only the Nuffield 'O' level course had more, and this only 15 per cent, of the marks for application and evaluation (Crellin, 1979). Others have made similar analyses over the years, (Jenkins, 1979; Spurgin, 1967; and Phillips, 1982), and came to similar conclusions; that the vast majority of marks for any 'O' level and CSE exam in physics are awarded for the 'knowledge and understanding' of physical facts and principles. The National Criteria for Physics sought to redress this balance when it stipulated that now only about 45 per cent of the marks must be awarded to knowledge and understanding, the rest to the practical and cognitive processes of doing physics (SEC, 1985 a, p. 4).

The emphasis on the assessment of pre-specified behavioural objectives, while causing examiners to be more specific and to open up the mysteries of the examination game so that everyone knew the rules, had the unfortunate disadvantage of fragmenting physics teaching into the mastery of a series of small tasks — a danger that became increasingly strong with the grade related criteria and the TAPS type practical assessments of the 1980s (Johnson, 1983; and Woolnough, 1985). The whole is greater than the sum of its parts, and was in danger of being lost by too much concentration on the parts. Too much concentration on reliability, which examination boards (aware of their responsibility for public credibility) inevitably rated most highly, could mean a reduction of validity which depended so much on individual professional judgment. Eric Rogers highlighted the danger in his inimitable way when he said

> it is fashionable in Europe now to carry out a meticulous analysis of separate objectives and outcomes of teaching and learning, so that they can be assessed in test. The 'taxonomy of educational values' grew in the work of Bloom and others in the United States twenty years ago. As it developed it was a valuable revolt about carelessness, vague planning and testing. But it concentrates attention on aspects that are clearly measurable and it misses some of the most important factors in our hopes for lasting benefits from Nuffield science — the enjoyment, ambition, pride, that we look for in 'wonder and delight and intellectual satisfaction'. (Rogers, 1977, p. 3)

If the form of the examination questions in physics has changed dramatically, and the questions seeking to test more for understanding than mere knowledge, the content of the syllabuses have changed less so. Syllabuses have become fuller and more explicit. More emphasis had been put on general principles, such as wave motion explaining light and sound and kinetic theory to explain the properties of solids, liquids and gases, and less on specific experimentation. Modern physics had come in, with the structure of the atom, electron physics, radioactivity, and most recently, electronics. Optics and calorimetry had been reduced and relative humidity, voltaic cells, Wheatstone bridges and dip-circles omitted completely. With the conversion to SI units, the measurement of the mechanical equivalent of heat had become redundant, if not meaningless. On the whole, however, teachers had been reluctant to allow a favourite topic to be dropped from the syllabus to make way for new topics or more thinking time, and it has needed a traumatic incentive to shift that conservatism. In the sixties that quantum leap came with Nuffield, in the eighties it has needed the National Criteria to insist on a reduced core.

Whether the physics exams had become more or less difficult, it is not easy to say; they were clearly measuring different aspects of the subject. What is certain is that the 'O' level examination in physics was more difficult than in other subjects. Along with chemistry and French, it was judged to be the most difficult subject, by approximately half a grade (Nuttall *et al.*, 1974; McVey, 1978). Furthermore it has been shown that this difficulty, and perceived difficulty, has been instrumental in deterring pupils, especially girls, from choosing to study physics (Ormerod and Duckworth, 1975). It has been consistently argued, both for this reason and that the physics should be simplified to be understood more meaningfully, that physics syllabuses are too difficult (Fairbrother, 1979) and should be reduced. With such evidence, it is perhaps only the desire to maintain the high-status, and exclusivity, of physics that has prevented a reduction in the exam syllabus for so long.

There was an innate conservatism in the very nature of the examination system which tended to maintain physics, along with other subjects, as an academic, knowledge-dominated subject used to grade pupils not only on their ability in physics but also, implicitly, on their overall ability and worth to society. Of the eight examination boards administering the GCE examinations in England and Wales, seven were based on universities with strong university representation on the various controlling councils, boards, advisory committees and examination panels. Oxford and Cambridge universities had a particular influence on the system, out of all proportion to the number of entrants for their exams. The total entry through the Oxford, Cambridge, and the Oxford and Cambridge boards was typically similar to the separate entries for the London and the Joint Matriculation Board (JMB), but the distribution among the different types of schools was quite different. The Oxford and Cambridge Board had a predominance of entries from the public schools, JMB from the Northern grammar schools, and the Associated Examining Board (AEB) growing with the uptake from the old secondary modern schools and FE. With the inevitable link with entrance to higher education, the older universities were able to influence the tone, and set a standard, for all the examinations. In particular, the Oxford and Cambridge Schools Examination Board, set up in 1873 on the recommendation of the Headmasters Conference to safeguard academic standards and prevent government interference in schools (Howat, 1973), still held the allegiance of the majority of the public, HMC schools. Though only representing about 5 per cent of the total GCE entries they represented a disproportionate number of university entrants; typically 30 per cent of the entrants to the University of Oxford had come from Oxford and Cambridge schools. Consequently the influence of the older universities in 'maintaining standards' was transferred down through the system, for no board was prepared to change their examinations in such a way that it might incur the displeasure of the universities and consequently disadvantage their candidates.

But each board had its own rigorous and elaborate system for defining its syllabuses and setting, and marking the exam papers. Though the chief examiner was responsible for the examination in physics, that title had a different meaning for different boards and the actual examination would be the composite product of the efforts of awarders, examiners, revisers, assessors, and even (for the multi choice paper) statisticians. The actual preparation of an examination would take about two years, so any change in the system would have this hysteresis effect (Lewis, 1977). Each stage in the development of a question paper, and each stage in the revision of an examination syllabus, was subject to checks and counter checks from the various interested parties of examiners, university lecturers and school teachers, from the examination board's organizational convenience, and, retrospectively, from the candidates' own teachers. Those involved with the examinations, whether from the schools or the universities, tended to be more concerned with 'maintaining the standards' than 'developing the curriculum'. The examination boards were commercial organizations with a financial imperative not to lose money and consequently they were wary of making any progressive changes which might lose them customers. And above all the physics teachers themselves were consistently a conservative restraint on change, evoking an anguished outcry at any suggestion of removing a favourite topic from the syllabus. The rules of the examination game forced teachers to act in a reactionary way. Physics teachers perceived their task as getting as many of their pupils through the examination as possible. They built up their skills in achieving success on the basis of teaching from past papers, and any radical change to the examination would inevitably threaten this expertise. The result was that the GCE examination system encouraged little radical change in the teaching of physics for most of the period. Though certain topics came and others disappeared, though the style of the questions changed, and though the exams became more perceptive testing more for understanding and less for mere factual recall, the overall effect on the physics curriculum was to maintain it as a knowledge-dominated, academic subject which emphasized the virtues of knowing rather than doing, and was ultimately shaped by a top-down, university dominated hierarchy.

While many had hoped that the CSE examination would introduce a broader approach both to curriculum development and to examining, and indeed many individual teachers did experiment imaginatively through the Mode 3 exam, the overwhelming pattern within CSE became simply a watered down GCE. Because of the high status of the GCE, and its sheer professionalism in examining techniques, many of the CSE examinations sought to copy the GCE model. The CSE physics examinations emphasized the physics content of the grammar-school tradition. But, because of the perceived lower ability of their clientele, there was a greater emphasis on straight recall and less on understanding. The result was an examination syllabus for the average pupils in the comprehensive schools that was even less stimulating and satisfying than the GCE was for the brighter pupils. There were creative teachers who recognized this and instituted their own syllabus and examination through Mode 3. The best of these were very good indeed showing a remarkable degree of imagination, industry and rigour in producing courses that were genuinely appropriate to the interests and aptitudes of their pupils, but there were also some very uninspired ones. It was inevitable that the vast amount of work demanded of an individual teacher to develop his own physics syllabus and examination (necessitating a one-man, unpaid, curriculum development and examination exercise to be done by an already overworked head of department in his 'spare' time) would produce many schemes that were not up to a professional standard, and were not redeemed by the various symbiotic moderation exercises set up by regional consortium. This variation caused the credibility of the CSE as a whole to be questioned, and further reinforced the differentiation between the high status GCE pupil and the low status CSE. It also produced either disenchantment, or promotion, among many physics teachers who had developed Mode 3 syllabuses, in either case dampening the creative innovations left in physics teaching itself. By the late seventies any creative head of steam in the CSE system had blown itself out.

But also through the seventies, born out of a desperation that the academic straitjacket which the examination system was imposing upon the school curriculum could not be reformed from within, came a series of movements to bypass the examination system by the introduction of alternative forms of pupil accreditation. Many hoped that the existing, bipartite, exam system would be destroyed altogether as it was fundamentally incompatible with the ideals of comprehensive education. Even the much advocated amalgamation of the GCE with the CSE to form a common system of examining, eventually accepted by Sir Keith Joseph in 1984 (SEC, 1984, p. 95), appeared only to be a way of papering over the cracks of an intrinsically inappropriate system. Though the effect on physics teaching of these new initiatives was still only slight by the end of our period, their implications were far reaching and represent an important strand in the argument about the nature of 'science for all' in comprehensive schools.

The aim of giving pupils due recognition for their achievement was not new. It had been advocated through much of the Schools Council's work, and had its genesis through modern languages and mathematics. The modern linguists, concerned that many of their pupils dropped their subject well before they were able to take an external GCE or CSE exam, instituted a whole series of lower level, graded language tests which it was expected the majority of pupils would be able to achieve by the end of the first, second and third years of their course. Such tests, were based on a more relevant, conversational form of language teaching and were built up from the lowest levels, to act as an accessible and therefore motivational incentive for all pupils. The Cockcroft report on maths education in schools also spoke of the harmful effect of the normal GCE assessment of pupils in which the standard was taken from the highest level and all pupils graded according to the degree to which they failed to attain those standards. Instead, it encouraged a 'bottom-up' approach in which standards were built up from the lower levels, and students awards recorded according to their level of positive achievement.

Thus the movement towards records of achievement, graded assessments, unit accreditation and criteria-referencing in science got underway; all of which involved a new and creative impetus to consider not only the best form of recording pupil achievement but also the very nature of the different subjects appropriate to the comprehensive school. Phrases stressing the importance of 'celebrating success', and the Secretary of State urging the Sheffield conference to find ways of acknowledging 'what the pupil knows, understands and can do' (Joseph, 1984), came to be the accepted wisdom. With the government's determination to take the initiative from the individual, obdurate examination boards by the imposition of National Criteria for all subjects, and by the setting up of the Secondary Examinations Council in 1982 under the leadership of Sir William Cockcroft (SEC, 1984), it became clear that a genuine reformation of the schools examination system was underway.

In science the initiative came through OCEA, set up in 1982 by the Director of the Oxford University Department of Educational Studies, the CEOs of Oxfordshire, Somerset, Leicestershire and Coventry, and the Secretary of the Oxford University Delegacy for Local Examinations (Josephy, 1986; Lock, 1987). This was a project devised to give public acknowledgement of all the worthwhile achievements of the pupil, through a formative personal report, through a record of examination successes and through the development and introduction of graded assessments in maths, English, modern languages and science. The assessment scheme for the OCEA science was based on science as a problem-solving activity, and stressed the processes of planning, performing, interpreting and communicating, independent of specific content. It was inferred that science would, ideally, be taught as a single subject up to the age of 16, though the framework would allow it to be taught as the separate subjects of physics, chemistry and biology. It was to be compatible with the new GCSE examinations; the patterns for the practical work assessment of which (Skevington, 1986) and the embryonic Grade Criteria for Physics (SEC, 1985 b) having themselves been influenced by the OCEA thinking. Following the OCEA developments, other LEAs were to produce similar ways of registering positive pupil achievement in science; the credit accumulation system in ILEA (GASP), the 'can do' tests and graded criteria assessments in Suffolk, and the gold and silver certificate awards for the achievement of certain scientific competencies in Avon (Armitage, 1984), all rewarded attainment. This latter project, was similar to the Scottish Techniques for Assessment of Practical Skills scheme (Bryce, 1984), both of which emphasized competencies in many specific scientific tasks. Though initially designed for the least able pupils, they gave an impetus to an atomistic approach to science teaching for all pupils which, while high on reliability, tended to be low on scientific validity.

All of these schemes, by emphasising the 'doing' rather than the 'knowing' of science, were redefining the nature of science in the secondary school. Inevitably, and deliberately, they devalued the emphasis given to the more academic virtues traditionally assessed in the GCE and CSE physics exams. This re-emphasis was to be introduced into the GCSE, with its obligatory assessment of practical work, and the encouragement that there should be practical of an investigational type with teacher assessment. Hence we had come full circle. The external examination system had traditionally been seen as the mechanism for maintaining a highly academic irrelevance in school physics teaching. Having despaired of changing the exam system, and deplored the quasi-centralist control of the exam boards, a thoroughly centralized system had used the National Criteria to change the examination system and forced both the boards, and consequently the teachers in the schools to make their physics teaching more practical and socially relevant to their pupils. The exam system which had been seen as a conservative, reactionary influence maintaining a grammar school curriculum had become the revolutionary mechanism for encouraging change.

References

ABBOTT, A.F. (1963–), *Ordinary Level Physics*, London, Heinemann.
ARMITAGE, P. (1984), 'Some evidence of success', *Times Educational Supplement* Extra, 21 September, p. 54.
AVISON, J. (1984), *The World of Physics*, London, Nelson.
BARNES, D., BRITTON, J.N. and ROSEN, H. (1971), *Language, the Learner and the School*, Harmondsworth, Penguin.
BELOE, R. (1960), *Secondary School Examination After the GCE*, London, HMSO.

BERNSTEIN, B. (1971), 'On the classification and framing of educational knowledge' in YOUNG, M.F.D. (Ed) *Knowledge and Control*, London, Collier Macmillan.
BLOOM, B.S. (1956), *Taxonomy of Educational Objectives, 1, The Cognitive Domain*, London, Longmans.
BOULIND, H.F. (1957), 'Accommodation and equipment' in PERKINS, W.H. (Ed) *Science in Schools*, London, Butterworth, pp. 62–81.
BRYCE, T.G.K., MCCALL, J., MACGREGOR, J., ROBERTSON, I.J. and WESTON, R.A.J. (1983), *Techniques for the Assessment of Practical Skills in Foundation Science*, London, Heinemann.
BRYCE, T. and ROBERTSON, I. (1984), 'Tried and tested', *Times Educational Supplement* Extra, 21 September.
CRELLIN, J.R., ORTON, R.J.J., and TAWNEY, D.A. (1979), 'Present day school physics syllabuses', *Progress in Physics*, 42, pp. 677–725.
DUNCAN T. (1968–70), *Exploring Physics, Books 1–5*, London, John Murray.
DUNCAN, T. (1978–), *Physics for Today and Tomorrow*, London, John Murray.
FAIRBROTHER, R.W. (1979), '*Physics is too difficult*' appendix to *Statistics Relating to Education and Physics*, London, Institute of Physics.
HALL, W.C., and MOWL, B.S. (1973), *Patterns*, Schools' Council Integrated Science Project, London, Longman and Penguin.
HMI (1960), *Science in Secondary Schools*, London, HMSO.
HOWAT, G.M.D. (1973), *Oxford and Cambridge Schools' Examination Board, 1873–1973*, Oxford, Oxford and Cambridge Schools Examination Board.
IAAM (1929), *Report on the Conditions of Science Teaching in Oxfordshire*, London, IAAM.
JARDINE, J. (1964–67), *Physics is Fun, Books 1–4*, London, Heinemann.
JENKINS, E.W. (1979), *From Armstrong to Nuffield*, London, John Murray.
JOHNSON, A.H. (1983), 'Criteria-referenced testing in science', *School Science Review*, 229, pp. 626–34.
JOHNSON, K. (1978 and 1980), *Physics for You*, London, Hutchinson.
JOHNSON, R.K. (1979), 'Readability', *School Science Review*, 212, pp. 562–8.
JOINT COUNCIL FOR 16+ NATIONAL CRITERIA (1981), *Draft National Criteria for Physics*, Manchester, JMB.
JOSEPH, K. (1983), Letter dated 8 March 1983 to Dr. Andrews, Joint Council of GCE and CSE Boards, Appendix SEC(83)19.
JOSEPH, K. (1984), speech to North of England Education Conference, Sheffield, 6 January, pp. 60–8 in *SEC Annual Report 1983–84*, London, SEC.
JOSEPHY, R. (1986), 'Assessment of practical and experimental work in physics through OCEA', *Physics Education*, 21.4, pp. 214–20.
LEE, R.M. (1977), 'JMB Physics papers 1951–1976', *Physics Education*, 12.1, pp. 20–23.
LEWIS, J.L. (1968–), *Longmans Physics Topics*, London, Longman.
LEWIS, J.L. (1969), 'From Daniell cell to the apparatus kit', *Physics Education*, 4.5, pp. 257–63.
LEWIS, J.L. (1977), 'Nuffield O level examining', *Physics Education*, 12.1, pp. 16–19.
LEWIS, J., FOXCROFT, G., MOTT, N. and PARKER, A. (1981), 'Physics 16+ criteria could lead to disaster', *Times Educational Supplement*, 4 December.
LOCK, R. (1987), 'OCEA — the development of a graded assessment scheme in

science (1982–84)', *School Science Review*, 68.224, pp. 570–575.
LUNZER, E.A. and GARDNER, W.K. (1979), *The Effective Use of Reading*, London, Heinemann.
MACINTOSH, H. (1981), '16–plus: naught for comfort', *Times Educational Supplement*, 16 October, p. 4.
MCKENZIE, A.E.E. (1948–), *Physics*, Cambridge, Cambridge University Press.
MCVEY, P.J. (1978), 'Are public examinations fair to science students', *Physics Education*, 13.1, pp. 28–32.
NOAKES, G.R. (1950–), *A Textbook of General Physics*, London, Macmillan.
NUTTALL, D.L., BACKHOUSE, J.K., and WILMOTT, A.S. (1974), *Comparibility of Standards between Subjects*, London, Evans/Methuen.
ORMEROD, M.B. and DUCKWORTH, D. (1975), *Pupils' Attitudes to Science: A Review*, Windsor, NFER.
PHILLIPS, R.F. (1982), 'Did the exams work? 1 and 2', *Education in Science*, 98, pp. 13–17, and 99, pp. 15–20.
POOLE, J. (1975), 'A summary of the developments of science teaching equipment 1950–72, appendix in the History of Philip Harris', unpublished mimeo.
PRESTT, B. (1980), *Language in Science*, Hatfield, ASE.
RAYNOR, J. and GRANT, N. (1972), *Patterns of Curriculum*, Milton Keynes, Open University Press.
ROGERS, E.M. (1966), 'Examinations' in *Physics Nuffield 'O' Level Teachers Guide 1*, London, Longman, pp. 79–99.
ROGERS, E.M. (1977), *Revised Nuffield Physics, General Introduction*, London, Longman.
SEC (1984), *Annual Report*, London, Secondary Examinations Council.
SEC (1985 a), *The National Criteria for Physics*, London, Secondary Examinations Council.
SEC (1985 b), *Draft Grade Criteria*, Physics, London, Secondary Examinations Council.
SKEVINGTON, J.H. (1986), 'Internal assessment of practical course work in GCSE', *Physics Education*, 21.4, pp. 204–11.
SPURGIN, C.B. (1967), 'What earns the marks?', *Physics Education*, 2.6, pp. 306–11.
THOMPSON, N. (1966), 'An experiment in examining at 'A' level standard (1)', *Physics Education*, 1.2, pp.107–13, and 'An Experiment in examining at 'A' level standard (2)' *Physics Education*, 1.3, pp. 163–9.
WALFORD, G. (1980), 'Sex bias in physics textbooks', *School Science Review*, 219, pp. 220–7.
WARING, M. (1979), *Social Pressures and Curriculum Innovations*, London, Methuen.
WARREN, J. (1965), *The Teaching of Physics*, London, Butterworth.
WOOLNOUGH, B.E. (1985), '... the sum of its parts. Practical work and its assessment', *Times Educational Supplement*, 22 March.

8 'Tightening the net' — Central Policy

DES Policy

In 1960, the classroom teacher had almost complete autonomy concerning the curriculum he taught. Within the constraints of any external examination syllabus, or any scheme that the school had developed for itself, the physics teacher was the final, the sole, arbiter of what was taught and how. Denis Lawton describes the period 1944–60 as the 'golden age of teacher control' of the curriculum (Lawton, 1981, p. 16). From that time central and local government became steadily more interventionist into the secret garden of the school curriculum. Though Macmillan, as Prime Minister, had little interest in interfering with the curriculum of the schools, his Minister of Education, David Eccles did and he established the Curriculum Study Group. This was opposed by the teachers' professional associations, on the grounds that it took to central government responsibility for matters that rightly belonged to the teachers. In 1964, it was replaced by a Schools Council for the Curriculum and Examination on the recommendation of Edward Boyle's Lockwood Committee. This Schools Council, which was firmly in the hands of teachers and the teacher unions, was responsible for a plethora of new curriculum and examination reports through the sixties and seventies. Though, until its eventual demise in 1983, it was responsible for stimulating and coordinating much teacher activity in curriculum development it never took the opportunity of developing a coherent, whole school curriculum policy. It was resolute that such decisions should be left in the hands of the individual school.

In the DES, meanwhile, concern was growing that central government should have more say in the content as well as the organization and buildings of education. As early as 1968 a paper was circulating in the DES on the need for pupil assessment in schools to prevent underachievement, and this was followed by a working group on measuring educational attainment which concluded in 1971 that 'regular assessment is desirable and feasible'; a recommendation which was to lead to the setting up of the Assessment of Performance Unit (APU) in 1974 (Egglestone, 1986). The political imperative for the APU was as an instrument of accountability whereby the teacher's performance could be called to account against their pupils' scores on the tests, hence controlling the curriculum centrally. In the event the APU science tests were designed so sensitively that the results were not accessible to be used to this end. By the time that the APU results were available, in the early 1980s, the government had found alternative ways of controlling the curriculum, largely by controlling the examination system, and so the looseness in the APU results did not matter.

Sir James Hamilton, the Permanent Secretary at the DES from 1976–83, was quite clear that 'in a country that has no tradition of national initiatives on curriculum policy, I was wholly prepared to use reforms of the exam system to bring about much needed changes in national attitude towards curriculum' (Hamilton, 1983, p. 11). To this end the government withdrew its support from the Schools Council and replaced it by the Secondary Examinations Council, which set up the Joint Council to establish National Criteria for the 16+ examinations and took responsibility for the GCSE examination which replaced the GCE and CSE. The SEC, set up in 1982 under Sir William Cockcroft, was to consist of the Secretary of State's appointees, without formal representatives of the teachers' unions. To this Council, all the examination groups would be answerable. Thus, the balance of power moved from the teachers and the autonomous examination boards to central government. Significantly the second council to replace the curriculum half of the Schools Council work was set up after the SEC, as the School Curriculum Development Committee (the SCDC), and was financed far less generously. Thus making the curriculum development always less influential than the examination development. The DES was using the examination tail to wag the curriculum dog.

The DES was to make a further bid to control the shape of the whole school curriculum through the examination system by proposing a distinction and merit certification for the GCSE which could only be obtained if the candidate had satisfactorily performed in a specified range of, largely academic, subjects (DES, 1984). There was considerable opposition to this blatant attempt to reimpose an essentially grammar school curriculum pattern onto the whole school system and, by the end of our period, this proposal had been taken no further.

However we are moving ahead of ourselves. There was to be much action from the DES, through its discussion and policy documents, to influence the curriculum directly. The whole DES involvement in the curriculum debate had become more overt, and more widely acceptable, after the Tyndale affair of 1974 had revealed how little control anyone had over irresponsible and incompetent teachers. Sir James Hamilton became the new Permanent Secretary of State at the DES in 1976 and was determined that the DES should become more interventionist and '... act not only through influence and example, but also more directly ...' in matters of curriculum policy (Hamilton, 1983, p. 10). He was only too willing to involve the public at large in the Great Debate on the state of school education, which followed in the wake of Callaghan's Ruskin speech of 1976. Though many saw this debate as an occasion to make schools the scapegoat for industry's failure ('schools must change to save industry'!), it provided the DES with widely accepted grounds, and a public climate, for actively stepping in to take control of the school curriculum.

Thereafter followed a torrent of papers emanating from the DES and HMI, background papers, discussion papers, consultative papers, policy papers, so that by the end of our period the government had established a formal policy document for science through the 5–16 age range, and had laid down broad guidelines for the curriculum as a whole.

The government policy for science developed as part of its thinking about the curriculum as a whole. Starting with *Educating our Children*, the background paper for the regional conferences of the Great Debate (DES, 1977 a), it spelt out some of the problems in the current school curriculum; the wide diversity of educational experience of children within schools and between schools, the overcrowded academic curriculum, and the perceived detachment of the school curriculum from the economic realities of the country. The excessive variety in the option system was deplored with a strong indication towards a more standardized, common curriculum. No solutions were proposed but the subsequent Green Paper, *Education in Schools* (DES, 1977 b) was 'clear that the time had come to try to establish generally accepted principles for the composition of the secondary curriculum for all pupils' and that 'science should find a secure place for all pupils at least to the age of 16' alongside maths and English. It was unwavering in its adherence to the comprehensive system, recognizing the 'importance of educating together young people from different backgrounds, as an essential preparation for a more united and understanding society'. It claimed confidently the right, nay the duty, to take the lead in establishing the required consensus — 'it would not be compatible with the duty of the Secretaries of State ... to abdicate from leadership on educational issues which have become a matter of lively concern'. Little was said about the content of the curriculum, save that it should be broad and balanced and form a preparation for working life. LEAs were to be 'invited' to submit a review of their curricular arrangements and policy in various areas, through Circular 14/77 (DES, 1977c), thereby reminding the LEAs that they too had a statutory responsibility for the curriculum in their schools. When the results were collated by the DES (DES, 1979) it became clear that many authorities had little knowledge of or policies for the curriculum in their schools.

By 1981 the DES in *The School Curriculum* was claiming an 'overwhelming case for providing all pupils between 11–16 with curricula of broadly common character' to ensure a balanced education and to prevent subsequent choices being restricted. Science was to be one common element for all, a science in which breadth and rigour were both important. Again, nothing specific was said about the science, nor any distinction made between the sciences, though it was accepted that the different sciences would still exist. The only suggestion about the time allocation for this science was that it should not make 'unacceptable demands on curriculum time'. The subsequent consultation lead to the policy statement of 1985, *Science 5–16*, (DES, 1985), a document which revealed both the development and consensus of scientific thinking in that time, but also the unresolved tensions.

The most significant aspect of the DES curriculum papers was not the subtlety of their content, (indeed some, like *The Organisation and Content of the 5–16 Curriculum* as late as 1984 (DES, 1984) were showing a surprising lack of understanding of some of the fundamental issues), but that their very existence projected the public message that central government, usually represented by the DES but increasingly by the MSC too, was taking the initiative for controlling the shape of the whole curriculum in schools. An initiative which neither the teachers, in their schools or through the Schools Council, nor the LEAs had taken for themselves.

Parallel to the DES papers on the curriculum were HMI papers which represented a rather more progressive approach. HMI had, in 1975, set up a nationwide survey of practice in schools, at a time 'when some stocktaking of the secondary scene seemed timely' (HMI, 1979, p. 1). The results of the three-year survey were published in *Aspects of Secondary Education in England* (HMI, 1979), and produced a comprehensive and critical analysis of the existing state of the schools. It was able to quantify, among other things, the enormous variety allowed and encouraged by the option system in the fourth and fifth forms and hence show more dramatically the need for reform. It showed, for instance, that while 51 per cent of boys were studying physics in the fourth form only 13 per cent of the girls were, and that only 7·5 per cent of pupils were studying three science subjects in the fourth form (10 per cent of the boys and 5 per cent of the girls) (p. 166). At the other extreme, over two-thirds of the fourth formers were studying only one science or none at all, and this consisted of 76 per cent of the girls who were predominently studying only biology and 58 per cent of the boys for whom physics was most likely to be their only science choice. Clearly such an unbalanced polarization of pupils was unsatisfactory and revealed that the schools were a long way from producing a balanced science education for all.

Something needed to be done, and HMI were ready with their solution. It had become clear that HMI, under the leadership of Norman Booth, were advocating integrated science for all, possibly along the lines of SCISP. In their appraisal of problems in some key subjects in *Maths, Science and Modern Languages in Maintained Schools* (HMI, 1977) they asked 'would it not be better to have a unified science course which taught the basic sciences of physics, chemistry and biology, augmented by units . . . which allowed for some treatment of . . . their impact on the environment, society and engineering?'. In the science working paper for *Curriculum 11–16*, the first of the curriculum red books (HMI, 1978), a common science approach was advocated including three aspects; first it should include science for enquiring minds plus science for action plus science for citizens; second science should be seen in terms of process; and third that a science education should cover a certain minimum content illustrated by a controversial list of key words that all pupils should understand. Although this paper was clearly a committee composite, (derivative from the ASE policy statement (ASE 1973) and the HMI criteria for good practice used in their secondary survey which defined school science in terms of the skills and processes (HMI, 1979, p. 194)), it made a positive contribution regarding the type of broad, balanced science that was appropriate. As to the amount of time and the structure for that science, HMI made clear their view in the secondary survey that 'it is difficult to justify the large time allowance (often twelve periods out of forty)' spent on studying three separate sciences and 'it seems more reasonable to ask for "double-subject" time for science in years 4 and 5' (p. 197). This was in line with the recommendation in the ASE *Alternatives for Science Education* published the same year which also argued for a maximum time allocation of 20 per cent.

Bob Doe, reporting the current position of science on the publication of the Green Paper (Doe, 1977), highlighted HMI's encouragement of integrated science courses on the lines of SCISP ('the aims of this new approach have never been officially announced') in place of the separate sciences because it facilitated a balanced curriculum and postponement of specialization. He quoted Norman Booth, Senior Inspector for Science, as repeatedly saying that integrated science was the logical thing up to the age of 16 and that 'straightforward physics or chemistry just won't do any longer'. Doe concluded that the majority of science teachers, with their inbuilt conservatism, would have to organize themselves pretty aggressively against the forces already mustered behind the move towards integration. 'Integrated science reduces timetabling problems, the apparent seriousness of specialized staff shortages like physics, the cost of labs and equipment and the likelihood of uneconomic option groups — in short it has on its side that most conclusive educational argument of them all, administrative convenience' (p. 7). HMI in general, and Norman Booth in particular, were clearly committed to integrated science as being more appropriate to the needs of all pupils in the comprehensive schools. He wanted to give more emphasis to 'science the useful' as well as 'science the beautiful' (Booth, 1979, pp. 153–56).

By the time the next DES consultative document, *Science Education in Schools* (DES, 1982), came out, Norman Booth had retired and been replaced as SI for Science by John Whinnerah, an ex-physics teacher of a more conservative and pragmatic inclination. Consequently the tone of that document, while still arguing for a broad science programme for all, was more cautious about the organization of science in the fourth and fifth form. It, acknowledged that it was still the 'subject of much current discussion, and ... no single model can be identified as providing a pattern suitable for all schools and all pupils' (p. 5). It was clearly still primarily concerned with the ablest pupils, 'that they acquire the grounding which will permit the maintenance of the highest standards now achieved in 'A' level work and beyond' and that all pupils learn 'the scientific basis of technology which pervades their lives and helps to create the country's wealth'. Clearly the more conservative politicians, teachers and scientific community were reacting to the perceived undue haste towards a single integrated science for schools. The Permanent Secretary at the DES himself had worries about the premature rejection of the separate sciences when he said, to the ASE Education Conference in 1983, 'I am bound to say that I share the Royal Society's reservations; I am sure that we are nowhere near being able to go for broke on an integrated science' (Hamilton, 1983, p. 13). This reaction was reflected in the time allocation for science in the document which had moved subtly, but significantly, from 20 per cent to 'about 20 per cent of the total curriculum time — eight or nine periods in a 40-period week', thus allowing the three sciences to continue as an option, alongside a double subject integrated science, as recommended by the Royal Society (Pitt, 1982).

This battle, as to whether the three separate subjects should be allowed, continued fiercely, and inconclusively, through to the final version of the DES policy statement in 1985 *Science 5–16: A Statement of Policy* (DES, 1985). Though this was a DES, not an HMI, paper its development had been very strongly influenced by the science HMI, now led by SI Vic Green. He was very much in the mould of Norman Booth and was strongly in favour of a common science course. The draft report was subject to continued rewriting, with the progressives wanting integrated science on general educational grounds and the establishment wanting to maintain the possibility of the separate sciences on vocational grounds. However the tension remained in the document, visible in the word 'about'. The time allocation permitted for the broad and balanced science education is, usually, given as 'about 20 per cent, eight or nine periods a week' (p. 20), and though other options are open, 'better coordinated teaching of the three separate subjects, or grouping these subjects into courses in physical science and biological science' it is clear that the message HMI want to get across is that the ideal broad and balanced science course is a single or a modular course of integrated science. 'The case for a move ... towards combined or integrated courses leading to double certification is a powerful one' (p. 23). The integrationalists had wanted 'a maximum of 20 per cent', in the end they had to compromise on 'about 20 per cent'.

However, the important message that comes through this final policy statement is not one about the organization of the science or sciences, but about the nature of that science. 'But the aims of this paper imply more radical changes for pupils of all abilities than simply pruning the content of existing physics, chemistry and biology courses to provide more room for investigative, applied and problem solving aspects, and then continue to teach those subjects in isolation from each other' (DES, 1985, p. 22). Indeed, the challenge for physics and science teachers in the next twenty-five years is to see how such an enlightened policy of 'investigative, applied, and problem solving' science, set into its personal, social, and technological context can actually be worked through into the classroom. Only then will the policy of 'science for all' have come of age.

HMI Policy

The relationship between the Inspectorate and the DES is a delicate, and important, one. Her Majesty's Inspectors are not DES civil servants, they are responsible not to the Secretary of State but to the Crown. Though they work very closely with the DES, and advise teachers, LEAs and the DES and 'report to the Secretary of State on the efficiency of the educational system', they are rightly proud of their independence and the consequent professional objectivity of the advice they can give. On the other hand they have no statutory power, they can advise but not direct, and so the effectiveness and credibility of their advice both to teachers and the DES has to be nurtured carefully.

HMI's influence on the educational scene comes in various forms. They regularly run DES courses and these, especially in those run by Tricker in the pre-Nuffield days, have been particularly effective in encouraging and disseminating good practice among a potentially influential cadre of teachers. They publish, from time to time, teacher handbooks, pamphlets and discussion papers to help and stimulate better teaching. They inspect schools and offer advice to the teachers and, since 1983, publish the reports of those school inspections. They are represented on the steering committees and working parties of all the significant educational developments in curriculum and assessment and, though often present in an observer's capacity, are able to contribute much important advice from the wealth of their experience in the educational scene. And they report to the DES and the Secretary of State on matters of practice and of policy, drafting and reacting to drafts of DES papers. During the first half of our period, the Inspectorate kept a low profile, influencing individual schools and teachers, making important contributions to the new curriculum development packages, but in general working behind the scenes and projecting a very quiet public image. Since Tyndale, when the DES was determined to play a more active role, HMI, under the leadership of Sheila Brown, also raised the level of their visibility and public activity. Though the style and flavour of the DES and the HMI publications on the curriculum has been distinctive, the growing interaction between them has increasingly produced a coherence; by 1985 the DES policy document on *Science 5–16* showed a very close matching to HMI thought.

The size of the Inspectorate is, and has been, small compared to the magnitude of their important tasks, a view confirmed by the Raynor study on their work set up by Margaret Thatcher's government in 1981 to try to find ways 'to achieve savings and increased efficiency and effectiveness' (Raynor, 1982). Some saw a touch of 'who will rid me of this turbulent priest?' in the survey, but in the event they reported very positively about the work of the Inspectorate. 'We have received widespread and virtually unanimous evidence of the high regard in which HM Inspectorate is held' they asserted (p. 9), and made few recommendations for change, save that they should be supplied with more ancillary support. The scale of the HMI activity was reported: 2202 secondary schools visited in 1979, (54 per cent of the total), 2979 visited in 1980, over 100 in-service courses arranged by HMI each year, HMI acting as assessors or observers on some 700 different outside bodies, and forty-one reports or discussion papers published by HMI from 1973 to 1981. And, additionally, they reported to and advised the Secretary of State for Education. The total number of inspectors in England around 1980 was just over 400, having fallen from over 450 in the early seventies. There were, typically in 1971, twenty-four science inspectors. For an individual subject, such as physics, there might have been as few as six, each of whom will have a three-fold responsibility; to the subject, to a regional area and to a cross-curriculum specialism such as assessment or multicultural education.

Leading the team of science inspectors has been the Staff Inspector for Science, and this has been a key and increasingly influential position. The different personalities, styles and inclination of these men had a considerable effect of their contributions. By 1960, Dr R.A.R. Tricker had already been SI for Science for fifteen years. He was an incisive, scholarly, rather patrician man with a deep commitment that pupils should learn science by doing it through practical, research-type investigations. A physicist by background, he maintained a lively personal interest in astronomy and the physics of sports, and published important works in these areas (Tricker, 1967 and 1973). His influence on the early development of the Nuffield 'O' level physics course was important, insisting that even the modern physics was to be taught through experimentation.

In 1962 he was succeeded by V.J. (Dick) Long who had also been a staunch supporter of the Nuffield 'O' level physics project and a member of the Modern Physics Committee. He was another good physicist, with a belief in the value of student investigations. He was chosen as Director of the Nuffield 'A' level physics course, and set the pattern for the whole project. However, partly through his frankness in discussing publicly the problems of the project, he lost the confidence of the university academics on the Steering Committee and was obliged to resign. They felt that in trying to introduce such modern physics as wave mechanics he was, in Mott's words, 'trying to turn 'A' level physics into a Third Programme type of physics'. The tensions between the university and school perceptions of school physics were clearly revealed here, and the power of the academics to influence the direction of school physics demonstrated (Fuller and Malvern, 1986). When Paul Black was given the directorship of the project, with Jon Ogborn, he immediately gained the confidence of the academics as he was himself a first rate physicist, being a Reader in Physics at the University of Birmingham. Interestingly, the scheme they developed was no less 'Third Programme' than that proposed by Dick Long, but, propogated with more authority and enthusiasm, it quelled all further criticism. They were to acknowledge their gratitude and indebtedness to Dick Long, for his part in starting and developing the project, for his continued 'acute, perceptive and sympathetic criticism and advice' (Black and Ogborn, 1971, p. viii). 'The overall shape of the course owes much to his original conception of it'.

When Dick Long left to run the East African Science Project, he was succeeded, in 1964, by Norman Booth, a warm, forthright, maverick character. He was to do much to move science education away from academic study of separate subjects towards a genuine science for all, a science which was useful, applied and relevant to the pupil's life and the society in which they were living. A chemist by training, he was a strong advocate of integrated science, and was the instigator of SCISP, though he was disappointed in some of the ways in which the project developed. He stressed that science was a process rather than a collection of facts and theories, and made those processes explicit in the 'eight tests for good science' (Booth, 1975 and 1979). Perhaps his ideas and enthusiasms were too advanced for the time for, on his retirement a more cautious, academic, conservative physicist was appointed in John Whinnerah, who was rather less enthusiastic about integrated science. His style, though approved of by his political masters and the professional institutions, was found to be very frustrating by those supporting the Alternatives for Science thinking who saw his pragmatism as reactionary and restrictive (Whinnerah, 1980). John Whinnerah was replaced by Vic Green, another chemist, who though quite different in style to Norman Booth was like-minded in his approach to science education. He was a reserved, courteous, highly able and diplomatic man with the ability to get the best out of the people he worked with. His appointment was welcomed both by his colleagues in the Inspectorate and others in the science education business. Without ever appearing a charismatic or a dominant leader, he gained widespread respect by his ability and patient persuasion. He made balanced science sound less threatening then integrated science, more important still he was able to stress the content, rather than the label of science; the centrality of the investigational approach and the importance of the applications and implications of science in society. Though he had only been in post for less than three years by the end of our period, already his quiet influence was being felt on policy, especially in the DES policy statement for science and the inclusion of science in the national priority areas for INSET.

LEA Policy and Science Advisers

Of more direct concern to the physics teacher in his school than HMI was the local science adviser, who could, and often did, have a significant influence on the way that science was taught in that school. Few teachers would know, or have met, their local science HMI, but most would be quite familiar with their LEA science adviser and would contact him, or rarely her, when they wanted advice or money. But science advisers, as advisers in other subjects, were not widely in post until the late sixties, though some of the larger LEAs had a long tradition of using science advisers. Birmingham, for instance, was using science inspectors before the first world war as 'a kind of mobile resource service. Lessons were prepared and packed in boxes on Friday afternoons and on Monday morning four trunks laden with apparatus and pulled by four porters left for various parts of the city. Each trunk contained material for two science lessons and demonstrators ready to teach greeted the trunks as they arrived at the schools' (Winkley, 1985, p. 25). Clearly the shortage of apparatus and science teachers in schools is no new phenomenon!

But the growth of advisers, or inspectors as they were called in some LEAs, began in earnest in the late sixties, in response to school reorganization, the expansion of school buildings and facilities and the proliferation of new curriculum. In the sixties the specialist advisers were appointed *ad hoc*, to organize PE, home economics or music. By the mid-1970s most LEAs were offering a comprehensive service of specialist and general advisers, most of the subjects in the school curriculum would have their own adviser. Into the 1980s some LEAs were beginning to reorganize their advisers into teams, acting on the whole curriculum. In 1974 there were 1849 advisers in England, rising to about 2000 on reorganization the following year. By 1981 this number had fallen back to 1850, of whom seventy-nine were science advisers (Raynor, 1982). This overall provision, however, masked an enormous variation across the 100 or so LEAs. One LEA had 121 inspectors (ILEA), while six LEAs had eight or less.

The work of the advisers was always varied and hectic (Milbourn, 1975; Bolam *et al*, 1978; Walker, 1979; and Winkley, 1985). Through the expansion of the late sixties, advisers 'described the whirlwind life of planning, ordering equipment, meeting with architects, commercial agencies and so on to keep the programme rolling' (Winkley, 1985, p. 34), leading to the crises of reorganization in the early seventies and recession, falling rolls and the problems of redeployment in the eighties. All advisers, including the science advisers, were caught up in this climate of reacting to crises as they arose and so few had the time or opportunity to develop a coherent curriculum policy for their subject, a fact revealed by the DES survey of the LEAs' curriculum provision in 1977 (DES, 1979). It would not be true to say, however, that some science advisers did not affect the science teaching in their county; far from it.

Science advisers could influence the way science was taught through each of their different activities. The building of new labs and the provision of new equipment gave a great impetus to the spread of the Nuffield physics apparatus in the schools, if not always of the Nuffield philosophy. Some science advisers would award extra money to schools preferentially if they used it to introduce Nuffield courses. Subsequently a few other LEAs imposed the same inducement to introduce SCISP, a fact that teachers and the abnormally high uptake of SCISP in Hampshire will attest to. If a teacher wanted money or promotion it was advisable to follow the line being advocated by the adviser. The adviser was also influential in the appointment and promotion of science staff, thus increasing the proportion of like minded staff in the county. For those staff in post there was the provision of resources, the involvement with curriculum working parties, and the possibility of INSET courses, (in the late sixties Kent provided INSET courses on Nuffield for all of their science staff), or even secondment onto short or long courses, with the science adviser's approval. Over the years, an adviser was able to impose a distinctive pattern of science through the schools in his county; either through overt pressure, or by more subtle means, some would move their teachers in a particular direction. Others with a policy of *laissez-faire* would find the majority of their schools remaining in a traditional, under-resourced style of teaching.

Each science adviser was unique and had almost unlimited freedom in the type of science he encouraged. Though technically accountable to the CEO or senior adviser his autonomy was rarely challenged. Nevertheless the majority of the advisers were, to a greater or lesser degree, in favour of integrated science. The very fact that they were science advisers, and not physics, chemistry or biology advisers, gave then an in-built bias towards grouping the sciences together, for administrative convenience if not for sound educational reasons. In the late sixties, a science advisers group (SAG) was formed at the ASE and there, meeting informally each year, they encouraged each other in following the ASE line towards integrated science. When the SSCR was launched in 1982, the science advisers were encouraged to support and initiate local activities in line with the project's philosophy (SSCR, 1982) and this the majority did with enthusiasm. In all eighty-seven of the 102 LEAs supported some 270 groups to develop different aspects of the science curriculum through local working groups. In some LEAs such activities formed a coherent whole as part of their ongoing INSET. In Leicestershire, for instance, under their Senior Science Adviser Jeff Kirkham (who was in 1986 to take over the directorship of SSCR), a full series of nine booklets was produced by working groups of teachers which covered every aspect of the teaching and assessment of school science from 5 to 16. In Suffolk, the SSCR team produced a balanced science course for the 13–16 age range that could be used throughout the county. In other counties, the advisers merely encouraged specific initiatives such as developing curriculum material specifically for the less able, for multicultural situations, or the assessment of practical skills.

The overall influence of the science advisers has undoubtedly been to encourage integrated science in the schools. After the initial support for the separate Nuffield sciences in the late sixties, the prevailing trend was to support the move away from specialization and towards unifying the sciences. Prophetically, the ASE Education conference in 1969, while recognizing and welcoming this move towards the breaking down of barriers between the sciences, reported that 'whilst teachers were enthusiastic about the new approaches to science education (ie separate subject Nuffield), both in content and method there was a danger that over-enthusiasm might interfere with this trend (towards integration)' (Spears, 1969, pp. 11–14). And indeed this did happen. The emphasis on the teaching of the separate sciences was certainly encouraged by the well produced Nuffield courses and though the science advisers encouraged the Nuffield Secondary Science and the SCISP courses as they came out, they never achieved the status and public acceptability to obtain widespread uptake (except in a few local areas with committed teachers and persuasive science advisers!). It was not until the end of our period, with the onset of GCSE and the encouragement of the DES as well as the ASE policy statement, that the science advisers began to make more headway with the introduction of balanced science courses when some of them started to produce on a county wide scale their own versions of modular science courses to meet the new exam. In 1985 it looked as if such balanced science courses would find a far greater acceptance in the schools than the integrated science course of SCISP did ten years earlier.

References

ASE (1973), *Science for the 13–16 Age Group,* Hatfield, ASE.
BLACK, P.J. and OGBORN, J. (1971), *Physics Teachers Handbook, Nuffield A Level,* Harmondsworth, Penguin.
BOLAM, R., SMITH, G. and CANTER, H. (1978), *LEA Advisers and the Mechanisms of Innovation,* Windsor, NFER.
BOOTH, N. (1975), 'The impact of science teaching projects on secondary education', *Education in Science,* 63, pp. 27–30.
BOOTH, N. (1979) 'What next? ASE presidential address', *School Science Review,* 214, pp. 153–6.
DES (1977 a), *Educating our Children, Four Subjects for Debate,* London, HMSO.
DES (1977 b), *Education in Schools. A Consultative Document,* Cmnd 6869, London, HMSO.
DES (1977 c), *Local Education Arrangements for the School Curriculum,* Circular 14/77, London, HMSO.
DES (1979), *Local Authority Arrangements for the School Curriculum,* Report on Circular 14/77, London, HMSO.
DES (1981), *The School Curriculum,* London, HMSO.
DES (1982), *Science Education in Schools – A Consultative Document,* London, HMSO.
DES (1984), 'The organisation and content of the 5–16 curriculum' (a note by the DES) 115/84 press release, mimeo paper, London, DES.
DES (1985), *Science* 5–16. A Statement of Policy, London, HMSO.
DOE, R. (1977), 'Focus on science', *Times Educational Supplement,* 29 July, p. 7.
EGGLESTONE, J. (1986), Personal communication on unpublished evaluation of APU, 9 September.

FULLER, K.D. and MALVERN, D.D. (1986), 'One don, one beak — University pressures and curriculum development in the first Nuffield A-level physics project', *British Journal of Educational Studies*, XXXIV.3, pp. 219–34.
HAMILTON, J. (1983), 'The nature and problem of curriculum development', *Education in Science*, 103, pp. 10–14.
HMI (1977), *Mathematics, Science and Modern Languages in Maintained Schools in England*, London, DES.
HMI (1978), *Curriculum 11–16: Working Papers by HMI*, London, HMSO.
HMI (1979), *Aspects of Secondary Education in England*, London, HMSO.
LAWTON, D. (1981), *An Introduction to Teaching and Learning*, London, Hodder and Stoughton.
MILBOURN, J.J. (1975), 'The role of the science adviser', *School Science Review*, 199, pp. 285–8.
PITT, H. (1982), *Science Education 11–18 in England and Wales*, London, Royal Society.
RAYNOR, D.G. (1982), *The Study of HM Inspectorate in England and Wales*, London, HMSO.
SSCR (1982), 'SSCR development programme 1983–1986, *Science Advisers Bulletin No. 1*, mimeo paper, London, Secondary Science Curriculum Review.
SPEARS, T. (1969), 'The fifth annual education conference', *Education in Science*, 33, pp. 11–14.
TRICKER, R.A.R. (1967), *The Path of the Planets*, London, Mills and Boon.
TRICKER, R.A.R. (1973), 'Place of astronomy in school physics', *Physics Education*, 8. 7, pp. 449–54.
TRICKER, R.A.R. and TRICKER, B.J.K. (1967), *The Science of Movement*, London, Mills and Boon.
WALKER, R. (1979), *The Observational Work of LEA Inspectors and Advisers*, Norwich, University of East Anglia Press.
WHINNERAH, J.B. (1980), 'Balanced science approaches', *Education in Science*, 86, pp. 24–6.
WINKLEY, D. (1985), *Diplomat and Detectives, LEA Advisers at Work*, London, Robert Royce.

9 'Labouring in the Fields' — Five School Cameos

From Rhetoric to Reality

In the previous chapters we have considered the developments in physics teaching from the national perspective. This does not, however, give a full picture of what actually was happening to physics teaching in the classrooms and laboratories of the schools. In this chapter we will try to add flesh and blood to the story, and see how such macroscopic changes have been interpreted in the reality of schools, how physics teaching has developed 'at the chalk-face'.

To obtain such insights we will look at five schools to see how the physics teachers there have translated and reflected the wider policies and trends. The choice of 'typical' schools in a system as diverse as that in England is not easy. Every school is different, because it is an autonomous, human institution consisting of many and varied teachers. Consequently any insights from a particular school can only be illustrative of particular issues and never definitive. Different types of school will also have different perceptions of the way that physics can be taught and the fundamental aims for teaching physics. Because of this, the five schools chosen each represent a different type, each with a different history. King Arthur's School was a grammar school, and Riverside a secondary modern before they each went comprehensive. Camford was, and remained, a selective school and as such represents the academic tradition in both the state and the private system. Windmill Hill School was another secondary modern school, but kept a limited age range of 11–16 when it became a comprehensive school. The sixth form college, Brunel College, grew out of a traditional grammar school.

There will be many schools which do not fit readily into these patterns, but I believe that they are sufficiently comprehensive and typical to allow

Of People, Policy and Power

the most significant issues to be highlighted. Each cameo will develop the story of the changes in that school with emphasis on those issues which have been the central themes of this book. The cameos are not case studies in the formal sense of the word for, although each is based on a real school, licence has been taken in selection of the aspects discussed and, in insignificant ways, names and details have been changed. I hope, however, that the cameos will 'ring true' both to those in the actual schools and to those who know schools like them. I hope too, that the reality in the schools will give deeper significance to the rhetoric of national policy and curriculum issues.

King Arthur's School (Grammar School turned Comprehensive)

King Arthur's School was founded nearly 400 years ago and was well known and well regarded by the community. Most of the local establishment had been through the school, and many of the present scholars had had their parents, perhaps even their grandparents, at the school before them. The end-of-term carol service in the parish church was a splendid occasion and signalled the start of the Christmas festivities for many in the town. The school was, understandably and popularly, a conservative institution. But, for the school as for the local community, things were to change. The town which had a population of 4000 in 1960 was to grow rapidly through the mid-sixties and seventies until, by 1985, it had risen to 16,000. Housing estates had sprung up to serve the new industries and to act as dormitories for those working in the neighbouring towns and London.

The school, a voluntary controlled boys' grammar school, had only a one form entry in 1960, but this had grown to two in 1965 and to a three form entry by 1970, the year before it went comprehensive and coeducational. The reorganization consisted of King Arthur's merging with the local secondary modern school and importing the girls from a neighbouring grammar school which was also going comprehensive. The amalgamation was made on a single day in September 1971, bringing together pupils into the new system consisting of two lower schools, catering for the first three years which fed into an upper school for the fourth, fifth and sixth forms. By the end of the seventies the school had grown to accommodate 2000 pupils and had established an enviable reputation both locally and nationally. The charismatic head at the time of the reorganization, a linguist appointed from a well known public school six years earlier, had built up the school through good management, imaginative staff appointments and a flair for publicity. His vision for King Arthur's was that it should provide a grammar school, even a public school, education for all, and he spared no effort to see that this happened. By publicly proclaiming that his was the school that parents moved house to get their children into, he caused it to happen on an increasing scale and soon established a well-deserved reputation for the school, especially in music and drama which had been developed to a very high standard. By the time he left the school in 1980 it was a thoroughly well established comprehensive school in which many lively young teachers had developed their teaching expertise, and from which they had spread their influence as they had been promoted to posts of responsibility in other schools. It had been a popular school as a small boys' grammar school. It had become equally acceptable and successful as a large coeducational comprehensive.

The science department had effected a similar development over this period. In 1960 there were three science teachers in the school, all graduates. Len Norman, the physicist, had graduated from Cambridge and taught in Bedfordshire and the Army before coming to King Arthur's in 1957. He was to stay in the school for twenty-five years, formally taking over the direction of the science department in 1965, as well as taking responsibility for the school's resources and the CCF. Apart from his love of teaching, he was an enthusiastic photographer and radio man, interests which were freely demonstrated in the room in which he did all his teaching. As the school grew, so did the number of science staff. It was normal for the head to appoint graduate staff, though there was one exception in the physics department when, in 1975, a non-graduate was appointed straight from training on the personal recommendation of the course tutor; he was to be responsible for the low ability classes. Though it was never easy to fill the physics posts, the reputation of the school ensured that staffing was always adequate and often very good, sometimes with industrial experience. Many stayed a few years and then moved on to run their own departments elsewhere. By 1979, when Dr David Pearce was appointed, the physics staff had grown to four. Dr Pearce had ten years successful research experience behind him when he decided to enter teaching and took the MSC training grant for the PGCE. His ability was soon being applied in the school and after two years he took over the physics department and after two more became Head of Science, responsible now for the direction of seventeen science teachers and seventeen labs.

In 1960 Len Norman taught all the physics in the school. Physics was taught as a separate subject from year 1 leading on to the 'O' level exam which all the boys would be expected to take, and most of them pass. About six or seven boys would continue to study physics in the sixth form but as the upper and lower sixth forms were taught together the teaching group consisted of about a dozen lively and well motivated students, most of whom would go on to university to read physics, engineering or medicine. Len's aim in teaching was to instil into pupils a love and enthusiasm for physics, an aim he applied equally to the less able pupils he was to meet later. His own mixture of enthusiasm and showmanship ensured that his physics lessons were remembered well after their physics content had been forgotten. Many an old boy would recount the memory of their first physics lesson in which Len came in, drew a picture of a crane on the blackboard and proceeded to hang his coat on the hook he had just chalked (not noticing the strategically placed, invisible, tack on the board), or subsequent lessons in which his spectacular presentation of the demonstration transformer culminated in all the class holding hands to receive a frightening but, not quite, lethal electric shock. His classroom itself was a living demonstration of physics. Not only was it filled with equipment but he had even had the walls painted in the colours, red, green and blue for three walls, the floor yellow and the ceiling white! Such idiosyncrasies were not to continue as the lab space grew from one room in 1960, to one lab and a room in 1970 to a suite of three labs by 1985.

When the school went comprehensive in 1971, and embraced the staff from the secondary modern who had been teaching elementary science only, the curriculum changed so that all pupils took combined science for the first two years, separate sciences in the third year before having the option of choosing physics from the option blocks in years 4 and 5. Only 'O' level classes were offered in physics, Len believing that it was not a suitable subject for the less able who could continue with their physics as part of a non-examined science class. But when the joint 16+ examination was proposed in 1975 King Arthur's became a pilot school. Subsequently the number of students studying physics increased from about forty-five to 100, clearly tapping, and successfully, a much greater pool of students for whom physics was appropriate. King Arthur's has continued with the 16+ physics ever since, finding it possible, and desirable, to teach the pupils in non-streamed classes. By 1985 about 45 per cent of the age group were choosing to study physics to 16+, and of these 140 pupils typically thirty-five would continue it into the sixth form. The courses taught were to the traditional syllabuses, neither Len or David believing that the Nuffield courses would improve their teaching which relied a lot on personal enthusiasm, lively class teaching and demonstration. It would be wrong to suggest, however, that the pupils were expected to be passive receptors of knowledge, indeed the increasing independence of the pupils for their own learning was encouraged, especially in the sixth form where a weekly work programme was provided for the students to enable them to regulate their own learning.

The relationship of physics to the other sciences had developed pragmatically. The staff appointed throughout had been specialists in their own science, and enthusiasts for it. They did not find it difficult to take that enthusiasm across to the other sciences when teaching combined science in the first two years, a policy readily agreed to at comprehensivization to enable the teachers more easily to get to know their pupils who they would teach for five rather than two periods a week. Beyond year 2, however, there was no enthusiasm for teachers to teach outside their own subject, each science had its own head of department, its own laboratories, and its own traditions. It was not until the 1980s, when David Pearce was appointed as Head of the Science Faculty and started to hold meetings to discuss issues of common concern, that the staff began to consider that they might indeed share common aims. Inevitably, it forced David, himself a physicist to the core, to share the interests of the other sciences. As he and his colleagues began to consider the discussion and policy papers of the ASE, HMI and the DES, as they became involved in courses run by HMI, by the county science adviser and by the science staff of the local UDE, they became slowly more sympathetic to balanced science in the fourths and fifths.

Even more fundamentally, their concept of the nature of science teaching was changing from academic sciences for a few, to appropriate and human science for all. Nowhere was this more clearly evidenced than in the matter of girls and physics. David realized that the physics sets contained few girls, probably less than 20 per cent. He raised this at departmental meetings, circulating data and articles published on the issue by Jan Harding and the Institute of Physics. As a department, they resolved to change the situation and this caused them to consider not just the packing, but the content of the parcel. In particular they realized the need to increase the personal aspects of physics in the third year course, to make it more interesting, to include more social aspects and to use more discussion and, particularly, more co-operative activities. These aims were then incorporated into all of their courses, and the teachers became more aware of the wider, more human, aspects of their courses for all, not just the girls. All this, together with positive careers advice by a very lively, woman, science teacher who argued that their life chances would be severely limited if they dropped physics, caused the percentage of girls studying physics to increase steadily, from about 20 to 35 per cent. One year they tried an experiment of teaching boys and girls in separate groups and, though persuaded that it allowed the girls more freedom to talk more, they were not persuaded that there was any consequent improvement in their learning of physics. In their hearts they were uneasy about this separation which was contrary to their underlying philosophy of comprehensive education and so, after the one year experiment which had shown no significant improvement, the idea was quietly dropped.

The links that the physics department had with technology had fluctuated over the years. Informally, the electronics and the photographic clubs had always flourished and enabled many students to develop technological hobbies in their own time. Little of the electronics had gone into the physics courses, however, because they were not included in the exam syllabuses. It had lately been introduced into the third year course and as an option in the new 16+ course. David Pearce recently changed the examination board for his 'A' level examination to enable more electronics to be examined, as well as preferring their overall pattern of examining. After discussions and working parties with other teachers and tutors from the local UDE, and with the active involvement of a new teacher appointed to the physics department with a technology brief, the science syllabus for years 1 and 2 was examined to see if technological activities could be introduced there. It was agreed, though not without battles, that the existing course content could be reduced to allow a module of problem-solving activities to be introduced. This discussion also encouraged the writers of other modules to modify their units to make them more technologically flavoured. Formal links with the CDT department were never easy. The CDT department had built up a first rate reputation for excellence in craft work, and were suspicious that they might lose this if moved to a more technological approach. A courtship between the departments developed while the teacher with the technology brief was still in the physics department, when he left the separate departments went their separate ways. By this time the former Head of the Craft Department had retired and two new graduate technologists had been appointed to the CDT department. They were now able to offer the modular technology course and staff it from their own department, with only informal advice coming from the physics department to help with the electronics module.

One of the important strengths in King Arthur's physics department had always been their involvement with other local science teachers. Back in the early sixties, Len Norman along with the heads of physics at two other local grammar schools, went to lobby the local education authority for more money for their schools. They had been excited by the *Teaching of Modern Physics* report emanating from Malvern and armed with this they persuaded the LEA to provide more money for their science. Initially it was for their schools only but subsequently to other local schools. At this time the LEA did not have a science adviser, but the Deputy Education Officer, himself once a physics teacher, used this trio as the basis for a science advisory group of local heads of science. This group was to have an important role in developing science policy in the county even after the appointment of a science adviser, who was to work closely with it. Len Norman also worked closely with other teachers in the formation of a local physics centre, which subsequently developed into a science and technology centre, and with the local ASE group. Believing that no school should ever work in isolation he both gained and gave strength and support from such cross-fertilization. It was to prove important as science in the county moved into the comprehensive age.

King Arthur's also developed strong links with the local UDE. First through students on teaching practice and then as a founder member of a group of schools who, in 1974, developed an associated school scheme with the department to share more fully in the preparation and training of trainee physics teachers. Such links enabled further cross-fertilization of ideas, as well as the pick of good students looking for their first teaching appointments in the area!

Physics teaching at King Arthur's had been strong throughout the twenty-five years. It had been favoured with lively well qualified staff. It had seen the transition from a grammar school, concerned only for the able potential scientists, to a comprehensive school catering both for the needs of those who will do no more science after 16 and those who will carry it through to higher education. The department was continuously and professionally seeking ways to satisfy both aims, and doing so still to the satisfaction of the local community.

One worry, articulated by Dr Pearce however, still lingers as the school leaves 1985. Will King Arthur's be able to keep teachers of the academic quality that they have been used to? He, as a good creative scientist, sees himself still as a physicist with a responsibility to the scientific community, as well as to the pupils. At the moment he is well satisfied by the challenges in running the department, but is aware that this is taking him away from his first love, physics. Is he going to be satisfied, indeed are his talents being used to the best advantage, by spending so much time teaching pupils who are not going to become scientists or engineers? If not, should he be moving to the type of educational institution in which he can spend more of his time 'teaching physics, and helping provide the nation with the skilled manpower it requires'?

Riverside School (Secondary Modern turned Comprehensive)

By 1960 Riverside County Secondary School had been on its new site for only four years but already it had outgrown its original buildings. Designed for 550 boys and girls, it had now incorporated 'temporary accommodation' as the numbers approached 800. Though it was situated in a pleasant, semi-rural town, it could hardly have been considered as educationally favoured. Attracting the cream of the town's children were a boys' and a girls' direct grant grammar school, a new county grammar school, a convent school and another secondary modern school which was situated in the more desirable part of town. Riverside drew its clientele from that part of the town that contained a council estate built for slum clearance families, an RAF camp and some neighbouring villages. The RAF station, with its constantly changing personnel, brought problems of continuity and insecurity. The large, poor families from the council estate, with its reputation for lawlessness and internecine feuding, brought their problems into the school too. And yet the school was a relatively stable and well-ordered community from which little was asked and not much, at least academically, given. The vast majority of the pupils left school at 15, after four years of an 'all-round, bread and butter' curriculum based largely on traditional academic subjects. Many would have done no public examinations, some would have taken UEI exams in a variety of subjects, and a few of the most able would have been persuaded to stay on for an extra year to take GCE exams before going on to further study at the local FE college. Parents had few expectations of the school and little contact with it, content that their children be 'looked after' until they were 15. If they could get a job in agriculture, the local factories or the retail trade, as most of them did, they were more than satisfied.

The staff at Riverside, who were largely college-trained, had remained fairly constant since the end of the war. The teaching was largely formal, to classes of thirty-five to forty docile pupils who still accepted the authority of their teachers. The classrooms were furnished with rows of desks and a blackboard. The 'modern labs', though fitted with laboratory benches, were equipped mainly with apparatus for teacher demonstration. The workshops were, however, well stocked with tools and machines. Overall, however, the resourcing was by modern standards very limited. It was the time in which the Chairman of the Education Committee for that county could, and did, say that 'all you need for teaching is a teacher, a piece of chalk and a nissan hut'!

The science staff (it would be inappropriately suggestive to call it a science department) were headed by Mr Cox, an ex-fitter electrician from the Royal Army Corps who had taken a two year teacher-training course to 'give him time after the war to look for something better'. He had, by 1960, been in the school for two years, having previously taught for ten years in another secondary modern school in the West Country. There were three other science teachers, each with a specialism of physics, chemistry or biology — 'always a woman for biology'. Mr Cox's job, apart from teaching general science with a physics bias to the first three years, physics in year 4 ('very formally to get pupils through UEI exams') and a few extra physics classes for the GCE elite, was to keep the laboratories and the apparatus in good order and to decide, unilaterally, what science should be taught throughout the school. In the two years he had been in the school, he had got the work schemes organized for himself and his colleagues and life ran smoothly and uneventfully. He taught his classes of twenty pupils — he had persuaded the head that because of the practical work that needed to be done, and the flexibility required, it was necessary to teach science in half-sized classes — in a clearly structured way. Based around the knowledge that had to be learnt, he used simple class experiments, demonstrations, dictated notes and chalk and talk. Yet through his own enthusiasm and intrinsic interest in physics and applied science he conveyed science as a living thing to many children. The pre-CSE exams supplied by UEI were very content-based and exerted a restrictive straitjacket for those studying physics in the fourth year. His non-examination groups in their last year, however, were able to enjoy much more open constructional and investigational work as they learnt the skills of photography, of building and modifying go-carts and generally 'doing science'. He 'did his own thing' in the classroom and planned the science curriculum as a 'one man band'. His strengths and enthusiasms were reflected in his teaching and, in a much diluted form, throughout the school.

But life in this academic backwater, which took care of the children that no-one else wanted, was to change radically. Through the restless, expansionist sixties, staff turnover at the school was rapid, especially among the physics staff who would stay for only a year or two before moving on to promotion in a more stimulating environment. In 1967, following the government's Circular 10/65, the county Education Committee decided that all the secondary schools in the county should go comprehensive. On the retirement of the Headmaster of Riverside, rather tired after twenty-eight years in the school, a young, energetic man was appointed specifically to take the school into the promised land and re-organize it along comprehensive lines. This process was to start in 1973 when the first comprehensive intake, drawn from a more balanced catchment area, entered the school. The new head saw the need for a clear management structure in both the pastoral and the academic fields. He recognized the need to raise the academic standards and status of the staff and made a number of imports of good graduates to head up the departments. Such a one was Mr Evans who, as a biologist, was appointed Head of Science in 1973 over the head of the non-graduate Mr Cox, who was moved sideways, taking responsibility for the physics department and various administrative tasks. The pastoral side of the school was organized on the year group basis, with each year having its own year head. The pastoral posts were largely taken by the ex-secondary modern staff who were able to retain the status in the pastoral hierarchy that they had lost in the academic.

In the event, the whole tone of the school tightened up sharply as the optimism associated with teaching brighter pupils was harnessed by a purposeful, if bureaucratic head. Staffing structures were initiated, with patterns spelt out on triangular shaped paper for both the academic and the pastoral sides. Posts of responsibility were designated, and individual responsibilities defined. Heads of faculties and heads of years organized their teams, held meetings, planned courses, and articulated their curriculum through shared activity. The new physics teacher was no longer alone to do his own thing, but a member of a science department, and of a year group, from both of which he received support and to both of whom he gave his commitment and time. With the raising of the school leaving age in 1974, and the introduction of comprehensivization, new structures, new laboratories and a new curriculum all needed to be organized.

Throughout the sixties, the science curriculum had been developing indirectly on the back of Nuffield. One influence of the new courses was to loosen the purse strings of the LEA and so Riverside was able to buy kits of apparatus for class experiments where previously there was a single piece of apparatus for demonstration. At first these were calorimeters, glass blocks and meters for standard experiments, it was not until the mid-70s that the more exotic ripple tanks, dynamics trolleys and radioactivity apparatus found their way into the school. Inevitably the science lessons became more based on pupil experiment than on formal demonstrations. Syllabuses and work schemes became more structured and standardized to enable all of the expanding science department to cover the same material. All pupils took a combined science course for their first three years, and then had to select one, two or three science subjects from the fourth and fifth form option system.

The new CSE exam had been introduced in 1965, when the school was still a secondary modern and, although they presented new challenges for both teacher and pupil as they sought to assess understanding and pupil achievement, they were heavily influenced by the grammar school curriculum from the GCE. However freedom to innovate was allowed, even encouraged in this hey-day of the Schools Council, and Mr Cox as 'supremo' of the science exams in the local area consortium was at one time overseeing forty different types of science exam from fourteen schools involved. Riverside, however, offered only physics, chemistry and biology at CSE, and these catered for about 40 per cent, 20 per cent, and 60 per cent respectively of the pupils in their last two years of compulsory schooling.

Though the school went comprehensive in 1973, it was not until five years later that the first comprehensive intake reached the 16+ exams, and the first time that a whole class of pupils took the 'O' level in physics. Thereafter this was to be the norm, with about seventeen pupils passing 'O' level physics each year and about forty, from two sets, successfully taking it at CSE. Another set of about twenty would take the CSE physical science exam. Mr Knight was appointed in 1976 to build up the physics academically and was given the brief 'to get the top set through "O" level and persuade them to opt for "A" level physics, if he wanted to teach sixth form physics subsequently'. In this he succeeded and produced a sixth form physics group which would thereafter produce about eight to ten 'A' level passes per year, about half of whom would continue with their physics into higher education, perhaps three into engineering courses and one into physics itself. Mr Knight, having earned not only the sixth form teaching, but also the headship of the physics department on the retirement of Mr Cox in 1981, then left the school in 1984 to take up a head of science post in a neighbouring comprehensive. His post was not refilled, however, due to a shortage of points in the school at the time; the school with its elaborate management structure and static teaching force had already tied up too many scale points for the school with its falling roll. Fortunately the newly appointed Deputy Head, Dr Pipe, was a physicist and formerly a head of science so was able to take on the running of the physics department under the overall science umbrella of Mr Evans. A lively young engineering graduate, with two years industrial experience and a PGCE, was appointed to teach physics at the same time. When the college trained physical science teacher was seconded a year later, after sixteen years in this his only school, and was replaced by a probationary teacher with a PhD from Cambridge (who needed to stay locally for reasons of the heart, but was to leave both the area and teaching during the year), the physics teaching force in the school had never looked stronger — inexperienced but with unusual qualifications and potential.

Physics teaching at Riverside had changed enormously over the twenty-five years. In 1960, the physics teaching was a straightforward, formal presentation of physics facts to undemanding youngsters with few aspirations of academic achievement, in a secondary modern school from which most pupils left at the age of 15 to enter directly into menial employment. The syllabus, and the exams, were idiosyncratic and the individualistic teaching relied for its strength and enthusiasms on the gifted amateur. By 1985, the school had become comprehensive and the whole business of physics teaching had become more professional. The quality of the teachers, of the curriculum, of the resources, of the departmental organization, yes and even of the exams, had improved out of all recognition. The original hope that a comprehensive school should provide a 'grammar school education for all' was very nearly fulfilled. All pupils stayed on to 16 and were being taught experimental physics in well equipped labs by a wholly graduate staff, who were thinking and planning their teaching departmentally. All pupils were exposed to physics for three years, over half for five years, and a dozen continuing it into the sixth form. The overall curriculum, for both physics and science, had been improved, made safer and more standardized to conform to the common good and the common exam syllabuses. In so doing, however, it had lost the opportunities for individuality, flair and opportunism that a freer, innovative teacher might have had twenty years earlier. Ironically, in the mid-eighties, when the science department was working with the CDT department to introduce technology, they found that, after much anguish and many working parties and draft papers, they were moving towards the sort of activity that Mr Cox was getting his non-examination pupils involved in twenty-five years earlier. *Plus ca change, plus c'est la meme chose!*

Throughout the period, however, underlying changes in the attitudes of society in general and of young people in particular had made the task and context of physics teaching quite different. Social problems, antisocial attitudes, bureaucratic administration had all entered into the daily life of the physics teacher to the extent that, in Mr Cox's words, 'the teaching of physics has almost become a part time activity, what you get around to when all the pastoral, discipline and administrative tasks have been done'. His life in 1960 was ordered, relaxed and simple. He taught his classes the way he thought best and the vast majority of pupils accepted his authority with little demur. If they had any personal problems, as many of them did, they kept them at home — Mr Cox found little difficulty in containing them in school. He went home around 4.00 pm, with the little marking and preparation required already done, and forgot about school until the next day. With comprehensivization came professionalism, administration and corporate planning, and a lot more time spent on paperwork and at meetings. Following the permissive sixties, with the growth of personal problems, the universal questioning of authority and the school more consciously embracing the pupils social problems into the pastoral system, the lot of the teacher of physics, as of other subjects, became more emotionally demanding. He was likely to spend more time quelling riotous teenagers or consoling pregnant fifth formers in his tutor group than solving 'A' level physics questions or devising demonstration experiments. At the end of his emotionally draining day at school, he would have had a full set of books to mark, lessons and experiments to prepare for the next day, and a departmental meeting in which to plan the latest form of teacher assessment of pupils course work for the GCSE. He was unlikely to forget about school in the evening.

As to whether the school was meeting the needs of scoiety better, the issues are far from clear. Society might ask two things of science education in its schools, that it should help all pupils to become scientifically literate and that it help produce the scientific and technological manpower that it requires. In both of these respects Riverside had improved vastly, though some might question whether the output in terms of producing physicists and engineers for higher education, just three or four per year from an initial cohort of 180, was commensurate with the resources put in. And yet, in some ways, the school was satisfying the needs of society better in 1960 than in 1985! In 1960, the expressed needs of society were very small and easily met. This was to keep a large number of under-privileged youngsters off the streets until they were 15, and then to release them to fill their appropriate, menial role in life. In 1985 the expectations of parents and pupils were so much higher: that ALL pupils should be scientifically literate and obtain a satisfying and fulfilling job. But, at the same time, society in the form of employing agencies, despite its protestations to the contrary, could not provide the job opportunities that many of the pupils now believed they had a right to. In some ways, the problem with Riverside School, as for so many other comprehensive schools, was that it had become too successful! In raising the life expectations of all of its pupils above that which the hierarchical and materialistic society of 1985 could fulfil, it has produced frustrated youngsters. In providing a grammar school education for all, in a society which could not provide grammar school jobs for all, in raising expectations of equality in a society which remains fundamentally unequal, it had raised the wind. The next challenge, which should be especially appropriate for physics teachers, is to learn how to harness it.

Camford School (Selective, Direct Grant Independent)

Camford was as proud of its direct grant grammar school, as Camford School was of its traditions and its links with the town. Though some claimed that the school could trace its history back to pre-Norman times, it had been rebuilt on its present site in 1870. By 1960 the school contained 600 boys, one-third of whom were boarders. The school was a happy and contented one, with a full range of academic, cultural and sporting activities. The presence of the boarders, while doing little to enhance the academic record of the school, did ensure that the school was alive seven days a week and that the tradition of extra-curricular activities remained strong. The head, a distinguished classicist who had taken the school into the Headmasters Conference, had come to the school soon after the Second World War and was pleased to tell visitors that he was only the second headmaster that the school had had since before the First World War. For him, the school was his life and his family, and he showed this in the care with which he selected both his staff and his pupils, selecting on grounds of character and potential as well as proven ability. The staff and, in general, the boys, responded enthusiastically to the expectations and example he gave them.

Of People, Policy and Power

And so the school continued, growing slowly in size, and steadily in reputation until in 1971 the head retired. Shortly after the arrival of the next head, another outstanding young scholar, the school, with sad reluctance, changed its status. From 1974, the direct grant was steadily phased out until by 1980 it had become fully independent; 700 strong with the boarding side reduced to 100, and a 'local catchment area' from which it could select of about twenty miles radius. Apart from a few partial scholarships financed from its own endowments, it was also able to recruit twelve boys for assisted places each year, about 10 per cent of its intake. The school prospectus in 1985 stressed that 'the emphasis placed on the pursuit of excellence, with teaching done in a moderately traditional style which we believe is suited to the requirements of pupils selected for their academic ability'. As a result of this policy, and the increased pressure from fee-paying parents, the academic achievements of the school measured in 'A' level results and university entrants rose to an impressive level.

Physics had always held a strong, central position in the school with heads who, though not scientists themselves, recognized the importance of the subject for the boys and left the direction of the subject to the heads of department they had appointed. The school policy, throughout the twenty-five years, was that all boys should continue with physics up until the 'O' level at 16. A large fraction of the more able pupils continued it through to 'A' level. The three science departments in the school were and remained relatively autonomous, with each departmental head having freedom to do his own thing while negotiating amicably with the other scientists. The science department was to remain a federation of independent states, each in its own territory and each with its own budget. As the school grew, and also the demand for physics, so the physics staff grew from three in 1960, through three-and-a-half to four full-time physics staff in 1985. The staff were always graduate and often professionally trained. Over the years, the physics department encompassed a range of talents and enthusiasms, apart from the specialisms in physics. Whether it was acting, singing, orienteering, scouting, computing, rowing or mountain climbing, the physics staff were consistently involved with a range of school activities. The school had been fortunate in holding its physics staff for good lengths of time. David Johnson headed the department from 1954–64; Peter Bryant from 1965–73; and Alan Davidson from 1973 onwards. Throughout the whole of that period, John Rogers, an Oxford graduate, had served the school in teaching physics, maths and cross-country as well as the numerous other tasks accruing to a committed teacher. Three other physicists had been in the department for more than ten years. There was a sense of continuity, many of the practices of 1985 would not have been unfamiliar to the physics teacher of 1960. The labs, though now extended, still had the same rows of fixed benches with uniformed boys sitting receptively behind them. The practical work, though with different apparatus, still had the same structure to illustrate the theoretical topic being studied. The 'O' and 'A' level examinations, though now containing more demanding questions, still were the focus and goal of much of the teaching. Even the text books, though now more lavishly illustrated, still contained very much the same content which had to be learnt and understood. But the department, if stable, had been far from static in that time.

The curriculum pattern in 1960 was that every boy should study combined science for the first two years, the three separate subjects in year 3, and physics definitely, chemistry probably and biology possibly, up to 'O' level at 16. They were then able to choose to study three or four 'A' level subjects from physics, chemistry, biology, maths and all the arts and language subjects. Many of the best students chose the sciences. This pattern has been modified over the years in various ways. In 1969 the Nuffield physical science course was introduced into the sixth form and taken by the good biologists along with maths. This had been taught successfully, jointly by a physicist and a chemist, and continued to attract a set of about a dozen pupils, many of whom were latterly taking it with maths and an arts subject. In 1970 biology became a compulsory subject up to 16, a policy merely formalizing the growing popularity of the subject, with chemistry also being taken by the majority of the boys. 10 per cent of the timetabled time was given to each subject so that through the seventies and the eighties, the majority of the boys would spend 30 per cent of their time in the fourth and fifth form doing sciences, to the detriment of time spent on the humanities and creative activities. In 1973 it was decided that the lower sets in the fourths and fifths were not coping satisfactorily with the three separate sciences, so they were entered for the double subject combined science, a practice that Alan Davidson, the new head of department, had brought from his previous school. In this way about two-thirds of the fifth form took all three sciences as separate subjects, while the lower third obtained their science through the more truncated combined science. All the boys got 'balanced science', but they took 30 per cent of the timetable to do it.

In the sixties, there were three 'A' level sets taking physics each year, with numbers varying between thirty-six and forty-eight. There would be a good set, a reasonable set and a set of biologists who needed physics as a third subject for medicine. Most of the top two sets would go to university or polytechnic, with subjects being equally shared between the pure and the applied sciences. The number studying physics remained fairly constant throughout the seventies, though with the advent of physical science only two sets were doing physics *per se*. In the eighties, however, the demand for physics grew again and a third set had to be introduced. Through the seventies and eighties, the career aspirations of the sixth forms became steadily more vocational, and the balance between pure and applied degree courses swung decidedly towards the latter. The introduction of both the combined science and the physical science exams had been done at the instigation of one or two members of staff, who persuaded their colleagues and the head to acquiesce. The next, and more difficult task, was to persuade the parents to accept it too and the staff did have a battle with some parents in the initial stages. However, staff determination, supported by evidence stating that the universities would accept them, eventually won the day and after a few years in practice, it was only the most belligerent parents who would complain — and for them there was always the alternative of separate sciences.

Throughout the twenty-five years, the physics staff at Camford School had developed a comfortable accommodation with the exam system. They did not find the syllabuses constricting; their teaching would be wider than the bare necessities anyway. On the whole, what they wanted to teach was what was in the exam syllabus and this provided a useful framework for the teachers and a most helpful incentive to the pupils. The teachers and the pupils became increasingly successful at playing the exam game, with both teacher and pupil working together to beat the examiner. There was no ambiguity of the teachers' role, there was no teacher assessment, the teachers were clearly on the side of the pupils. In 1985, with the GCSE only twelve months away, the staff were still not persuaded that there was any need to change the system and, as far as their pupils were concerned, there probably wasn't. The very fact that pupils in other schools found the 'O' level examination inappropriate and divisive, was the very reason that Camford School liked it; it did separate their pupils from the rest, and thus justified the price of the school fee. Their pupils were successful in it and so attained the 'glittering prizes' more readily. There was no doubt that the very good teaching at the school was successful at 'A' level. In the sixties, the 'A' level pass rate in physics would be between 60 per cent and 80 per cent, with between a quarter and a third of the candidates getting grade A or B. This standard improved steadily through the seventies until in the eighties they would expect a pass rate of more than 90 per cent, with over half of them getting grade A or B. With a dozen boys getting three A grades each year it was not surprising that they got an increasing number of boys into Oxbridge. From an upper sixth of nearly 100 they would hope for twenty places in a good year. In the sixties the school was pleased to get into double figures.

In spite of all the academic pressure in the school there had always been a 'thin red line' of technological activities in one form or another. The involvement of the physics staff, and their relationship with other subjects in the technology teaching, illustrates well the different approaches and how they reflect the personalities and inclinations of the people involved. David Johnson would have considered himself a pure physicist and this was reflected in his physics teaching. The practical work was standard and the only freedom to experiment came in the science club, the photographic club, the small, and sporadic, astronomical club and the CCF field days. The only craft work being done by the pupils was some very basic woodwork by the less able pupils in a dingy shed at the back of the kitchens.

In the summer of 1966, at the end of Peter Bryant's first year as head of physics, he reflected on the goals he hoped the pupils would have achieved from doing practical physics and on the actual practicals he had done, and realized that the two did not match. He heard a lecture at an ASE day conference on project work in physics being done at a neighbouring FE college and his imagination was fired. He resolved, and effected, that he would have his sixth formers doing open-ended projects in their physics lessons. Cutting out some of the standard cookery book experiments he used the time to get the pupils working on their own projects, often around a common theme. With string and sealing wax, and the simplest of tools, the students spent time testing the strength of paper, glass, copper, elastic etc., and studying its creep, its dependence on temperature and its breaking strain. After considering Newton's laws of motion with the lower sixth, they spent two weeks investigating different properties of firework rockets; their force/time characteristic, their calorific value, the impulse delivered and their trajectory. Using the new strobe-flash boys devised ways of studying the life of a milk splash and the deformation of a golf ball when struck. Working with the new PE teacher, recently appointed from Loughborough and keen on ergonomics, they studied the motion of weight-lifters with multishot photography and heart-rate under exercise with simple ESGs. Linking with a local scientific establishment, they studied the mechanical and thermal properties of samples of resin that were to be used for mounting super-conducting magnets which would hopefully not crack when submerged in liquid nitrogen. Most of these were done by lower sixth formers, in their normal physics lessons, though not all in the same year! They often spread out into the student's own time, they were channelled into the exhibitions for the school open day, and taken to local science fairs. Some were to be developed as projects at the Welsh farm that the school purchased and used for ten years in the late sixties and early seventies. The normal labs were far from ideal for such projects, though not impossible. But when a nearby Nissen hut became free, it had been the day-boys' changing room, this was commandeered and converted by the boys and the staff into a projects lab. Soon the smell of sweat and linament was being replaced by the smell of firework exhausts and of capacitors discharging across the wires of a linear induction motor. But the roof continued to leak and when the biologists moved out of their small lab into some new ones, the old biology lab was converted into a projects lab instead.

But, in 1965, Peter Bryant left and Alan Davidson took over the physics department. Within a year the messy and chaotic projects lab had been reconverted into a normal teaching room. Alan Davidson was a more ordered man, and a computing and electronics expert to boot. Soon Apple computers were becoming a normal part of physics lessons, and home-made programmes and interfaces were springing up to meet particular needs. He wanted to introduce more electronics into the physics syllabuses, and devised his own schemes and kits, later to be developed commercially with colleagues in other schools. These units he put first into the third form physics course, as a module, then into the science courses for the first two years, and then developed material for the fourth and fifth forms too. As the exams change at 'A' level and GCSE he will find ways of incorporating more electronics there. Hence all pupils would meet a coordinated programme of electronics in their physics courses, as well as in the electronic club and informally after school.

Alongside the development of the electronics in the physics department, there had been rapid changes in the craft area too. On the retirement of the old woodwork teacher in the late seventies, Don Millar was appointed to teach design. Don was an exceptional man with an unconventional background, trained in and previously teaching English, his hobby of making harpsichords had become his obsession and he wanted to share it with boys through design in wood. In 1980 he introduced a design course for 'O' level and two years later a few boys started an 'A' level in design. Two years after Don arrived, he appointed Alf Field, a technology teacher with industrial experience. Quickly the art, craft and design department blossomed around these two men, and the subject took over the old art lessons to introduce boys to as many different processes and materials through design as possible. Boys also made good use of the department out of lesson time and it soon became clear that more facilities were needed. The case was made by the ACD department, along with Alan Davidson from physics, that a new technology centre be set up. An appeal for money from the parents realized enough to convert the old warehouse into a technology centre, which was to be used for lessons, hobbies, and as the base for the new modular technology course introduced in 1984.

In all of these different ways, and in a school traditionally committed to academic studies, many boys had been introduced to aspects of technology through the inspiration and determination of different members of staff. Each, in their own way, had different perceptions of technology, there was no standard package to be bought off the shelf. Perhaps because of this, and the personal commitment that the teachers brought to their own schemes, they were each in their own way a stimulus to many boys, providing a rare opportunity for creativity and self-expression in a normally conformist environment.

Windmill Hill School (Secondary Modern gone 11–16 Comprehensive)

It had been many years since the rise on which Windmill Hill School was built had last seen a windmill. Indeed, had one been there now, the surrounding houses and blocks of flats would have shielded it from any prevailing winds that might have made it an effective source of power for the local industry. By 1960 the school was a well-established secondary modern school satisfactorily meeting the needs of 500 boys and girls, most of whom left school at 15 to start work in the local shops, businesses and factories. In 1967 it became an 11–16, coeducational, comprehensive feeding into a sixth form college and the nearby technical college. Not too far away were two 11–18 comprehensives and these were able to attract the children from some of the more ambitious families until the zoning arrangements in the area were tightened up. It remained a four form entry school for the first ten years of its existence as a comprehensive school, and then as a result of further reorganization in the area it grew to a six form entry of 900 pupils. With the arrival of a new head in the early eighties, the school began to offer its facilities more to the local community, using its workshops, classrooms and sports facilities for evening classes and offering a creche and luncheon service for local 'mums'. Though it was now called Windmill Hill Secondary School and Community Centre (WHSSCC for short!) it was still a school at heart, though one which saw itself as serving its local community, even if the actuality of that service out of school time was modest.

The science taught by the three science teachers in the secondary modern days was pedestrian and book-orientated. There was no set syllabus, and each teacher taught from his or her own interests and the text book available. For physics, this began with rather old copies of Harrison's *Elementary General Science* followed by equally battered copies of McKenzie's *General Physics*. It was difficult to get or retain well-trained staff, and for physics it was almost impossible. Though physics was taught, it often had to be done by a biologist, a subject in which the school regularly had a surplus. Even when the school changed its name to comprehensive in 1967, and started receiving pupils from a slightly wider ability range, the situation in the science department did not change to any noticeable extent. The staff remained the same, the facilities remained the same and, in a very large measure, the teaching remained the same. There was virtually no departmental policy, each teacher did their own thing, the emphasis and quality of which depended on the specialism and the quality of the teacher. Peter Edwards, who as Head of the Science Department, had to take the physics even though he was a biologist by training, did introduce an individualized work scheme for the fourth and fifth form physicists in the mid-seventies when such schemes were fashionable. He even went around speaking of it to groups of local teachers, but in truth it did not amount to much. He set up a series of simple experiments to illustrate basic physics and provided a recipe to be followed by the pupils to ensure they did the right thing; he provided quarter-class sets of each experiment so that there would be four different experiments going on at the same time. But the physics was not very good, the experiments not very exciting and the organization casual. Indeed, when Dick Barrett was interviewed for a post at the school in 1978 he was advised, by a chemistry teacher whose department was better organized, that 'teaching physics in this school is inventing as many lessons as possible with a weight and a piece of string'. Peter Edwards had, however, bought a number of expensive pieces of physics apparatus to use for demonstrations; a spectrometer, a projection microscope, a chart recorder, even a pulse electrometer, and these were found in the cupboards by Dick Barrett after his appointment, unused and still in their original wrappings.

By 1978, even the head was dissatisfied with the way that the science department was developing and Peter Edwards was called in, firmly admonished, and challenged to decide whether he wanted to teach biology or physics. Having chosen the former, the head advertised for a scale 3 physicist, and appointed Dick Barrett to 'shake up the science department in general and the head of department in particular'. This he did to such good effect that within twelve months he had been given full responsibility for the direction of the department, when Peter Edwards was moved sideways into remedial work, (a move made easier and more pressing for the headmaster following a nasty accident that Peter had in the laboratory with a Winchester of concentrated acid!). Dick was a physics graduate from Portsmouth Polytechnic, and had taken his first teaching post in a grammar school in the same town. There he had learnt his craft in a well-organized science department of twelve scientists and gained useful experience when he was given the responsibility of reorganizing the first two years combined science course when the school went comprehensive. He was not yet 30 when he moved to Windmill Hill, but he was determined and wise beyond his years. This wisdom, and tact, were to be utilized to the full in the following years as he sought to bring together the science teachers to form a team with a common, and appropriate science policy for the pupils. Not the least of his problems was Gill Read who, as an untrained Oxford physicist with a first class honours degree and a Mensa badge, had been appointed as a probationer to teach physics twelve months earlier. It took him a further twelve months to persuade her and the authorities that she was an irremediable disaster in the classroom, when having been passed her probationary year against his advice, she eventually realized for herself that teaching was not for her. The physics department, with only twelve out of 150 pupils opting to do physics in the fourth year, was, as the estate agents would say, 'ripe for improvement'!

Perhaps the most interesting, certainly the most radical, changes in the physics and the science curriculum came in the last seven years, after the arrival of Dick Barrett in 1978. Up until then, though the status of the school had changed, the nature of the science taught in the school had changed very little. Despite the 'curriculum revolution' of the previous fifteen years, the science taught was still based on transferring the content of the 'O' level syllabus, or, in the case of the CSE, a watered down 'O' level syllabus, to the pupils in a rather didactic, academic style. Such a physics appeared to have little to do with the pupils' lives or to engage with their concerns. Perhaps even worse, it was not being taught well. When Dick Barrett arrived at Windmill Hill, he was still thinking as a physicist, he liked his subject and wanted to teach it enthusiastically so that more pupils would enjoy it too. It was not until later that his perception of the needs of the pupils became central and his thinking and planning developed around the meaning of 'science for all'. Pre-1978, the teaching of years 1 and 2 had been left to the individual whims of the teachers, Dick saw the need to standardize the syllabus so that all pupils would have a common foundation, and all the science teachers would be able to work together in a mutually supportive way. After a series of science department meetings, and with the agreement of his colleagues, he introduced the scheme based on the science for the seventies that he had developed and found successful in his previous schools. He had also been persuaded of the virtues of Nuffield 'O' level physics by his previous experience and resolved to introduce that for years 3, 4 and 5. He had seen the gain in pupil-motivation and achievement when his school in Portsmouth had changed from 'trad' to Nuffield, and was able to impress his new head that such a change to a more experimentally-based course would have the same effect at Windmill Hill. It was not difficult to persuade the head of the need for more money to equip the course, as he had already acknowledged the paucity of the present provision. As this coincided with the building of new laboratories to cope with the increased numbers, money was freely available for him to buy complete class sets, and any other equipment that he wanted. On top of the normal capitation, he obtained £1700 from the PTA and a further £5000 over two years from the LEA as the labs were being built.

By 1980, the science department had gained its new look, and new spirit. Aims and objectives had been agreed by the staff, and courses established throughout the five years. Though there was modification of the courses to match the individuality of the school and the teachers, the courses were at that stage essentially 'off the peg', and centrally produced. The school was entering pupils for 'O' level and CSE in physics, chemistry and biology, and human biology. There were no Mode 3s and no combined or integrated sciences offered. The physics department had certainly been revived, and physics was becoming an increasingly popular subject. Within two years the numbers opting for physics in the fourth form had risen from twelve to twenty-five to seventy-five, which represented about 50 per cent of the year group, and this proportion remained fairly constant providing three physics sets each year. The proportion of girls choosing physics was quite high, about half of the 'O' level set and a quarter of the CSE set were girls, a proportion not entirely unrelated to the charm and sensitivity of teaching of Dick Barrett and his physics colleague Will Stevenson, newly-appointed in 1979. But Dick and his colleagues were not satisfied with this considerably improved state of affairs. Once into the habit of questioning and discussing the suitability of their courses to the pupils' needs, they realized that they were still far from perfect.

Two problems came to the fore in these discussions. The first, an organizational one, related to the choices that the pupils had to make at 14; they had to choose from the separate sciences scattered through five option blocks and, though a few chose all three sciences, the vast majority chose only two or one of the sciences and thus finished up with an unbalanced diet, and one which inevitably precluded certain career choices. The second problem was more fundamental; was the type of science being offered, an essentially academic, content-dominated science, really appropriate for their pupils for the majority of whom this school science would be the only scientific education they would ever receive? Was the science that the pupils were receiving really the best way of preparing scientifically literate citizens for tomorrow's world?

The first of these problems was tackled through physical science. In 1980 a Mode 3 physical science course was introduced into the option system, initially for those who would have found the separate sciences too demanding. It was a modular course, and had been developed by the new Head of Chemistry in his previous school. Initially it was only one group, alongside 'O' level and CSE levels in physics and chemistry, but by 1983, when an 'O' level in physical science had been introduced, there was one set in 'O' level physics (and one in 'O' level chemistry), one set in 'O' level physical science and four sets in Mode 3 CSE physical science. In this way the school was getting close to its aim of getting every pupil to have a balanced science course by doing physical science and biology and using only two option blocks, or 20 per cent of the time. It was still possible to do physics and chemistry as separate subjects, but only those with definite and appropriate sixth form aspirations were allowed to do so. All those with any uncertainty in their minds, and all those who were considering doing three sciences at 'A' level, were encouraged to take physical science, with biology, to keep their options open. Before introducing this policy, Dick Barrett had contacted the heads of science at the institutions to which his 16-year-old leavers would go, the local sixth form college and neighbouring 11–18 comprehensives. He asked what they wanted from his pupils, and whether they would accept 'O' level physical science as an entry for their 'A' level courses in physics and chemistry. In the event, they were most supportive and readily signed a letter giving their 'acceptance of students wishing to study physics, chemistry and biology 'A' levels if they possess 'O' levels in physical science and biology' — with the usual constraints of satisfactory pass grades. Armed with this letter, Dick Barrett had no difficulty in getting parents to accept this policy.

Alongside this development, and underpinning it, was a reconsideration of the content and teaching strategies for the courses. Dick had joined a working group of local teachers working with the local UDE on making the 11–13 science syllabus more 'technologically flavoured', indeed he was seconded to it for one-day-a-week for a year to develop curriculum material. Through this he introduced into his first two year science courses both problem-solving practical work and resource material for 'science in society' issues. Five small projects were written into each of the first two years, typically problems causing students to make clocks, towers, bridges, weighing machines or to investigate the best colour and type for warning notices. He was happy to omit traditional topics of physics, such as forces and electric circuitry from the syllabus believing that they could not be treated satisfactorily at this stage, and that formalizing them did nothing to add to the pupils tacit knowledge. He introduced readings about simple technological situations; saving energy, plastics, uses of technology, and used these along with extracts from *Reading About Science* as the basis of class discussion and individual exercises. He collected resources from organizations such as British Gas, the Electricity Council, and the Keep Britain Tidy Group, and used their material throughout the school as appropriate. Along with other members of the science department, he was building into all of the science courses a feel of relevance to everyday life and pupils' personal involvement and active engagement with their problems. Though such changes were easier to make for the 11–13 courses, the project component in the physical science exam and the development of the examination questions to assess more applications and comprehension exercises enabled this broader science for all to be developed right through, up to the age of 16.

The school as a whole, as well as the scientists, began to consider a co-ordinated, entitlement curriculum for the school, and grouping the sciences and technology together seemed more appropriate. In 1984 Dick Barrett was appointed the first Director of the CDST Department (craft, design, science and technology). This now included seven science teachers, three CDT and two teachers from the food and nutrition department who saw the new curriculum trends in their subject driving them closer towards the sciences too. Clearly there was much in common between some of the problem-solving approaches of the scientists and the CDT teachers, though their skills and traditions seemed likely to keep their subjects distinct for the foreseeable future. It was interesting to note that previously, the only link between the science and craft departments had been back in the seventies when Ben Charles, the rural scientist had linked himself and his finances to the CDT department, because he could not get on with the head of science at the time! Perhaps two main themes are illustrated by the developments at Windmill Hill. Firstly, that one person, with a clear commitment to improving the science education in a school, can make such a significant difference in a relatively short space of time and that the rate of change can be quicker and more radical when the teachers are not restrained and distracted by the influence of the more academic sixth-form teaching. And secondly, or so Dick Barrett would claim, that in considering primarily the scientific education of all pupils up to the age of 16, rather than the needs of the future specialist, you are developing courses of balanced science that also provides perfectly adequately, (even better?) for the potential physicist and engineer too.

Brunel College (Grammar School turned Sixth Form College)

The town in which Brunel College was situated was little more than 100 years old. A railway town, populated largely by London over-spill folk, it maintained a sense of left-wing, civic pride for which its grammar school had been a natural focus. There were, however, other grammar schools in the area with much longer traditions and much higher status. This resulted, through parental choice and the consequent pecking order, in the school containing pupils of good, rather than brilliant, ability, with utilitarian rather than imperial ambitions. Though there had been large cut-backs in the British Rail workshops in the 1970s, the area was still one of high employment with newer light industrial firms utilizing the technical traditions and expertise existing in the town. It was in 1971 that the country's educational policy caused the school to stop taking its grammar school input at 11, and by 1976 the school had become a full sixth form college. All the students from the nine 11–16 comprehensives in its ten-mile radius catchment area now came to Brunel College, or to the neighbouring FE college. The grammar school in the sixties normally had a four form entry, leading to a school of nearly 800 pupils. With a little rebuilding Brunel College was able to accommodate about 1000 students, though few would claim that the facilities for specialist subjects like physics were over-generous.

In the grammar school days, physics was taught throughout the school to all the pupils up to the age of 16. Thereafter, physics in the sixth form became increasingly popular, raising from one set of ten when John Alanson first came to the school to teach physics in 1962, until the time of reorganization, when about twenty-five students would study for 'A' level physics each year. After reorganization, that growth continued, from the sixty students taking physics at 'A' level in 1975 to rather more than twice that number ten years later. By this time, the physics department was, in addition to these eight sets of 'A' level physics, also teaching two sets of electronics systems to 'A' level, one set of 'AO' electronics and six sets for the one-year course leading to 'O' level physics. Corresponding to the increase in pupil numbers was the growth of the physics staff. In the grammar school days physics was taught by two graduate physicists, supplemented when necessary by the deputy head, himself a physicist. As the sixth form college developed, so it recruited graduates with a background of physics, engineering or electronics, forming a department of seven full-time, and one part-time, teachers with differing but complimentary experience.

The physics department had at its disposal five laboratories, three of which it devoted to 'A' level physics teaching, one to 'O' level physics and one kept exclusively for electronics; all were well resourced. The demand on these labs was such that not all the lessons could be taught in a laboratory, causing the practical work to be done in specific periods. The central physics prep-room also served as a social centre for the physics staff causing them to be a cohesive, if isolated team communicating easily and informally about professional and personal matters. There was general agreement about the aims and methods of their teaching, simplified by the limited number of goals facing the department; to prepare their students for higher education in physics or related subjects in the 'A' level courses, and to provide an 'O' level physics for those who needed that for entry to a job at the technician level. The teachers and their students saw their goals largely in vocational terms, and in this, as also with the teaching styles, there had been little change over the twenty-five years. Though the quantity and the quality of the teaching had increased over that period, much of the style and the content of the teaching remained the same.

The department had flirted with Nuffield 'A' level physics in the late 70s, and for three years had one set taking Nuffield as an alternative to the traditional 'A' level course. This was introduced, experimentally, in response to one feeder school who were doing Nuffield physics at 'O' level. But it did not prove popular with either the staff or the students, who would keep comparing their own progress with the apparently greater amount of physics being covered by their peers on the traditional course, and so after three years it was dropped. The natural enthusiasms of the department lay more with the structured content of formal physics and with electronics, than with what they perceived as the more tenuous outcomes of Nuffield. The thought of the problems inherent in having 120 students doing 120 different investigations in the limited laboratory space more used to handling practicals in pre-boxed form, also proved too traumatic to encourage a wholesale introduction of the Nuffield course.

Technology appeared in the college under various guises. Though there was little overt technology in the physics course itself, many 'A' level physicists were also studying electronic systems as an 'A' level, or computer studies in the maths department. It was also possible to study for a design course within the CDT department. The use of computers and electronics in the physics courses had been widely introduced by the head of physics, himself an 'electronics wizard'. He had started electronics as a club activity back in 1964, then introduced it into 'A' level physics and in an 'AO' electronics course, leading to the 'A' level electronic systems being introduced in 1978. As with many such innovations, its introduction was dependent on the enthusiasm and 'do-it-yourself' expertise of the staff 'over and above the call of duty'.

The strengths of the department are reflected in the destination of the students after college. In a typical year when 110 students studied 'A' level physics, about ninety would pass. Of these, about half would go onto higher education, twelve to read physics, sixteen into engineering of one form or another, six into electronics and four to computing. Others would go on to study chemistry, or biology or medicine. Of those not going onto higher education, the majority would be utilizing their physics in direct employment at one of the local industries, many of which had an electronic or scientific base.

The staff as a whole, while not complacent, were well satisfied with the job they were doing at Brunel College. A few, particularly the younger, more radical entrants to teaching, found the academic conservatism at the college restricting and moved to other, more open, institutions where they could work with a wider range of vocational and pre-vocational courses. As physicists, they found little difficulty in getting promoted posts elsewhere. But most had had experience of other types of school, of comprehensives or of grammar schools, and had little desire to return to them. They enjoyed the freer, more co-operative attitude of the students who were able to take a more independent responsibility for their work. They appreciated the strength that the cross-fertilization and mutual encouragement of a large team gave. And they found the sixth-form teaching, without significant distractions by pastoral involvement, both more challenging and more satisfying. Here was a group of teachers who found enjoyment in their subject. In the context of Brunel College they were able to carry that enjoyment into their teaching. Furthermore, they had the satisfaction of having the approval of their community by preparing and training large numbers of scientists and technologists for a technologically voracious society.

10 'The coat of many colours' — of People, Policy and Power?

Overall Trends in Physics Teaching

And so, as we come to the end of our study, we must look back, review the changes that have taken place and return to our original questions regarding the reasons for these developments. Who has been driving the bus? Can we make sense of the reasons behind the trends? How far have the agents for change been individual people, articulated policies or expressions of a political power struggle?

In considering the trends in physics teaching, we will consider three aspects. First the content of the subject and the way it has been taught, with particular consideration to the changes in practical work. Second the place and importance of physics in the school curriculum, and third the role of the physics teacher in school.

Changes in Content and Approach

Much of the content of physics has, unsurprisingly, stayed the same. Certain topics have fallen out of favour: Archimedes' principle, geometrical optics, calorimetry. Others, such as wave theory, photography, and electronics have been introduced. The style of teaching has, often, changed more radically. There has been, after Nuffield, a much greater emphasis on practical work, though there is evidence that the amount of practical work being done in the eighties may be decreasing again. After Nuffield, the thrust of the practical work was increasingly directed at discovering, rather than verifying, the underlying theory. Much of the Nuffield influence went towards reinforcing an academic, grammar school 'physics for the enquiring mind' approach and tended to make physics teaching more pure, concentrating on theory, and less applied. In one sense, Nuffield Physics could be considered as the end of a line, the culmination of physics as an intellectual study for able pupils in grammar schools, rather than as a staging post for a more appropriate type of relevant physics for typical pupils in comprehensive schools.

There were significant changes in the way that physics teaching was 'packaged' too. Text books in the last decade increasingly reflected physics as being relevant and important in real life. They were increasingly setting it into its human context through examples and photographs which involved real people. If the physics teaching of the sixties was about theory in a neutral, and self contained, academic context, by the late seventies its usefulness in application was being re-established, and illustrated as being relevant to both men and women. Physics had moved some way towards being part of Layton's 'science for the people'. Some text books also reflected the change from physics teaching being a matter of the transfer of knowledge to passive, absorbing pupils to it being a matter of the acquisition of understanding and appreciation of physics by active, learning pupils. Other text books, however, still reflected the continuing practice of physics being taught as the passive learning of predigested information.

Perhaps more interesting than the changes that did occur, were those that did not. For while so much was changing radically in both society and in schooling throughout twenty-five years, much in school physics teaching had changed not at all. Much of the content was the same, and much of the content seemed irrelevant to the pupils. Much of the practical activity was still perceived as being trivial and incomprehensible. Most motivation (for pupils, parents and teachers) came through examination targets, to which society still gave high currency for physics. Schools were still short of good physics teachers. Pupils still did their physics in short periods, in classes of about twenty-five pupils, all studying the same topic or doing the same experiment, in rooms and laboratories with a single teacher qualified as a teacher of physics. *Plus ca change, plus la meme chose!*

Yet, despite all the pressures for a more relevant science, and all the encouragements for moving away from separate sciences to an integrated science, physics itself had become increasingly popular in terms of its uptake at 'O' and CSE levels. The amount of physics had increased enormously through the period; from being taught only to a majority of the most able boys and very few girls, to being taught to the majority of all boys and a smaller, but increasing proportion of girls. In many schools the physics teaching had been untouched by central initiatives such as the Nuffield courses, SCISP and ILIS, or by insights that had been provided about cognitive development, sex stereotyping or the role of language in learning. On the other hand, in many schools the physics teaching continued to be rigorous and stimulating, providing a sound base for future study and for careers in sicence or engineering. The quality of the teaching, as for any other subject, depended on the quality of the individual physics teacher, and as this varied so the range of teaching within, and between schools varied enormously. Yet, with the provision of so many resources in books, apparatus and teaching schemes, it had become increasingly unlikely to find physics being taught really badly; which was, of course, one of the aims of the Nuffield project.

Changes in Practical Work

Central to the whole of physics teaching in England, to a degree more dominant than in any other country, is the role of the practical. The most powerful tradition in English science education, asserts Mary Waring (1985), has been that of individual practical work. More significantly 'the outcome has been a deeply-entrenched faith in a tradition which has assumed the status of an absolute, and a fundamental conservatism about what school science is, and should be' (p. 139). For many teachers physics teaching is doing practical work. It is in this area that some of the most fundamental battles and more interesting and revealing changes have taken place.

In the early 1960s, Professor Kerr carried out a seminal enquiry into the nature and purpose of practical work in school science (Kerr, 1963). He found that physics teachers put much emphasis on pupils carrying out standard practical experiments, often as quantitative verifications, rarely as qualitative introductions. A lot of demonstration work was done, especially with the younger classes, but very little use was made of independent investigations. Subsequently, other surveys (Thompson, 1975; Eggleston, Galton and Jones, 1976, HMI, 1979; Beatty and Woolnough, 1982; APU 1982) have traced a growing emphasis on practical work but less significant changes than might have been expected. After Nuffield, standard experiments to verify theory were to some extent replaced by standard experiments to discover theory. Demonstrations became less popular. Investigational projects remained unpopular. In the words of HMI 'many science teachers recognize the important of practical work ... (they) believed that pupils should have first hand practical experience in laboratories in order to acquire skills in handling apparatus, to measure constants and to illustrate concepts and principles. Unfortunately practical work often did not go further than this and few opportunities were provided for pupils to conduct challenging experimental investigations' (HMI, 1979, p. 184). Through the seventies there was a growing move to 'guided discovery' experiments, often relying on highly structured work sheets to guide the pupil to the required 'right answer'. Most of the practical work was linked closely to the theoretical content of the course, and determined by it, though towards the end of our period, there was a growing emphasis on using practical work to develop the skills and processes of science, for their own sake.

Though most teachers relied on standard, convergent, content-led practicals, there was a 'thin red line' throughout the period in which investigational practical work was encouraged and practised. HMI, under the leadership of Dr Tricker, were advocating the introduction of original, pupil investigations before Nuffield (HMI, 1960, pp. 62–5), as were the authors of the Kerr report. The Editor of the *ASE Bulletin* was inviting 'a new approach to science teaching ... based on problem solving activities and experimental investigations' (ASE, 1963, p. 8) and this was supported by physics teachers in, significantly, the technical and FE sectors (Bolton, 1963; Tuff, 1963). The Nuffield 'O' level physics project did not follow this approach, all of its practical experiments were much more directed by the theoretical outcomes. The Nuffield Secondary Science course, however, aimed at the less able pupils, laid great stress on the essential part played by the pupils' own investigations, 'open-ended investigations which involve responsibility for the pupils in devising methods of investigating problems they have themselves posed and identified as important' (Misslebrook, 1970, p. 19), and this was to prove very successful for the few students who followed this course. Certain CSE courses also gave encouragement to pupil investigations (for example, Bloom, 1969) as did project technology (Marshall, 1974), but while there were physics teachers involved with such technological projects, it was to remain very much a minority activity throughout physics training as a whole.

There was to remain an influential legacy of the traditional grammar school/secondary modern school split in this aspect. The high status, theory-led, grammar school tradition maintained the convergent standard experiments to elucidate the theory. The open-ended, investigational practical work, leading to the development of relevant skills and knowledge, was to flourish only among the lower status, lower ability and technically-minded pupils. Physics teachers persisted in giving those aims of practical work related to creative, investigational objectives a very low rating (Kerr, 1963; Holley, 1974, Beatty and Woolnough, 1982). Even the inclusion of investigational practical work as an assessed part of the Nuffield 'A' level physics course, (Black and Ogborn, 1971) under the influence of Bill Bolton and Bill Trotter, did little to raise its public status as it was not reflected in the physics practical laboratories of the most prestigious universities. Where such investigational work was being done, its quality was self-evidently excellent. But it was not until the end of our period, under the combined onslaught of the APU rationale, the DES and HMI exhortations, and the

GCSE's allowance that there were signs that investigational practical work might become widely accepted.

The confusion over the role of practical work arose, and remained, because of lack of clarity about its aims, especially in its relationship to theory. It was widely accepted throughout our period that the practical should be inextricably tied to the theory; its main, often its only, purpose was to illustrate, discover or clarify the underlying theory. Even Kerr, in defending himself against '... seeming to suggest a division between theory and practice' said 'such a divorce is not implied; each must support the other to form an integrated experience' (Kerr, 1963, p. 21). The Nuffield project was surprisingly inexplicit about its rationale for practical work, but implicitly made the practical linked with, and subservient to, the theory by setting the practicals into the context of the theoretical guidelines.

When teachers were asked about their aims for doing practical work in surveys from Oxford following up Kerr's earlier work (Thompson, 1975; Beatty and Woolnough, 1982; Thomas, 1983) an important change was noted between the pre- and post-Nuffield time. There was more confidence that practical work was good for discovering and elucidating theoretical work in 1963 than there was after more than a decade of Nuffield experience. One might have expected the opposite. It could be explained, as Professor Kerr hypothesized in discussion, that it was the former results of 1963, in the heady, idealistic days leading into the Nuffield courses that were misleading and that the later, more realistic opinions were more valid. Then teachers were claiming that practicals were good for developing practical skills, for giving an increased feel for the physical phenomena, and for arousing and maintaining interest. By the late 1970s, there seemed to be a growing recognition that there was more to doing practicals than discovering or elucidating theoretical concepts.

This is not the place for a full critique of much of the practical work done in school physics over the period; that has been done elsewhere (Woolnough and Allsop, 1985). Suffice to say that there was a growing dissatisfaction with much of current practice through the 1960s and 1970s, with the 'guided discovery' and 'getting the right answer' syndrome. The description of Tigger's adventures in the House at Pooh Corner provides a not inappropriate parallel to much pupil practical activity in schools; '... and with one loud worra worra worra worra worra, he jumped at the end of the tablecloth, pulled it to the ground, wrapped himself up in it three times, rolled to the other end of the room, and, after a terrible struggle, got his head into the daylight again, and said cheerfully: "have I won?"' (Milne, 1926)!

At the root of much of the criticism lay a growing doubt about the efficacy and validity of the discovery method in science teaching, (for example, Ausubel, Novak and Hanesian 1978; Swatrz 1974; Stevens, 1978; Driver, 1983; Moore and Thomas, 1983) and the value of integrating the practical so much with the theory (Layton, 1973; and Woolnough, 1983). David Layton, in his book *Science for the People*, was arguing that it was '. . . difficult to see how both objectives, an understanding of the mature concepts of science and an understanding of the processes by which scientific knowledge grow, can be achieved simultaneously. We ought to attend to process as a separate objective, important in its own right, alongside content. The problem of reconciling these objectives in school science teaching', he maintained, 'has been considerably underestimated' (p. 176). Such messages were not heard, however, by most physics teachers, and, though the CSE assessment schemes for practical work did concentrate on the skills, most of these were at a very casual and pragmatic level. It was not until the APU team, under Paul Black and David Layton, developed their framework for scientific activity in terms of science as a problem solving activity (APU, 1984, p. 28) that a basis for validating the processes of science was given authority.

Undoubtedly the absence of any assessment for practical work in the 'O' level Nuffield physics, as indeed for other 'O' level physics courses, prevented serious thought being given to the objectives of practical work. Even Bloom's taxonomies of educational objectives, increasingly used by the examination boards for their mark schemes in the latter part of the 1970s, never developed the scheme for the psychomotor domain, and certainly did not try to analyze the linkage between the psychomotor and the cognitive and affective domains. The assessment of practical work looked set to become one of the most significant battle grounds for the future. Some insisted that a practical investigation could and should be assessed as a whole, and had been doing it for Nuffield 'A' level physics and some Mode 3 CSE schemes for some time. Others, suspicious about the lack of reliable moderation of such schemes, which depended ultimately on the teachers professional judgment, devised more reliable, atomistic, teacher-proof schemes. Schemes such as TAPS (Bryce, 1985) and the Avon Skills awards (Armitage, 1985) set out to test the pupil's competence in many separate practical skills, such as the ability to use a thermometer or to light a bunsen. Such schemes aimed both to be motivational to the weaker pupil and to be highly reliable. But they often tended to make science very mechanistic and introduced the danger of reducing scientific activity to a series of trivial tasks (Woolnough, 1985). The holistic nature of genuine scientific activity, with its dependence on Polanyi's tacit knowledge, on 'personal knowledge of particular things and a subtle judgement of their properties' (Ravetz, 1971, p. 15) was in danger of being destroyed. But then, such subversive, unfashionable thinking, with its language of craft, personal, tacit knowing rather than academic, objective, explicit knowledge was only just beginning to gain acceptance in the literature accessible to school teachers (Head, 1985; Woolnough and Allsop, 1985) and would need to withstand some cold, conventional winds if it was to survive the next twenty-five years.

Changes in the Place of Physics in the Curriculum

As the content of the physics courses had changed so little, so, until the last few years of our period, had the place and importance of the subject in the school curriculum. Whilst grammar and secondary modern schools became comprehensives, physics maintained its status in the curricular pecking order. While, as the senior HMI for science could say as late as 1980 that, 'the maintainance of study of five subjects, maths, English, French, chemistry and physics up to the age of 16, would provide adequate provision for every likely career path', the status of physics in both the selective and the ambitious comprehensive school remained strong. It provided a valuable ticket for pupils keen to obtain employment. The relative status of combined and integrated science, and also of CDT, remained weak both as currency on the external job market and also in not having any 'academic base' in higher education or the professional bodies to define its validity or give it credibility.

But in the last decade of our period, especially in the second half of that decade, the situation in the school curriculum changed significantly. The initial change to comprehensivization had led to the introduction of option systems which offered as wide a choice of subjects to all pupils at the age of 14 as possible. In such an *a la carte* restaurant, the battle for the choice of the more able pupils was easily won by subjects, like physics, with their established status and powerful departmental structure. It was not until the curriculum was considered as a whole, with a view to establishing an educational *table d'hote* menu, and the curriculum decisions taken not by the head of physics, or even by the head of science, but by a director of studies seeking to provide a balanced curriculum for all, that the freedom of physics to cultivate its own corner of the flower-bed was constrained. Directors of studies, especially when supported by HMI, science advisers and ultimately by DES policy statements, began to speak of the need for science, not the sciences, and sought advice from the head of science and listened to messages from the Association for Science Education. It became administratively convenient, especially when rolls were falling and physics teachers were in short supply, to contract the sciences into one subject, science, and give it 10–20 per cent of the curriculum time. Thus the in-school status of physics with respect to science was undermined.

Of course, this weakening of the boundaries of physics was not unique to physics. Once consideration was given to the curriculum as a whole, as distinct from how the existing subjects could be best put together to form the most satisfactory (or the least unsatisfactory!) composite, the independent strength of each and every subject was undermined. Cross-curricular considerations, modular curricular and central and local government edits on curriculum issues were all to threaten the autonomy of the individual subjects. And, as our period ends, the possibility of a collegiate pay structure replacing the traditional hierarchical one, would further erode the strength of the separate subjects through whose hierarchy teachers had established their promotion prospects and status. Thus physics was becoming more answerable, and subservient, to the needs of science and, subsequently, the curriculum as a whole. The days of separate physics departments, headed by powerful and well established physics teachers, fighting independent battles in the unregulated curriculum garden were ending.

And yet, as we leave 1985, the curricular messages for physics, with respect to science and even more with respect to technology, are far from clear. Messages from ASE, the science advisers, the SCDC, HMI and that branch of the DES responsible for the policy statement, see physics as subservient to science, and science and technology as being a unified whole, (rather like Williamandmary!). On the other hand, messages from the SEC give preference to the separate sciences and make a clear distinction between science and technology, by providing different national criteria for each. Furthermore, that branch of the DES responsible for the supply of teachers is quite clear that the shortage area is for teachers of physics not science (it is only potential teachers of physics, not of chemistry or biology, that will receive the £1200 bursary). The £1200 bursary is available for potential teachers of CDT too. The DES plans for their proposed city technical colleges also make a clear curriculum distinction between science and technology. So the position of physics in the curriculum, as an independent subject, as part of science or as linked with technology, remains far from unambiguous. What is certain is that physics has an important role to play in both science and technology and that unless science and technology are able to come together as a coherent unit, probably containing a range of modules, then the remaining physics teachers in schools will face as divided a future as did King Solomon's baby!

Changes in the Role of the Physics Teacher

It is in the physics teachers' role, and the tasks they have had to fulfil, that some of the most far reaching changes have occurred. It was not uncommon in 1960 for physics teachers to teach physics only to able, well-motivated pupils, and for this subject to absorb their most creative energies. Increasingly, this single-mindedness of purpose had been dissipated, first to teaching combined science to the first two years, often in mixed ability groups, then to teaching science or physics to poorly motivated pupils in their last two years of compulsory schooling, and latterly being encouraged to teach biology and chemistry to pupils up to the age of 16 as part of integrated science. Starting as physicists teaching physics they became science teachers with a physics background. Their own interests and expertise gained on degree studies, also led them into teaching some of the electronics, computer studies and technology courses that were to emerge in the 1980s. Inevitably, the singlemindedness of physicists towards their subject was diluted. Furthermore, the tasks and contexts of teaching as a whole changed, with the pupils' personal problems and pastoral responsibilities making ever increasing demands on the teachers' life. In 1960, the teachers' role would have been of a teacher of physics, first, who also had normal school responsibilities and took an interest in the pupils' welfare. By 1985, the emphasis would have changed to being a teacher of pupils, first, who as a member of the whole school staff would teach physics and other subjects as appropriate to the needs of the school and the LEA.

Of course, such generalizations are superficial. The actual situation varied enormously from school to school, as the school cameos illustrated. In 1960, the school system was unashamedly divided; physics was generally taught well in the (boys') grammar, independent, direct grant and technical schools, it was unusual to find it taught well in the secondary modern or the girls' schools. Through the 60s and 70s, schooling was becoming more similar with the introduction of, largely coeducational comprehensive schools and the abolition of the direct grant status in 1975. The roles of physics teachers in the comprehensive schools became wider, though for the physics teachers in the independent schools and the remaining grammar schools the situation was largely unchanged. By the latter years of our period, the role of the physics teachers, as for the pupils, was becoming increasingly polarised again. The independent schools were becoming stronger, as the government reinforced them with the Assisted Places Scheme, as they became better resourced through parental contributions, and as the teachers' industrial action caused increasing parental dissatisfaction with what the state schools could offer. The state comprehensive schools were to be increasingly affected by the cuts in government spending, by the public disparagement by the government and vilification by the press, and by the restrictions caused by the contraction of the system along with falling rolls. Already, by the end of our period, there were signs that we were getting an increasingly divided educational system again, with the rich and the very able catered for in the private sector and the rest, looked after in the comprehensive schools, which were becoming the folk school for the masses.

The differing role of the teacher of physics in the two types of school was becoming wider, and reminiscent of the 1960s again. In the independent schools, the physics teacher was teaching the high status physics still with good equipment and well motivated pupils, while in the comprehensive schools, the physics teachers were moving, headlong, towards balanced science and science studies as 'science for the people' and to teach this low status subject with inadequate provisions to less able or motivated pupils. Ironically, the left-wing advocation of integrated science had increased, not reduced, the dangers of stratification by curriculum. Alongside this devalued science were coming the technological subjects, with the new status which is linked with vocational training and lavish MSC funding. For many physicists the attractions of the 'dry' and well resourced sciences in the technology/TVEI/CDT area were becoming more attractive than the 'wet' sciences with biology and chemistry. Increasingly, physics teachers were seeing their role more in technology than in science.

Models for Change

The Horticultural Model

We started this discussion of curriculum change by thinking of an horticultural model. We saw the physics teaching as the plant growing in the garden (no longer hidden!) of the whole school curriculum. Different schemes have been developed, first in the rich conditions of the originator's greenhouse, and then transplanted into the normal school where conditions in the open field have not always been sympathetic to healthy growth. (It is not only with commercial products that the picture on the seed packet bears little resemblance to the plants that eventually grow, or fail to flourish!). The curriculum plants have been sown in lines defined by the examinations, and tended and nurtured by advisers, HMI, text book writers, apparatus manufacturers and the professional institutions and associations. Other plants have been sown in the flower bed, some weeds too, and the competition for survival ensued; in the later half of our period more selectivity has been applied to the cultivation of an overall pleasing effect than was evident in the earlier years. The economic and political climate has helped or, more lately, hindered the growth of the plant. At certain times the garden was laid out to produce pleasing educational flowers, in harsher times the demand was for more useful vocational flowers. There were certain natural seasons when the school was ready for growth and others when recuperation was in order. Above all, there were certain curricular plants, certain innovations, that took root because they had a natural affinity for that environment. Others, no matter how eagerly they were propagated would not flourish without constant, artificial attention.

In hindsight, it is clear that some of the finer points of Nuffield physics, developed in the rich seed beds of selective schools with dedicated gardeners, were too rarefied for the everyday, outdoor conditions of the average pupil with the average teacher in the average school. But the very real success it had in producing schemes and ideas that were transplantable derived from the fact that the originators were themselves teachers who had developed their own thinking with pupils in schools. The experimental equipment that they produced met a natural response and flourished well in most classrooms, especially as it was promoted by so many persuasive and commercially-motivated salesmen. SCISP was altogether too exotic a plant to blossom naturally, and too lacking in commercial value to warrant expensive husbandry. Nuffield Secondary Science, and the early technology courses, were producing wholesome vegetables at a time when the demand was for decorative flowers. It remains to be seen whether the new integrated or balanced science courses will prove to be a healthy mixture of compatible flowers or an unnatural hybrid readily susceptible to the vagaries of climate and an hostile environment. It also remains to be seen whether the TVEI intrusions are able to produce a healthy plant when the excessive attentions and enriched nourishment of the MSC gardener from next door are withdrawn. It is hoped that the picture of the divided garden, with a small, attractive flower bed at one end, carefully, lovingly and lavishly nurtured, and a large vegetable garden at the other, going to seed through lack of attention and nutrient, will not in the event develop.

The Mechanical Oscillator Model

There is, however, another model which is even more appropriate both to physics and to our understanding of the factors influencing curriculum development in physics. It is a model of the mechanical oscillator. In its simplest form, the system will consist of a massive body suspended on a spring. This system will have a certain natural frequency of oscillation, dependent on the mass of the body and the elastic properties of the spring. If an input is put into the system which has a frequency sympathetic to that of the natural frequency of the oscillator, then the oscillator will resonate, oscillations will build up and continue. If an input signal is imposed on the system which does not match its natural frequency, then no sympathetic oscillation will build up and the signal will die as soon as the forcing agent ceases its input. Fundamentally, the natural frequency of the oscillator depends on the properties of the mass and the spring in the system, it is not determined by the quality or properties of the input. 'No innovation, however well thought through, will appeal unless it already lurks in inchoate form in the minds of the community it is meant to serve' (Reed, 1986, p. 2). And, though the properties of the system might change over time, the mass might change or the suspension become less elastic, it is those properties of the system which determine whether an input signal takes or not. The analogy with curriculum innovation and dissemination is clear, and the questions concerning the factors affecting the changes in the curriculum become ones about who is putting the inputs into the system and what are the factors which determine its inertia and its natural frequency.

The model can be illustrated as we consider the question as to why change in the physics curriculum has taken place so slowly, what was the inertia and the 'elastic' constraints of the system, and then to consider how they were changing. The inertia of the English system, in which so much decision making has been devolved from the centre and the individual teacher and school have had so much autonomy, lay primarily with the teachers themselves. Teachers are by nature conservative, moulded by their own background and maintained by their own sub-cultures, and physics teachers are no exception. They have graduated through single subject honours degree courses, usually in physics or engineering, and will have taken their professional training through a PGCE which concentrated on the teaching of that subject. Few science teachers will have entered teaching with a first degree, or a professional training, in combined sciences. Having entered teaching as a physics specialist that specialism will have been reinforced by salary and departmental structures. Promotion and status have been accessible through the post of head of physics, and the teachers self-interest been linked to the developing of a strong departmental empire with status and power. Expertise, equipment, apparatus, textbooks and exam success have all been vested in the existing subject such as physics and given the system its inertia. Physics teachers, of which there was a relatively adequate supply, were satisfied, if not complacent, that they were meeting the needs of society in providing an increasing number of students qualified in physics.

The characteristics of the suspension supporting the mass of physics teachers also tended to have a high 'elastic constant' and thus to discourage the introduction of new, disturbing innovations. The pattern of the school curriculum was divided into separate, independent subjects. These divisions were reinforced by the external examination system in which physics, and other traditional subjects, always carried more status and vocational currency in the world of employment than such unconvincing upstarts as integrated science or technology. There was the natural support of higher education, with university physics departments giving validity, justification and unconscious reinforcement to school physics, and a professional institution in the Institute of Physics also underpinning and defending the place of physics in the curriculum. In the curricular free-market which existed throughout most of our period, with no central government control of what was taught in the schools, it was inevitable that the inertia of the system should be high and that introduction of innovations as forcing oscillations should be damped by the stiffness of the suspension. However, as we leave our period, in 1985, we find that we are moving into a system where the inertia of the mass is decreasing, the stiffness of the suspension is weakening, and the innovative agents more forceful. All of which could cause a change in the natural frequency of the oscillating system and a more likely resonance, or at least an easier and more energetic forcing of an unnatural oscillation! With the increasingly inadequate pool of strong, enthusiastic and well-qualified physics teachers in schools, and the subversion of physics into the science departments of schools with decreasing rolls and whole curricular planning, the strength and independence of the physics empire is being eroded; empires which will be completely destroyed as the salary scales and departmental structuring becomes more collegiate. As society increasingly demands vocational qualifications in technology, rather than physics or science, as external funding is pumped into such alternative subjects through TVEI, as examination groups start to produce and market better 'balanced science' and CDT courses, as the strength and status of physics in the validating bodies themselves (ie in universities and polytechnics) becomes weaker, so the linkage in the suspension becomes weaker and newer innovations from a more dirigist central government will be able to force greater disturbance on the system.

The Change Agents

Which brings us back to our underlying question: who, or what, are the change agents that have been influencing the teaching of physics and its place in the school curriculum over the twenty-five years since 1960? In a centralized educational system, such a question is relatively straightforward as the lines of decision making are clearly laid down; Rowell and Gaskell's (1986) perceptive study of the development of school physics in British Columbia for instance is able to concentrate on the development of, and teachers' reaction to, government authorized curriculum guides for physics. In the English system, 'a national system, locally administered' the lines of decision making, and the agents responsible for the changes, are far more diffuse. It also ensures that there is a considerable difference between the published statements of policy and courses and what actually occurs in practice in the school physics laboratory.

Some commentators in the 1970s, notably Bernstein and Young, saw the development of the subjects of the school curriculum almost entirely in terms of political power struggles. Bernstein (in Young, 1971, p. 47) asserted that 'How society selects, distributes, transmits and evaluates the educational knowledge it considers to be public, reflects both the distribution of power and the principle of social control' while Young argued that 'the power to define what counts as knowledge is a discussion about the status of knowledge with changes to the curricular *status quo* being resisted by those in the dominant social groupings'. Our story of the development of the physics curriculum in schools, especially in its relationship to, and competition with, a more general science course and technology, shows that there is much truth in this perspective. The position of a high status physics in the curriculum has been defended by the prestigious presence of the physics establishment external to schools, in the universities and the Institute of Physics. The difficulties that both integrated science and technology have had in gaining widespread acceptance has been due, in no little extent, to the absence of any such coordinated power grouping. There have been no university departments representing, defining and legitimating integrated science. The establishment that might have promoted technology was ineffective in that the university engineering departments were well satisfied with physics, and mathematics, as the well-tried basis for higher education, and the various engineering institutes were so independent and divided among themselves that they too were unable to define or discriminate between the many different types of technology courses blossoming in the schools.

However, it is easy to overemphasize the importance of such power struggles, and too simplistic to attribute all such changes, or lack of changes, in the physics curriculum to such political factors. Our story of the development of physics education has shown a more complex interaction, where individual people, often with quite different political persuasions or none, have worked together to influence policy and practice, and where economic and administrative expediency also have been highly significant in affecting change. That the political dimension was important, even if unconscious or covert, there can be no doubt. That all the changes can be explained in such terms, however, is very far from the truth. The development of physics education in schools has been the result of a subtle amalgam of people, policy and power working together in the social and economic climate of the time.

Of People

Perhaps the most striking aspect of these studies has been the enormous effect that individual people have had on the development of physics teaching, both at the local school and at the national development level. Certain individuals have had an influence over a longish period of time which was quite disproportionate to their number.

In the individual schools, a single person, usually the head of department, can have a quite distinctive influence on how physics is taught in that school, an influence which is largely independent of prevailing trends and fashions. In each of the cameo schools, the type and quality of the physics taught depended to a very large extent on the individual physics teachers in post. A determined head of department could maintain a traditional teaching style, irrespective of the temptations of Nuffield or the pressures of science advisers. An innovative physics teacher could introduce exciting project work or make the physics more relevant without any financial incentive or moral encouragement from anyone else. Clearly the prime factor was the energy, vision, and commitment of the teachers themselves, and in most cases that was unreasonably high. Physics teachers would have different backgrounds, different expertise, different perceptions of the nature of school science. An academic, convergent, conservative teacher would reflect those attitudes into the teaching. A teacher with, say, an industrial background or one who had become interested in electronics or computing during the degree course would find ways of incorporating such expertise into the physics lessons. Furthermore the stage in the teacher's, and the school's, educational history was significant. A teacher moving to a new school as head of department would be expected to make changes, to make a mark, and would have a honeymoon period in which to introduce new ideas, possibly gleaned from the previous school. A school which had recently expended a considerable amount of time, money and effort introducing a new curriculum would not be receptive to further changes for a few years, after which it would be ready for change. Younger, ambitious, teachers would welcome and initiate new developments as a means both of personal fulfilment and of publicly establishing themselves with a view to personal promotion. Older, more established, teachers would have vested interests in maintaining their existing pattern of teaching and less incentive for innovation. In the sixties and early seventies, the expansion of secondary education meant that the age profile of physics teachers was young, with many young teachers moving to become heads of department in different schools; providing opportunities for challenge and innovation. As the system contracted, movement became less, the teaching force — even in physics — became older and more stable, and intrinsic incentives for change became less. It also produced frustration as promotion ladders became blocked, and increased the wastage of physics teachers from the profession.

It may seem a truism, but one that needs stating as it encapsulates the most important factor in the teaching and development of physics in schools; the physics teaching was as good as the physics teacher. Though the provision of good courses and resources made it more difficult for a physics teacher to teach badly, good physics teaching was only done by good, high quality, teachers. Throughout our period, there were physics teachers of a very high quality, though never in numbers adequate to satisfy all schools. In the early years, especially, physicists of real distinction had come into teaching in the selective grammar and independent schools and found creative satisfaction and self-expression through curriculum development at the national and local level, as well as through the stimulation of teaching able pupils. With the growth of comprehensivization, the more obvious appeal of only teaching physics to bright pupils was decreased and the perceived pastoral problems were increased, thus making teaching a less attractive option for the physics graduate, though the total number of teachers teaching physics still increased up to the end of our period.

At the national level too, the influence of a few people was quite disproportionate to their number. Goodson (1984) speaks of the 'shifting amalgamations of subgroups and traditions' (p. 28) which act as the communities exerting influence on the way a subject develops, and it is true that such networks have existed for physics. Perhaps the strongest subgroup was the one growing out of the SMA Physical Sciences Sub-committee of the late 1950s and leading into the Nuffield 'O' level physics team. Led by John Lewis, this group of friends met socially and professionally and developed an understanding and working relationships which were to last throughout the twenty-five years. They represented the grammar school tradition of the honours physics graduate, entering physics teaching after the war with a love and enthusiasm for their subject and a high degree of professionalism. Ted Wenham, Geoffrey Foxcroft, John Osborne, Jim Jardine, Wilf Mace, Maureen Hurst, Bill Trotter, Eric Rogers, Geoffrey Dorling, Graham Verow, Donald McGill, Brian Chapman, David Chaundy, Wilfred Llowarch, Maurice Elwell, Dick Long and Henry Boulind all delighted in doing and thinking about physics, and all worked together on the original Nuffield course. Many of this group were still active and influential through the next two decades, supported and supplemented by similar, like-minded physicists such as Norman Clarke, Kevin Keohane, Nevill Mott, George Noakes, Donald Scott, Norman Thompson, Jon Ogborn, Paul Black, Fred Archenhold, Roy Schofield, Maurice Ebison, Charles Taylor. Though they all had a concern for education in its broadest sense, they were by training and by instinct physicists, with a love for their subject, and a personal commitment to ensuring its maintenance and welfare in the school curriculum.

Though the formal grouping through the Nuffield project was not to last beyond 1965, most of these people were active and influential throughout the next two decades. They continued their friendship and shared professional commitment in such activities as the meetings of the GCE examination boards, especially for the Nuffield examination, through the educational activities of the Institute of Physics, through the journal *Physics Education*, at the annual meetings of the ASE and ADEPT, and at an international level through the regular conferences of the ICPE and GIREP — at both of which the English physics educators were to make a leading and welcome contribution to encouraging physics education around the world. Such activities, by such physicists, were to have a very significant effect in stimulating and supporting those in physics teaching and to uphold, in Keohane's expression, the 'community spirit' among those involved in physics teaching. Indirectly, they consolidated a significant power base which maintained the position of physics as a discrete and lively subject for the school curriculum.

In a sense, such a group was anomalous and, arguably, detrimental to the development of a genuinely comprehensive curriculum, for they were all products of, and fashioned by, the old selective system. It will be a matter of later judgment to decide whether the rigour and analysis of their own training, and the restraint they undoubtedly put onto some of the wilder, premature adventures into comprehensive science curriculum, were beneficial or not. Though there were political implications in the maintainance of this type of high-status, essentially intellectual physics, these protagonists were largely unconscious of such and would have been very surprised to be accused of propagating a type of science which was politically and socially divisive. They saw themselves, and physics, as being apolitical. Indeed, Fensham in his perceptive, reflective essay reviewing the products of all the science curriculum movements of the 1960s and 1970s, throughout the world, said that 'they have been rightly criticized for so often behaving as if school and science education takes place in a social and political vacuum' (Fensham, 1985, p. 416). English physicists were not alone in being unaware of the covert political messages behind an apparently neutral science course. After the Nuffield physics project of the 1960s, the physicists had no coordinated pressure group for direct action within schools, merely the *ad hoc* activities of physicists as described above. Science, however, while weak in having no external validating authority to justify its existence, did have an increasingly coordinated voice from within teaching. The ASE, the science advisers group, and HMI under Norman

Booth and Vic Green, were strongly supportive of integrated science replacing the separate sciences up to the age of 16. Though there was little demand from the grass-roots teachers for integrated science, nor indeed from outside the schools, the message continued to be pressed until it became part of government policy in 1985. The people advocating integrated science were less easy to categorize than the physicists, but shared a common concern; that the average child should not suffer at the expense of the more able. Neither by failing at an inappropriate high status physics, nor by being offered a low status alternative science, should the average and less able child be prevented from having a meaningful scientific education or be cut off from future career opportunities and fixed into the lower strata in society. For some the motives were educational, others saw clearly and deliberately the political battle they were engaged in, and perceived it from a position at varying distances to the left of centre. Many of the integrationists did not have a strong personal commitment to any one of the sciences, but took a much broader view of the whole curriculum. The majority seemed to have had a background in chemistry, and seemed, for reasons so well articulated by Jenkins (1976) to have found it difficult to justify a place for their subject in the curriculum of the comprehensive school. Undoubtedly, Dick West was the leading and most articulate advocate of the need to radically reorganize science studies, a case well stated in *Alternatives for Science* and his role is discussed more fully in chapter 6. But he was well supported by others: Jeff Thompson, Kate Hinton, Kate Ellington, Mick Mitchell, Brian Atwood, Di Bentley, Bill Hall, Brian Mowl, John Bausor, Mike Lyth, John Heaney, Maurice Savory, Peter Scott, John Nellist, Hilda Misslebrook, Ray Leigh, and Beta Schofield as well as many of the science advisers and HMI.

But, although there were groups and subgroups working together encouraging either physics, on the one hand, or science studies on the other, there were two men who played an absolutely vital and unique role in each camp; John Lewis and Dick West. It would be easy, but misleading, to represent the developments in the physics v integrated science debate as a battle between two people representing the political right and left. On one side, we have John Lewis from his own public school background now teaching at Malvern College, working through the establishment of the Nuffield Foundation and the Institute of Physics to maintain an essentially elitist, intellectual physics. On the other side we have Dick West, from his working class background and teaching experience at Walworth School (an LCC school in the slums of SE London), fighting for the rights of the working class kids through the more democratic Schools Council and Association of Science Education to establish a more accessible, less divisive, popular science studies. Indeed, there is an element of truth in this caricature, though one which was not often consciously recognized. Though neither would ever wish to be, or to be seen as, representing one side or the other there was inevitably a cultural and political position which influenced their thinking and their actions.

It would be a gross oversimplification to suggest that such a political stance was ever the conscious thrust behind specific initiatives. Subconsciously, however, such personal views of society, and the role that education should play in it, inevitably influenced the position, commitment and response that different people had to the maintenance, or disturbance of the *status quo*. Most of the teachers involved with the different initiatives through the sixties and seventies were 'political innocents', we thought that we were concerned with the best way to teach physics or science to our pupils, we were surprised when we were told that we were actually involved in a political battle to change, or maintain, the social order of things.

Though there were considerable differences between John Lewis and Dick West in their characters, their backgrounds and their political world views, they did in fact have much in common. Both sincerely wanted to improve the education of all pupils, and worked through the subject they loved best to do it. Both wanted to broaden the teaching of science and move it away from academic irrelevances; John Lewis through his seminal *Science and Society* series and Dick West through his advocacy of science studies. Both were incredibly energetic and had the ability to keep on working when lesser mortals were flagging and craving for sleep. Both were very efficient political manipulators who knew how to use the existing organizational structures to further their goals. Both were charismatic leaders who collected a coterie of like-minded teachers around them, and elicited from them great loyalty and support. Needless to say, both were men of real ability and stature. And though at times they were working for different objectives, at others they worked well together. Certainly, they both held the other in high regard.

However, the success of an idea must be judged by the success in which it carries people, including people initially of a different persuasion, after the charisma of the leader and the momentum of the bandwagon has dispersed. Inevitably, the gap between the rhetoric of John Lewis and Dick West and the reality of the average classroom teacher was wide. This was recognized and led both, after their initial forays into changing teachers practice directly, to become more involved in changing practice through changing central policies. For John Lewis, this meant becoming involved with the examination system, which was being used as a means of controlling the curriculum. Initially this meant instituting, and subsequently leading a special Nuffield physics examination, (he was to be one of the chief examiners for Nuffield 'O' level Physics from the late sixties and throughout our period). Subsequently, he was able to influence examination procedures as a member of the Secondary Examination Council, and as chairman of their syllabus monitoring committees for GCSE Physics, for GCSE Science and for 18+ Physics from the inception of SEC in 1983 until 1986. For Dick West, this meant influencing ASE policy through the Ed(R) Committee, through the Alternatives for Science Education Working Party, through representation on the Schools Council, through the establishment and direction of the SSCR project, and ultimately as Senior Science Adviser to the ILEA. Both were able to influence ASE policy in their position as Chairman, John Lewis in 1977 and Dick West in 1978, though the ASE, with its teacher-dominated, democratic constitution, is an impossibly unwieldy organization to try and steer from the top (Layton, 1984). Both were, however, able to influence policy more directly as they, and the ASE, became more consciously involved in the corridors of power. Many late night conversations, as well as more formal presentations of evidence, were influential as the Inspectorate and the DES officers became more dirigist in determining curriculum policy.

For both John Lewis and Dick West, as for other would-be innovators, there was a fundamental tension in their own personal stance. On the one hand they believed in democracy and teacher autonomy, on the other they believed in an idea, in a way of teaching, that they wished to transfer to others. Nowhere was this dichotomy more clearly revealed than in the structure of the SSCR, of which John Lewis was a member of the Steering Committee and Dick West was its founding Director. It was set up, ostensibly, as a teacher-led, periphery model of curriculum development; it was to operate through many groups of teachers working independently throughout the country on problems and in ways peculiar to their local context. And yet, at the same time, it was clear that the Director, and his team, had a very clear view of the type of science that they wished to develop (the previous involvement of so many of the SSCR team with SCISP and with the ASE's Alternatives for Science Education was not coincidental or unnoticed). The hope was that 'the teachers working in the field would develop upwards and the team working at the centre would develop policy downwards and they would meet in the middle'. This hope was always, at the best, optimistic and at the worst unrealistically naive. It was expected that the central team would need to pull the various activities together at the end of the review with rather more autocratic selection than the public statements of the Director had earlier suggested. As the directorship of SSCR changed half-way through its four-year period, this was a tension that Dick West did not have to resolve himself! (Wilson, 1985).

Of Policy

There has been an increasingly widespread belief, especially over the last decade of our period, that changes in curriculum practice are brought about by changes of policy. First, a policy will be developed, driven forward either by logic in an educational expression of the strong anthropic principle or hammered out in horse-trading between committed protagonists with their own, often hidden, vested interests. This policy will then be articulated and disseminated and implemented by the classroom teacher. Hence practice will be changed and, hopefully, improved. We have seen expressions of this with the development of policy statements from the ASE, from HMI and the DES, and from the SEC with their national criteria for examinations. Though not formalized by the word 'policy', we have seen a similar intent with the development and dissemination of the Nuffield courses and SCISP.

We have seen in earlier chapters something of the way that the different policies have developed; established by a dominant group acquiring a consensus agreement within a network of appropriate subgroups. The degree to which these policies have affected the practice in schools depended, in our mechanical oscillator model, on the 'rightness' of the policy, the degree to which it matched the natural frequency of the system, and the force with which the policy was applied. With the English system having so much teacher autonomy, there was little direct pressure that could be directed at the schools to enforce the adoption of a particular policy. Certainly, neither the ASE or the Nuffield Foundation ever had any such power. HMI and science advisers could only advise, and even the final DES policy statement of 1985 had no binding status and could not enforce a school, to say, teach balanced science to all its pupils for 20 per cent of their time. There were only indirect pressures that could be applied to 'encourage' a certain policy, by providing discriminative resourcing, promotion and in-service training. Consequently any policy being advocated would only be adopted if it 'rang true' in the school.

For many the policies advocating integrated science just did not ring true, they did not resonate with the system. David Layton (1984) speaking about the SMAs advocation of general science in the 1920s said that one of its major characteristics was 'its lack of precise definition' which was 'at once both a weakness and a strength' (p. 203). Such a criticism could be made, and has been made, of the integrated science courses being produced through the seventies (Brown, 1977; and Black, 1986). It was a strength in that it could have a superficial appeal to a wide range of people, and provided an elusive target when under attack. It was a fundamental weakness in that it lacked any incisive thrust when trying to make entry into the school curriculum against physics and the other well established, high-status subjects; an entry which 'will be resisted in so far as they are perceived to undermine the values, relative power and privileges of the dominant groups involved' (Bernstein in Young, 1971, p. 34). This lack of definition and focus was also true for technology, when a myriad of different approaches, all under the name of technology, were being advocated indiscriminately. As for integrated science, this lack of a clear, resonant definition was to prove an immense barrier to its acceptance both inside and outside schools (Woolnough, 1975; Nash, Allsop and Woolnough, 1985). Though it is equally true that it was no easier to produce a 'precise definition' for physics either, that did not matter because teachers, schools, and society 'knew' what physics was by its historical place as a discipline legitimated by the physics establishment.

The policy of 'science for all' was unexceptional, but such a universal cry still covered the ambiguities which remained throughout the period. There were four questions unresolved. What sort of 'science for all'? Was it to be the same type of science for all pupils? Was one type of science appropriate for all the scientific needs of society? What was the relationship of science to technology?

There was a growing consensus about the sort of science for all; a wide acceptance that a policy of moving away from the dry, academic sciences to include more about the social, human and technological relevance and more problem solving activity. Bondi (1982) saw 'the very essence of science as its questioning nature, its inherent uncertainty, its utter dependence on constant and intense communication', but found school science 'a fraud' in comparison. His plea was to 'make science more attractive ... by teaching it as it really is, as a human endeavour' (p. 4). Though such rhetoric found resonance in the minds of science teachers, the practical constraints in the school made it more difficult to implement.

There was less agreement about the second question concerning whether the same type of science was appropriate for all. Having agreed that 'grammar school science' was not appropriate for all, having been persuaded that any differentiation between different types of science would cause social stratification of the pupils, having agreed that science for all should become more socially applicable and investigative, teachers were, by 1985, about to wonder whether the same sort of science, as singly defined in the national criteria, was really equally suitable for the most able and the least able.

There was also beginning to be a requestioning as to whether one type of science was suitable to meet all the needs that society demanded of science. Fensham (1985) asserted, as had Bondi, that there were two demands that society made of school science, to provide specialist manpower and to provide a scientifically literate citizenry. He suggested that 'these two demands are conflicting and not complementary as was almost universally assumed in the first wave of the science curriculum movement' (p. 417). But such questioning opened up the spectre of pupil stratification and separation again, and most teachers were not in tune with that yet, though the government policy makers were.

The fourth unresolved question arising from lack of clear definition in policy statements concerned the relationship between science and technology; should technology be subsumed in science or kept separate from it? This was a question of increasing significance to physicists. In the policy statements of the ASE in 1973, 1979 and 1981 and the DES in 1985, science and technology are usually linked together. Since science, after APU (1984), was now seen as a problem-solving process and this was almost identical to the 'process of technology' (Marshall, 1974), since science was to be concerned with technological applications, and since so much of the content of technology coincided with that of science, particularly physics, [for example, electricity, energy, structures, pneumatics], it seemed only sensible that science and technology should be taught together as a coordinated whole. Many of the more creative physicists certainly found sympathy with the approach and activities being introduced into CDT departments. However, the policy of SEC in introducing quite different sets of national criteria for CDT than for science, clearly separated the technology from the science. And such a separation was encouraged by the CDT teachers and their advisers who now saw a way of building up their own departmental status, and did not want the physicists stealing their golden goose.

Interestingly, though this is not the place to discuss the factors affecting the development of technology in the curriculum, we do have now, at the end of our period, signs that externally imposed policies are able to increase the standing in the school curriculum of a 'low-status' subject like CDT. With the SEC-policy defining CDT through their national criteria, and thereby building a strong defensive wall around it, with the government policy of pouring financial resources into it through the MSO's TVEI scheme, and with the DES giving validation to it through establishing 'technology' as one of the eight 'areas of experience and learning' in its policy statement for the *Science 5–16* (DES, 1985), the curriculum garden had been well planted, fed and tended. It is still too early to tell whether this new plant will continue to flourish when the beneficent gardener has left. Or to use our other model, though there is little indication that technology matches the natural frequency of the school curriculum, it may be that with such vigorous policy inputs, the system might start oscillating in a different, harmonic phase!

In relation to the battle to replace the grammar-school sciences of physics, chemistry and biology by the integrated science of the comprehensive, the policy statements appear to have had little direct and immediate effect. Nearly all HMI and DES policy statements since 1977, and all the ASE policy statements since 1971, have spoken almost entirely in terms of science, with only a few, incidental, references to physics and the other sciences. Though the separate sciences may have been tolerated, it was clear, though never justified, that science was to be treated as a unity. There has never been an ASE, or DES policy statement for physics since *Physics for Grammar Schools* (SMA and AWST, 1961). And yet the separate sciences have maintained their position. Apparently, the policy statements have lacked conviction and have not found resonance in the schools system.

Or perhaps oscillations just take time to build up. It is often said that an innovation takes twenty years before it becomes accepted in a school, but the general science movement has been active throughout the century (Layton, 1984; and Jenkins, 1979). History reflects the tendency to favour general science on educational grounds when the social climate is easy, but to revert to the separate sciences on vocational grounds when the economic times get hard. Fensham spoke of the twin demands for science education, to produce a scientifically literate citizenry and as manpower provision for a technological society, and doubted that the two could be satisfied together. It appears that while a more liberal peoples science may satisfy the former, physics is maintained to fulfil this latter demand.

Policy of Expediency

There is, of course, another type of policy which affects change; the policy of expediency, of the possible, of administrative convenience. It is clear that such a policy has been very significant in the development of physics. The curriculum itself, and the relationship of physics to science, has been strongly influenced by the availability of money, of laboratories, of teachers and of pupils and by staffing and salary structures.

When money was in short supply, as in the early sixties, emphasis was put more on didactic teaching, relying more on the cheaper spoken and written word. When money became available, commercially produced apparatus could be purchased and standardized practical work could develop in physics. As resources became short again, in the later decade, physics teachers either reverted to more didactic practices or, in line with

Rutherford's splendid adage when asked for more resources said, 'we haven't the money so we'll have to think'! Expediency encourage them to think of cheaper, more open-ended and creative investigational practical work, using cheap equipment and the environment, and of more effective ways of teaching physics, such as discussion and case study, which was not dependent on expensive apparatus. Similarly, when central money became available for specific expenditure, for buying Nuffield apparatus, computers or TVEI equipment, it was expedient policy for physics teachers to avail themselves of that, with the consequent influence on teaching styles.

As new schools were built, new laboratories were built around the existing subject structures and consequently distinct laboratories were built for physics and the other separate sciences, strengthening the distinct sub-cultures of each.

When an adequate supply of teachers was coming from the pool of physics graduates, it was expedient and natural for such teachers to teach their own subject. As there were very few graduate scientists entering teaching with a broad science degree, there was less internal pressure to teach science as an unified subject. As physics graduates entering teaching brought with them computing and electronic skills, so this influenced the way they taught. When, and where, the supply of graduate physics teachers became inadequate, it became expedient to heads to cover the deficiency in physics by teaching only science, as biologists or chemists could satisfactorily be described as science teachers. Such a practice became more common in the latter years of our period when falling rolls in the schools reduced the total size of the science teaching force and made it more difficult to maintain an adequate balance of physics teachers. The consequent converting of the sciences on the curriculum to a single science further increased the problem of recruiting physicists. When it would appear to a physics graduate that physics was not taught in the school, and that integrated science included biology and chemistry, the post became less attractive. Hence a change from teaching the sciences separately to teaching a single science on grounds of expediency, was to have a more permanent effect on the shape of the curriculum.

The changes in pupil population over the period affected the school structures in ways that also affected the status of physics. As schools grew, with the population explosion of the late sixties, so the size of the schools and the variety of subject provision encouraged the existence of many different, independent subjects. As the populations contracted into the eighties, schools were reorganized to make viable-sized units and sixth forms became detached from 11–18 schools into sixth form or tertiary colleges. The affect of this on the attractiveness of the 11–16 schools for physics graduates, with little physics teaching as such and no sixth form stimulation, was to further denude such schools of qualified physics teachers and to hasten the introduction of more generalized science courses.

The change of salary and staffing structures over the period was also to have a significant effect on physics. The introduction of the Burnham salary with, first, their special responsibility allowances and, subsequently, their hierarchical scales, encouraged the establishment of many independent subjects which became defined and solidified by heads of department locked onto scale posts. Physics became stronger with a head of department on a scale 3 or 4 post. As grammar and secondary modern schools merged to form comprehensives, the heads of subject departments invariably went to the grammar school staff necessitating a parallel pastoral hierarchy to satisfy and maintain the status of the senior staff from the secondary moderns. Hence the total points score of the school was divided between the curriculum and the pastoral staff and the points available for running the separate subjects decreased. A head of physics would often be appointed only on a scale 2 and his position and status, and that of the subject, much weakened in relation to the head of science overlord on a scale 4. The opportunities for a physicist to be promoted onto a scale 4 post in the eighties was to become greater through the CDT departments, especially with the TVEI money providing greater provision for higher scale appointments, and this was to take many physicists away from the science team and hence hasten, through default, the introduction of a unified science course. The encouragement of a more collegiate salary scale and staffing structure towards the end of our period would, undoubtedly, have the corresponding effect of removing any financial status for a head of physics and destroying the remaining physics empires in the curriculum, making that subject totally subservient to the head of science and the director of studies.

In such ways, administrative changes could, and did, have considerable, often unintentional, effects on the curriculum. In the first half of our period they encouraged the independence of physics, but in the latter half they combined to weaken the position of physics in the curriculum and to favour the introduction of science as a single subject. The policy of expediency could be very persuasive to both a head and the LEA.

Power

The power struggles that were influencing the teaching of physics in schools, and indeed the whole comprehensivizing curriculum, were taking place at various levels. Teachers were fighting their own battles in the schools, while around them, and sometimes interacting with them, there were battles at local and national government level and within the various organizations, all seeking to influence policy and practice. Many of the battles for control of the curriculum were not consciously political. Some were, however, and all, even if not articulated, were political in their outcome and represented certain political perspectives for society.

The power struggles within the school have been touched on in the previous section, and they should not be underestimated. The position and status of a head of physics department, and consequently of that subject, is not readily given up. Many physics teachers had built up their professional satisfaction and self-image through that subject and, in remaining in a school for perhaps twenty years will have had much incentive to maintain that position. A physics empire, strong in territorial position and wealthy in resources and status, with powerful friends in the universities, industry and the professional institutes, was readily set up and not easily dislodged. From such a position, against a weak attack from the advocates of integrated science and with little threat from anyone seeking a whole curriculum policy, the inertia in the system preserved the territorial boundaries with little difficulty. It was only in the last few years of our period that the attacks, and the prevailing winds, had become coordinated.

At the organizational level, the ASE, the Institute of Physics and the Royal Society had no direct power, they could only exhort, demonstrate and encourage 'good practice', and apply what leverage they could to influence the policy decisions of those who had more direct influence. The Schools Council's position was even more ineffective because of its fundamental weakness in being totally committed to the principle of teacher autonomy. With no overall, coherent curriculum policy, merely one of 'letting a hundred flowers grow', it could not expect to disturb the inertia in the system or to compete with those determined to put forward a more powerful and coherent input.

The influence of the local government on the school curriculum, which was almost non-existent in most authorities at the beginning of our period, was to grow through the institution of the science advisers. For most of that time, and in most counties, that influence was subtle and benign; encouraging and supporting science teachers in their different initiatives. Indeed, a chief education officer was stating even at the end of our period, in opposing any centralized direction on the school curriculum (by central government) that his county's 'practice was to have a simple statement saying schools should provide a balanced curriculum, should evaluate themselves and should continually stimulate teachers to think' (Brighouse, 1986). And yet, the influence was real and demonstrated by the quite distinctive character of the science teaching in different LEAs, due to the encouragement, with a greater or lesser degree of indirect pressure, of the science advisers. By the end of our period, for instance, SCISP was well established in Hampshire, the separate sciences still strong in Bucks, investigational practical work increasing in Oxfordshire, process science in Leicestershire, coordinated science in Norfolk and multi-cultural science studies in the ILEA. By 1985, the science advisers, as a group, were becoming increasingly influential and self-confident and looked likely to be increasingly effective in their coordinated policy of enforcing 20 per cent balanced science on all schools. By their control of finances and promotion paths, with the support of the DES policy statement, and through the expediency of staffing for science as distinct from the sciences, their increasingly coordinated attack on the existence of physics as a separate subject looked more ominous.

At the national level, where the government's concern in the first half of our period had been only at the organizational level, the determination to intrude into and control the secret garden of the curriculum was expressed with increasing effect in the period heralded by 'the great debate' of 1973. Such intervention was part of the overall power struggle between central and local government, and as such, reflected the growing dominance of central government. It was to have a significant effect on physics in the curriculum, for whereas local government initiatives generally encouraged the introduction of science, many of the national government initiatives were to maintain the status of physics as a separate subject. Such a distinction was most noticeable, and significant in our discussion of the political implications of the place of physics in the curriculum, with a right wing central government and left wing local governments. A Tory government was not unhappy with the divisive stratification of society that a high status physics in the curriculum might encourage, whereas a socialist local council would wish to encourage a more egalitarian people's science for all.

It was ironic that despite the Labour parties more eloquent rhetoric concerning the need to provide a good education for all, it was the Conservative governments who were to be more effective in making significant changes. Indeed it could be argued that the Conservatives were the party that took education more seriously as evidenced by the continuity of service of the respective secretaries of state — in Labour's eleven years of government, they had seven secretaries of state for education; in the Conservative's fourteen years they were to have only five. It was, however, the last period of Conservative government since 1979, under Margaret Thatcher and (since 1981) Keith Joseph, that has seen the most direct expression of government power for intervention. In the best traditions of Orwell's Ministry of Truth, the government which came to power on the rhetoric of devolving power to the people, and of less government interference in individuals' lives, was to make greater inroads into controlling the practice and curriculum of schools than any other previous government. In the words of the *THES* 'no previous government has so successfully aggrandized the power of the state while simultaneously and loudly proclaiming its deepest wish to roll back its frontiers' (THES, 1984).

Recognizing that the 1944 Education Act prevented central government from controlling the curriculum directly, it set about a series of initiatives which taken together, were to become increasingly powerful. The deluge of publications emanating from the DES and HMI on every aspect of the curriculum established the climate that the DES should provide direct guidance on all such matters, though their status could be no more than an advisory one. More authoritative, however, were the national criteria set up to control the GCSE examinations, and therefore to control the curriculum indirectly. Though there was no centralized mechanism for assessing individual teachers, the control of teacher supply could be, and was, controlled by the setting up of CATE in 1984 which was to pass judgment on all teacher training courses before government approval was given to the providing institutions. Similarly, the DES began to take more central control of the INSET for teachers by defining which priority areas should be funded by central government, hence limiting the LEA's freedom of choice. When linked to the reduction of the rate support grant for the LEAs by central government, this provided a very significant shift in control of the training and retraining of teachers. TVEI was introduced through the MSC. The Assisted Places Scheme syphoned off some of the most able pupils into the independent sector and underminded the morale and the resourcing of the state system.

In the debate about the position of physics in the curriculum, these various initiatives tended to given an uncertain message. The DES policy statements moved, under pressure from HMI, ASE and the science advisers, towards subsuming physics as part of a balanced science course, with a maximum of 20 per cent curriculum time. The SEC, however, reinforced the position of physics and the other sciences by establishing their national criteria a year before integrated science. CATE too, in insisting on at least two years of higher education in the subject the student was training to teach, reinforced the separate subjects. The 4/84 type INSET training courses were firmly committed to furthering the policy of balanced science for all. The Assisted Places Scheme was reinforcing the independent schools practice of teaching the separate sciences, while the TVEI scheme introduced its own divisiveness into the system and distracted many physicists away from balanced science. By the end of the seventies, there was among many educators inside and outside schools a growing consensus towards the type of curriculum, an entitlement curriculum, that was appropriate for the education of all pupils in comprehensive schools. Such a growing consensus was rudely disturbed by strong initiatives from central government which had the effect, probably a deliberate effect, of creating a much more divided system. The elite out into the independent schools doing high status physics in high status schools. The rest, either doing a low status science studies in the comprehensive schools or receiving a more vocationally directed technical training through TVEI.

Clearly if, at a time of economic stringency, sufficient money could not be made available to provide a good education for all pupils then resources would have to be provided selectively. The criteria for establishment of priorities were to be made, overtly, in terms of economic return through vocational training. In the words of an anonymous DES official, 'we have to select: to ration the educational opportunities so that society can cope with the output of education' (quoted in Simon, 1985, p. 223). Less overtly, the criteria that seems to have been used were those of re-establishing a divided and stratified system on political lines. Simon sees this fundamentally as an ideological battle; 'The present government is mounting a carefully designed and relentless struggle to strengthen centralised control over all areas of education, clearly realising the crucial role education plays, both ideological and structural, in the maintenance of existing class and social relations' (p. 234) and argues that such government intervention had become necessary because the comprehensive school system had become too successful, in over-educating young people in a contracting job market by creating 'aspirations which society cannot match'. He quotes the DES official as saying '... if we have a highly educated and idle population we may possibly anticipate more serious social conflict. People must be educated once more to know their place' (p. 223). Such a hypothesis; of a central government using its power to reintroduce a divided and stratified educational system along class, or at least manpower-planning, lines has become increasingly convincing by the developments of the last few years of our period. Ironically, the action of the left wing reformers in seeking to introduce a people's science while leaving the high status physics in the independent schools, has helped to hasten the very divisiveness they set out to oppose.

Poacher Turned Gamekeeper

Before leaving the discussion of the factors which have influenced change, it is worth reflecting on which of them have been conservative and which progressive influences, using both of those terms in a non-judgmental sense. In the event we will see that many of them have, at different times and in different contexts, changed from one to the other.

It would be easy to label as conservative factors, the physics teachers themselves, the professional institutions, the text book writers, the examination bodies and the DES. Similarly we could label as progressive influences the Nuffield team, the teacher trainers, the science advisers and the ASE. But this would be too simplistic.

Though the background and culture of most physics teachers inclined them to conserve an academic, grammar-school type physics, it was from among these teachers that the curriculum innovators came. All the Nuffield development team were, or had been, school physics teachers and their proposals were very progressive at the time. Yet the Nuffield 'O' level course became the new orthodoxy and helped to conserve the position of academic physics in the curriculum. The same could be said of the apparatus manufacturers. In the early sixties, their developments were vitally important for the introduction of the new, more practically based, courses and yet they too were to have a vested interest in conserving that approach through the profit from sales of such items as ripple tanks and ticker-timers. The text book publishers provided support for both progressive and conservative teaching. Considering the financial risks in publishing books ahead of the market, they did much to change the image of physics through their support of authors such as Jardine, Duncan and Keith Johnson.

The examination system is traditionally seen as a conservative influence on the curriculum, but even this has been used progressively through our period. The 'O' level Nuffield examination in physics continued to emphasize and act as an exemplar for understanding rather than merely learning physics. Later, as the examination boards became subject to the national criteria, they were obliged to encourage investigative practical work for all pupils by assessing it on the basis of broad processes, one of which was the planning of investigations. The national criteria, monitored by the SEC, was beginning to use the examination system to change practice in schools, by emphasizing process and reducing the content recall. It imposed on the autonomous and rarely progressive examination boards criteria which would move them, and through them the schools, in a new direction.

Many of the academic physicists, more recently accused of being reactionary conservatives, were within their sphere of activity, continually creative. Archetypically, John Lewis not only helped to transform physics teaching through the Nuffield project of the sixties, but continued to innovate through the seventies with the development of the Science in Society project, which was to pioneer a new market both in this country and abroad. Though still keeping his roots in physics, he was able to encourage 'good' balanced science and physics courses through his continuing involvement with the examination scene and SEC. The physics tutors in the UDEs were, by nature, innovative and progressive teachers but they, by their position as trainers of physics teachers, were to help conserve the existence of physics as a separate subject. Undoubtedly, there were others who were advocating science studies and process science, through the ASE, SCISP, OCEA and the SSCR, including Dick West, and some of the advisers and inspectors would be labelled as progressives. But there were, in 1986, already signs that this, too, might become the new rigidly structured orthodoxy. This, in its turn, would discourage experimentation, criticism and non-conformity, and might as a reaction reinforce the conservation of 'traditional' physics teaching in the independent system.

The Institute of Physics, which through its existence was inevitably conservative about the position of physics in the curriculum, was progressive in encouraging good practice through Physics Education and its various educational activities. The Royal Society, also, increasingly gave encouragement to science as a social activity, while being reluctant to lose physics as a separate subject until a convincing alternative was available.

The DES, largely neutral in the early period and active only through the stimulation provided by such HMI as Dr Tricker and Dick Long, was moving towards a more centralist position with a natural tendency for conservatism, if not retrogression. However, because the manifestation of any DES policy was in the hands of sympathetic and liberal people, such as Paul Black (through APU and SCDC), John Lewis (through SEC), and Vic Green (leading HMI), even such a dirigist system could be made into a framework in which good science of all types could develop.

Through all these change agents, there was a mixture of progression and conservatism. There is a natural tendency, spelt out lucidly in de Bono's book on lateral thinking, for the progressive young turks of one generation to become the reactionary establishment figures of the next. Having built up their reputation and expertise in one field there is a natural reluctance to jettison it in favour of a new fashion. Consequently one generation of innovators will need to be replaced by another. Perhaps the wonder is that there has been so much continued flexibility by so many people in physics education throughout our period.

Conclusion

What then can we conclude about the factors that have shaped the physics curriculum, as we try to make sense of what has happened to physics teaching in schools over the period 1960–85? It would be nice if we could isolate one factor which has been the key determinant of change. It would be satisfying if we could explain all the developments in terms of one particular perspective. Unfortunately, life is not as simple as that and the story of the development of physics teaching illustrates a splendid interaction of a variety of particular determinants. Particular people with their own histories and perspectives were working out the teaching and development of their subject as they saw fit, influenced inevitably by the social and educational climate of the time. Policies were developed, partly as a result of horse-trading between different pressure groups and partly as a logical necessity to match the changing situation in schools, and these policies were to have some, if not a great, influence on the way that physics was taught in the schools. Power struggles were being fought on the larger political scene and these too affected the way in which physics were perceived and challenged, as the pivotal element in the ideological debate about whether the curriculum should be common or differentiated. It is not possible to explain the developments in terms of one of these factors as change agents, alone. It is the cumulative effect of people, policies and power perspectives that gave us the typically English, piece-meal development of physics teaching from 1960–85.

We have seen in the horticultural model, how certain curriculum developments will grow, if planted and tended under certain conditions in the prevailing climate. The mechanical oscillator model illustrates how it is the characteristics of a school, its inertia and constraints, which determine whether or not an initiative takes and resonates. No matter how eagerly a scheme is promoted, whether by Nuffield salesmen or DES policy makers, that initiative will only be accepted and sustained if it matches the appropriate characteristics of the schools.

If there is one single theme which permeates the whole story, it is the vital importance of the individual in all aspects of physics teaching. Both at the national and at the school level, we have seen how individual people can have a remarkable effect on developments. Able, committed, energetic individuals have played a vital role in shaping physics teaching and the physics curriculum; they have had distinctive, unique contributions to make and have not been mere pawns in a political power game. Physics teaching has developed as individuals have made it develop. Physics teaching has been as good as the people involved in physics teaching. For this reason, much of this story has had to be not just about the development of physics teaching in an objective sense but about the people involved in physics teaching. And that I find a heartening conclusion. Of course, social and political climates help to shape developments in physics as in other aspects of the curriculum. But, in the first and last resort, teaching remains a human interaction between teachers and pupils. The natural creativity, resilience and humanity of physics teachers will prevent that ever becoming merely an impersonal product of the political system.

References

APU (1982), *Science in Schools, Report no. 1, Age 11+, Age 13+, Age 15+*, London, DES.
APU (1984), *Science in Schools, Report no. 2, Age 15*, London, DES.
ARMITAGE, P. (1984), 'Some evidence of success', *Times Educational Supplement Extra, Science*, 21, September, p. 54.
ASE (1963), 'A new approach to science teaching', *ASE Bulletin*, 6, p. 8.
AUSUBEL, D.P., NOVAK, J.D., and HANESIAN, H. (1978), *Educational Psychology, A Cognitive View*, London, Holt, Rinehart and Winston.
BEATTY, J.W., and WOOLNOUGH, B.E. (1982), 'Why do practical work in 11–13 science?', *School Science Review*, 225, pp. 768–770.
BLACK, P. (1986), 'Integrated or co-ordinated science? Presidential address', *School Science Review*, 241, pp. 669–81.
BLACK, P.J., and OGBORN, J. (1971), *Physics Teachers Handbook. Nuffield A Level*, Harmondsworth, Penguin.
BLOOM, J.D. (1969), 'Towards a new course and examination in science', *Education in Science*, 32, pp. 27–8.
BOLTON, W. (1963), 'Physics projects', *ASE Bulletin*, 7, pp. 27–8.
BONDI, H. (1982), 'Why science must go under the microscope', *Times Educational Supplement*, 10 September, p. 4.
BRIGHOUSE, T. (1986), 'Curriculum plan a danger', *Oxford Times*, 12 December.
BROWN, S. (1977), 'A review of the meaning of, and arguments for, integrated science', *Studies in Science Education*, 4, pp. 31–62.
BRYCE, T.G.K., MCCALL, J., MACGREGOR, J., ROBERTSON, I.J. and WESTON, R.A.J. (1983), *Techniques for the Assessment of Practical Skills in Foundation Science*, London, Heinemann.
BRYCE, T., and ROBERTSON, I. (1984), 'Tried and tested', Times Educational Supplement, Extra, Science, 21 September.
DES (1985), *Science 5–16. A Statement of Policy*, London, HMSO.
DRIVER, R. (1983), *The Pupil as Scientist?*, Milton Keynes, Open University Press.
EGGLESTON, J.F., GALTON, M.J., and JONES, M.E. (1976), *Processes and Products of Science Teaching*, London, Macmillan.
FENSHAM, P.J. (1985), 'Science for all: A reflective essay', *Journal of Curriculum Studies*, 17.4, pp. 415–35.
GOODSON, I. and BALL, S. (1984), *Defining the Curriculum; Histories and Ethnographies of School Subjects*, Lewes, Falmer Press.
HEAD, J. (1985), *The Personal Response to Science*, Cambridge, Cambridge University Press.
HMI (1960), *Science in Secondary Schools*, London, HMSO.
HMI (1979), *Aspects of Secondary Education in England*, London, HMSO.
HOLLEY, B.J. (1974), *A–level Syllabus Studies: History and Physics*, London, Macmillan.
JENKINS, E.W. (1976), 'Education through chemistry — an unanswered challenge', *Education in Chemistry*, 13.3, pp. 84–5.
JENKINS, E.W. (1979), 'Methods and examinations' in *From Armstrong to Nuffield*, London, John Murray, pp. 290–309.
KEOHANE, K.W. (1966), 'Editorial', *Physics Education*, 1.1, p. 1.
KERR, J.F. (1963), *Practical Work in School Science*, Leicester, Leicester University Press.

LAYTON, D. (1973), *Science for the People*, London, George Allen and Unwin.
LAYTON, D. (1984), *Interpreters of Science*, London, John Murray/ASE.
MARSHALL, A.R. (1974), *School Technology in Action*, London, English University Press.
MILNE, A.A. (1926), *The House at Pooh Corner*, London, Methuen.
MISSLEBROOK, H. (1970), *Nuffield Secondary Science, Teachers Guide*, London, Longman.
MOORE, J.L. and THOMAS, F.H. (1983), 'Computer simulation of experiments; A valuable alternative to traditional laboratory work for secondary science teaching', *School Science Review*, 229, pp. 641–55.
NASH, M., ALLSOP, R.T., and WOOLNOUGH, B.E. (1985), *Factors Affecting the Uptake of Technology in Schools*, Oxford, Oxford University Department of Educational Studies.
RAVETZ, J. (1971), *Scientific Knowledge and its Social Problems*, New York, Oxford University Press.
REED, T.J. (1986), 'A sense of outrage', *Oxford Magazine*, 5.
ROWELL, P.M., and GASKELL, P.J. (1986), 'Tensions and re-alignments; school physics in British Columbia' in GOODSON, I. (Ed) *International Perspectives in Curriculum History*, London, Croom Helm.
SCHWAB, J.J. (1964), 'Structure of the discipline; meaning and significances' in FORD, G.W. and PUGNO, L. (Eds) *The Structure of Knowledge and the Curriculum*, Chicago, Rand McNally.
SIMON, B. (1985), *Does Education Matter?* London, Lawrence and Wishart.
SMA/AWST (1961), *Physics for Grammar Schools*, London, John Murray.
STEVENS, P. (1978), 'On the Nuffield philosophy of science', *Journal of Philosophy of Education*, 12, pp. 99–111.
SWARTZ, C.E., with KICE, J.S. (1975), 'Why don't physics teachers teach something useful', *Physics Teacher*, 13, p. 134.'
THES (1984), *Leader*, 8 June, p. 229.
THOMAS, D.E. (1983), 'Practical work in secondary school physcial science; an investigation into the aims and objectives of 4th and 5th form physics and chemistry teachers in Bedfordshire', unpublished MSc dissertation, Oxford University Department of Educational Studies.
THOMPSON, J.J. (1975), *Practical Work in Sixth Form Science*, Oxford, Oxford University Department of Educational Studies.
TUFF, S.M. (1963), '6th form investigations in physics', *ASE Bulletin*, 5, pp. 34–46.
WARING, M. (1985), 'Elementary school science teaching 1870–1904' in GOODSON, I.F. (Ed) *Social Histories of the Secondary Curriculum*, Lewes, Falmer Press.
WILSON, C. (1985), 'The SSCR — a lookback and the way ahead', *Education in Science*, 114, pp. 17–18.
WOOLNOUGH, B.E. (1975), 'The place of technology in schools', *School Science Reivew*, 196, pp. 443–8.
WOOLNOUGH, B.E. (1983), 'Exercises, investigations and experiences', *Physics Education*, 18.2, pp. 60–3.
WOOLNOUGH, B.E. (1985), '. . . the sum of its parts, practical work and its assessment', *Times Educational Supplement*, Extra, Science, 22 March, p. 43.
WOOLNOUGH, B.E. and ALLSOP, R.T. (1985), *Practical Work in Science*, Cambridge, Cambridge University Press.
YOUNG, M.F.D. (1971), *Knowledge and Control*, London, Collier Macmillan.

Index

Page numbers followed by 'r' refer to references.

Abbott, A.F. 160, 161, 162, 163, 178r
ADEPT *see* Association for Department of Education Physics Tutors
Adey, P 103, 112, 115r
Alanson, John 219
Allanson, Professor 113
Allsop, R.T. 62r, 227, 229, 244, 257r
Alternatives for Science Education (ASE) 147–9, 155, 185, 240, 242
Anderson, C.A. 20r
apparatus 29, 163–7, 204
   demonstrations 142–3
   manufacturers 165, 253
   Nuffield 29, 58, 100, 105, 165–7
   science advisers and 191
   TVEI scheme, for 167
   see also practical work
applied sciences *see* technology
APU *see* Assessment of Performance Unit
Archenhold, Fred 82, 102, 113, 129, 130, 156, 238
Armitage, P. 228, 256r
Artus, R.E. 121
ASE *see* Association for Science Education
ASE Bulletin 226
ASET 81
Aspects of Secondary Education in England (HMI) 184
assessment, 171, 172–3, 178
   practical work 228–9
   pupil accreditation 176–7, 178
   to prevent underachieving 181–2

Assessment of Performance Unit (APU) 7, 15, 50, 61r, 89, 182, 225, 228, 256r
assisted places scheme 35, 74, 208, 251
Associated Examining Board 174
Association for Department of Education Physics Tutors 76, 81, 82
Association for Science Education (ASE) 3, 6, 7, 20r, 65, 67, 74, 82, 88, 90, 101, 114r, 137–57, 170, 185, 193r
   Education Committees 154, 155, 242
   LAMP project 46, 60, 140, 141, 147
   members and meetings 141–4
   objectives 153–4
   policy 144–53
      mixed ability classes and 145–6
      power of policy determination 153–6
   publications 139–41, 226
   Science Advisers Group 192
Association of Women Science Teachers 86, 137, 144, 157r, 246, 257r
Attenborough, Sir David 121
Atwood, Brian 137, 155, 240
Ausubel, D.P. 228, 256
Avison, John 161, 178r
Avon Skills awards 228
AWST *see* Association of Women Science Teachers

Backhouse, J.K. 180r
Baker, K. 32, 61r
Ball, S. 45, 61r, 256r
Barnes, D. 106, 114r, 162, 178r

Index

Barrett, Dick 214–15, 216, 217, 218
Barton, A.W. 66, 73, 83r
Bausor, John 240
BBC TV Computer Literacy project 53
Beatty, J.W. 54, 61r, 225, 226, 227, 256r
Beloe, R. 168, 178r
Beloe Report 14, 168
Bentley, Di 240
Berkin, A.J. 118
Bernstein, B. 10, 20r, 147, 126, 178r, 236, 244
Bingham, Charles 111
biology 43, 45
Bishop, Andrew 139, 155
Black, Prof Paul J 2, 20r, 47, 61r, 82, 126, 169, 170, 189, 193r, 226, 228, 238, 243, 254, 256r
Blin-Stoyle, Prof R.J. 72, 83r, 118, 120, 121
Bloom, Benjamin S. 172, 173, 179r
Bloom, J.D. 226, 228, 256r
Bodmer, W.F. 121, 135r
Bolam, R. 191, 193r
Bolton, W. (Bill) 226, 256r
Bondi, H. 244, 245, 256r
Booth, Norman 55, 59, 61r, 73, 111, 113, 114r, 185, 186, 189–90, 193r, 239–40
botany 45
Boulind, Henry 82, 87, 89, 90, 97, 99–100, 102, 104, 154, 155, 163, 164, 179r, 238
Boyle, Edward 14, 181
Boyson, Dr Rhodes 73
Bragg, Sir Lawrence 94
Brighouse, T. 249, 256r
British Association for the Advancement of Science 49, 61r,m 65, 66, 86
British Committee on Physics Education 118, 126, 128
Britton, J.N. 106, 114r, 178r
Broad, H.F. 88
Brown, Sally 3, 20r, 47, 61r, 243, 256r
Brown, Sheila 188
Brunel College 195, 218–21
Bruner, J.S. 7, 8–9, 20r
Bryant, Peter 208, 211, 212
Bryce, T.G.K. 179r, 228, 256r
Burchan, Prof W.E. 118
Burge, Prof E.J. 126
Butler, Dr C.C. 95, 119

Callaghan, James 14, 183
Camford School 195, 207–13
Canter, H. 193r
case studies
   Brunel College 195, 218–21
   Camord School 195, 207–13
   King Arthur's School 195, 196–201
   Riverside School 195, 201–7
   Windmill Hill School 195, 213–18
CATE *see* Council for the Accreditation of Teacher Education
causation, correlation and 18
Cawthorne, R.G. 75, 83r
CDT *see* Craft, Design and Technology
Certificate of Secondary Education (CSE) 14, 42, 169, 171, 175–6
   Mode 3 syllabus 59, 60, 171, 175, 176, 218
chance 17–18
change
   agents of 235–6
   content and approach 223–5
   horticultural model 19–20, 232–3
   mechanical oscillator model 233–5
   place of physics in curriculum 229–30
   policy 243–6
   practical work 223, 225–9
   teachers role in 230–2, 237–42, 252–4
Chapman, Brian R. 73, 82, 83r, 102, 156, 157r, 238
Charles, Ben 218
Chaundy, David 192, 96, 102, 238
chemistry 44, 109–10
   integrated science and 48, 155–6
Clark, R.W. 87, 93, 94, 108, 114r
Clarke, Norman 88, 95, 102, 114r, 124, 238
Clegg, Dr J.A. 118, 124–5
'cock-up' theory 16
Cockcroft, Sir John 161
Cockcroft, Sir William 177, 182
Cockcroft Report 177
coincidence 17–18
combined science, Nuffield 110–2
comprehensive schools, introduction 9–10, 30–2
Computer Literacy project 53
computer studies 53
   see also electronics

260

Index

Conference of Educational Associations 29
'conspiracy' theory 16
correlation, causation and 18
Coulson, E.H. 88
Council for the Accreditation of
    Teacher Education 77, 251
courses
    for 4th and 5th formers 56–60
    modular science 60
    open science 60
    primary school approach 56
    science 5 to 13 course 56, 112
    science at work 46, 60, 61
    science for the 70s 56
    work-sheet dominated 55
    see also curriculum; general science;
        Nuffield Foundation
Cox, Mr 202, 203, 205, 206
Cox, C.B. 20r
Craft, Design and Technology 49–50, 52,
    153, 200, 212, 218, 220, 229, 245, 254
credit accumulation 176–7, 178
Crellin, J.R. 171, 172, 179r
Crook, Dick 165
CSE *see* Certificate of Secondary
    Education
curriculum 85–115
    accountability 13
    DES and 181–4
    government intervention 14, 181–4,
        250–2
    high and low status areas 10–11
    HMI and 184–90
    new courses, impact of 54–61
    physics, place in 229–30
    reduced core 173–4
    science 20% of time 60, 146, 151, 185,
        187, 251
    teacher-based 13–14
    see also courses; National Criteria;
        Nuffield Foundation
Curriculum 11–16 (HMI) 185
Curriculum Study Group 181

Dainton, Dr Frederick 41, 43, 61r
Dainton Report 65, 119
Davidson, Alan 208, 209, 212

Davies, Brian 125
Deeson, E. 129, 130, 135r
Department of Education and Science
    3, 6, 7, 15, 20r, 27, 35, 52, 67, 71, 74,
    150, 157r, 193r, 245, 256r
    policy 181–7
Department of Industry 53
Department of Trade and Industry 26, 53
desertation rate 69, 71
direct grant schools 14, 34
Doe, R. 185–6, 193
Donnison, Prof D. 34, 61r
Dorling, Geoffrey 238
Douse, M. 35, 61r
Dowdeswell, W.H. 88
Driver, Ros 46, 61r, 82, 140, 157r, 228,
    256r
Duckworth, D. 43, 61r, 174, 180r
Duff, A.R. 99, 114r
Duke of Edinburgh's Study Commission
    123
Duncan, Tom 107, 114r, 160–1, 179r, 253
Durham, Sir Kenneth 121
Dyball, R.H. 139
Dyson, A.E. 20r

Eaborn, Prof 120
Ebbutt, D. 151, 157r
Ebison, Maurice 125, 238
Eccles, David 181
Educating our Children (DES) 183
education
    changes *see* changes
    national developments *see* national
        developments
    tutors 75–7, 80–2
Education in Schools (DES) 183
Education in Science (ASE) 101, 139
Education Through Science (ASE) 149–50
Edwards, Peter 214
Egglestone, J.F. 3, 20r, 58r, 61r, 182,
    193r, 225, 256r
electronics 212, 220
Ellington, Kate 147, 240
Ellis, John 147
Elton, Prof Lewis 74–5, 83, 88
Elvins, Prof H.L. 29, 34, 61r
Elwell, Maurice 96–7, 102, 111, 238

261

Index

engineering sciences 49–50
   see also technology
English Culture and the Decline of the Industrial Spirit (Wiener) 13
Ennever, L. 112, 114r, 146, 157r
Entry to Physics Courses at the Tertiary Level 119
Erasmus 72
Evans, Mr 203, 205
Evatt, S. 151, 157r
examinations 167–78
   'A' level, numbers 43–4
   Boards, 174–5, 253
   CSE 42, 169, 171, 178–9, 218
   curriculum control by 251, 253
   GCE 42, 168–9, 171
   GCSE 169, 171, 177–8, 182, 251
   Nuffield 104, 172, 242, 253
   teacher assessment 171, 172–3, 176–7, 178
   UEI 202, 203
Expansion and Teachers Guide to Physics for Grammar Schools, An 144
expediency 246–8
expenditure 29
   see also funding
experimental guides, Nuffield 99
experiments *see* practical work
Exploring Physics (Duncan) 107, 160–1

Fairbrother, R.W. 82, 174, 179r
Farrer-Brown, Leslie 93, 94, 108
fee-paying schools *see* public schools
Fensham, P.J. 239, 245, 256r
Field, Alf 212
Fleck, Sir Alexander 66
Flood, J. 20r
Flowerday, Peter 125
Foxcroft, Geoffrey E. 92, 96, 102, 104, 105, 115, 143, 179r, 238
Framnework for Expansion, A 14
Fuller, K.D. 189, 194r
funding 29–30
   Industrial Fund 96, 92, 94, 115r, 164

Gagné, R.M. 113, 114r
Galton, M.J. 20r, 225, 256r
Gardner, W.K. 162, 179r

Gaskell, P.J. 235, 257r
Gavin, M.R. 113, 126
GCE *see* General Certificate of Education
GCSE *see* General Certificate of Secondary Education
gender differences 36, 37–8, 39, 45, 119, 199
   sex bias in textbooks 162–3
General Certificate of Education (GCE) 42, 168–9, 171
General Certificate of Secondary Education 169, 171, 177–8, 182, 251
   distinctions and merit awards 182
General Physics (MacKenzie) 159
general science 36, 45–8, 240
   chemists in favour of 48, 155–6
   HMI advocation of 185–6
   politics of integration 148–51
   Science for the 70s 56
   status 229
   see also Nuffield Foundation, combined science *and* secondary science; Schools Council Integrated Science Project
Girls and Physics 119
Goddard, John 125, 126
Goodier, Jack, 89, 96, 102, 127, 129, 130, 135r, 164
Goodson, I. 45, 61r, 238, 256r
government intervention 14, 181–4, 250–2
Grade Criteria for Physics (SEC) 178
Graduate Teacher Training Registry 67
grammar schools 28, 34
   pupils in 32
Grant, N. 10, 21r, 168, 180
Green, Eric 12
Green, G. 111, 114r
Green, Vic 186, 240, 254
GTTR *see* Graduate Teacher Training Registry

Half Our Future (Newsom) 108
Hall, Alan 156
Hall, W.C. (Bill) 112, 113, 115r, 172, 179r, 240
Halsey, A.H. 9, 20r
Hamilton, Sir James 182, 183, 186, 194r
Hanesian, H. 228, 256r
Harding, D. 86, 115r

Index

Harding, D.W. 98
Harding, Jan 199
Harlen, W. 112, 114r, 146, 157r
Harlow, David 122–3
Harrap, Martin 89
Harris, John 82
Harris, Philip 100
Harrison, G.B. 61r, 102, 153, 157r
Hartley, Sir Harold 123
Hattersley, Roy 34
Hayson, J.T. 78, 83r
Head, J. 229, 256r
Head of Science and the Task of Management, The (Siddle) 140
Heaney, John 155, 240
Heath, Edward 14
Heath government 30
Heavens, Prof O.S. 126
Her Majesty's Inspectorate 3, 7, 9, 20r, 38, 51, 56, 89, 108, 115r, 170, 179r, 194r, 225, 256r
   curriculum and 184–90
   policy 187–90
   Staff Inspector for Science 189
Heyworth, P. 62r
Hine, R.J. 12, 20r
Hinton, Kate 147, 240
Hirst, P.H. 6, 20r
HMI *see* Her Majesty's Inspectorate
Holley, B.J. 226, 256
Holman, John 141, 157r
Holt, Prof J.R. 118
Holt, Maurice 38
Hooper, D. 65, 83r
horticultural model 19–20, 232–3
Hoskyns, A. 12, 20r
Houghton award 69
Howat, G.M.D. 174, 179r
Hudson, J. 49, 61r
Hudson, L. 5, 21r
Hull, Richard 82
Hurst, Maureen 238
Hutchins, D.W. 49, 62r

IAAM 168, 179r
Independent Learning in Science Movement (ILIS) 12
independent schools *see* public schools
Independent Schools Information Service 34, 35, 62r
Industrial Fund 86, 92, 94, 115r, 164
industry, hostility to 49
Ingle, R. 54, 62r, 87–115r
INSET 190, 192, 251
Institute of Mathematics and its Applications 124
Institute of Mechanical Engineers 51
Institute of Physics 3, 7, 10, 21r, 65, 67, 69, 72, 83r, 123–9, 170, 249, 254
   Affiliated Schools 125
   Education Committee 125–6
   Education Group Committee 73, 125, 170, 171
   influence on teaching 127–8
   publications 125, 127, 129–35
   small grants scheme 125
institutional influences 117–36
   see also Institute of Physics; Royal Society
integrated science *see* general science; Nuffield combined *and* secondary science; Schools Council Integrated Science Project
International Commission of Physics Education 124
Interpreters of Science (Layton) 153
Isenberg, Cyril 126
ISIS *see* Independent Schools Information Service

James, Ed 156
Jardine, Jim 97, 102, 143, 160, 164, 179r, 238, 253
Jenkins, E.W. 30, 48, 62r, 123, 136r, 159–60, 172, 179r, 240, 246, 256r
Jennings, A. 62r, 87, 115r
job satisfaction 72
Johnson, A.H. 173, 179r
Johnson, Colin 147
Johnson, David 208, 211
Johnson, Keith 161, 179r, 253
Johnson, R.K. 162, 179r
Joint Committee for Physics Education 118–19, 125
Joint Council for 16+ National Criteria 169, 170, 179r, 182

263

Index

see also National Criteria
Joint Matriculation Board 174
Jones, Gron 82
Jones, M.E. 20r, 225, 256r
Jones, Prof R.V. 95
Joseph, Sir Keith 15, 118, 169, 170–1, 176, 179r, 250
Josephy, R. 177, 179r
Judge, H.J. 2, 21r

Kahn, B. 53, 62r
Kelly, A. 39, 62r
Keohane, Prof Kevin W. 38, 62r, 113, 118, 127, 129–30, 135, 238, 239, 256r
Kerr, Prof J.F. 225, 226, 227, 256r
Kice, J.S. 257r
Kincaid, Doug 147
King, Prof R. 118
King Arthur's School 195, 196–201
Kirkham, Jeff 73, 83r, 146, 155, 192
Knight, Mr 205
knowledge, Hirst's seven forms of 6
Knowledge and Control (Young) 10
Kuhn, T.S. 7, 21r

laboratories 163–4
see also apparatus; practical work
LAMP see less academically motivated pupils
Lance, J.R. 111
language 106, 162
Language in Science (Presst) 140
latch key kids 25
Lawton, Denis 6, 8, 21r, 181, 194r
Layton, David 30, 45, 62r, 87, 90, 102, 115r, 123, 136r, 137, 142, 149, 153, 165, 157r, 224, 228, 242, 246, 257r
Lee, R.M. 172, 179r
Leigh, Ray 240
less academically motivated pupils 46, 60, 140, 141, 147
Lewis, C.S. 18, 21r
Lewis, John 17, 21r, 88, 89, 91–5, 96, 97, 98, 99, 102, 104, 105, 115r, 118, 126, 127, 128, 136r, 141, 143, 146, 153, 157r, 162, 164, 166, 169, 170, 172, 175, 179r, 238, 240, 241, 242, 253, 254

Leybold and Phywe 93
Lipson, Prof Henry 88, 124
Llowarch, Wilfred 82, 89, 91, 92, 98, 102, 164, 238
Local Education Authority 249–50, 251
science advisers and policy 190–3
Lock, R. 177, 179r
Lockwood Committee 181
London Board 175
Long, V.J. (Dick) 92, 102, 118, 189, 238, 254
Lunzer, E.A. 162, 179r
Lyth, Mike 240

McCall, J. 179r, 256r
McCulloch, G. 30, 62r, 123, 136r
Mace, Wilf 95, 102, 238
McGill, Donald 95–6, 102, 124, 128, 164, 238
MacGregor, J. 179r, 256r
Macintosh, H. 169, 179r
MacIntyre, D. 3, 20r
McKenzie, A.E.E. 159, 179r
Maclure, S. 32, 62
Macmillan, Sir Harold 9, 24, 181
McVey, P.J. 174, 179r
Maddox, John 96, 101, 106, 115r, 118
Malvern, D.D. 189, 194r
Malvern College 88, 91, 92, 93, 105
Manpower Services Commission 26, 184, 254, 251
Marshall, A.R. 51, 62r, 226, 245, 257r
Marwick, A. 23, 62r
Marx, G. 7, 21r
Mason, Sir John 121
Maths, Science and Modern Language in Maintained Schools (HMI) 185
mechanical oscillator model 233–5
Medawar, P.B. 17, 21r
Mendlesohn, Dr K.A.G. 118
MEP teacher training 53
metrication 119
Micros in Schools scheme 53
middle ability group 47
Milbourn, J.J. 191, 194r
Millar, Don 212
Millar, R. 5, 21r

264

Index

Ministry of Education 66, 83r, 95
Misselbrook, Hilda 108–9, 115r, 226, 240, 257r
Mitchell, Mick 240
mixed ability classes 145–6
modular science 60
Moore, J.L. 228, 257r
Morris Report 65
Mott, Sir Nevill 73, 83r, 94, 95, 101, 118, 120, 122, 123, 124, 126, 128, 136r, 170, 179r, 238
Mowl, B.S. 112, 113, 115r, 172, 179r, 240
Myers, F.C. 51, 62r

Nash, M. 52, 62r, 244, 257r
National Committee on Physics Teaching 95
National Criteria 169, 171, 173, 177, 253
  see also Joint Council for 16+ National Criteria
national development
  biology and chemistry 44–5
  educational context 26–30
  general science 45–8
  impact of new courses 54–61
  physics teaching pyramid 36–8
physics trends 38–44
  political context 23–6, 147–51, 236, 240–1
  school context 30–2
  social context 23–6
  technology 48–53
    see also technology
NCST networks 153
Nellist, John 240
Newsom, J. 34, 62r, 107, 115r
Nicol, A.D.I. 126
Noakes, George R. 159, 180r, 238
Non-streamed science, a Teacher's guide (Sturgess) 140
Norman, Len 197–8, 200
North Western Physics Centre 124
Novak, J.D. 228, 256r
Nuffield Foundation 7, 54, 86, 90, 93, 94, 223–4
  13–16 course 60
  'A' level 17, 56, 226

apparatus 29, 58, 100, 105, 165–7
biology 45
combined science 55, 110–12
CSE level 59
examinations 104, 172, 242, 253
junior science 112
'O' level 17, 33, 55, 56, 58–9, 226
  experimental guides 99
  formation of project 95–100
  impact 100–2
  influence of 102–7
  launch 98–100
  question books 99–100, 104
  teachers guides 99, 105
secondary science 59, 60, 89, 108–10, 226
Nuttall, D.L. 174, 180r

OCEA 177–8
Ogborn, Jon 7, 17, 21r, 82, 189, 193r, 226, 238, 256r
Ogborn, John M. 126
Oldham, F. 126
open science 60
option system 184, 229
Ordinary Level Physics (Abbott) 160, 161
Organisation and Content of 5–16 curriculum (DES) 184
Ormerod, M.B. 174, 180r
Orton, R.J.J. 179r
Osborn, John 89, 91, 92, 95, 96, 102, 238
Oxford and Cambridge Board 174

Page, G.T. 51, 62r
Page Report 51
Parker, A. 179r
Parsons, C. 62r
Patterns of Curriculum 10
pay 248
  differential, shortage subjects 71, 230
  Houghton award 69
Pearce, David 197, 198, 199, 200, 201
Perkins, W.H. 66, 86, 115r
Petford, S.K.C. 114r
Philip Harris 165, 166
Phillips, Sir David 120
Phillips, R.F. 172, 180r
Physical Society 123

265

Index

physics
  trends in 38–44
  see also under individual aspects e.g.
    political context; policy *etc*
Physics Bulletin 127
Physics Education 125, 127, 129–35
Physics Education Committee 118, 128
Physics for Fun (Jardin) 160
Physics for Grammar Schools 7, 144, 146, 246
Physics for the Enquiring Mind 97, 98
Physics for Today and Tomorrow 161
Physics for You series (Johnson) 161
Piagetian thinking 103
Pidgeon, D.A. 30, 63r
Pillner, Mr 170
Pipe, Dr 205
Pipes, M.J. 126
Pitt, Sir Henry 119, 120, 136r, 186, 194r
Polanyi, M. 6, 21r
Polanyi's tacit learning 106, 228
policy 7–7, 181–94
  changes in 243–6
  DES 181–7
  expediency 246–8
  HMI 187–90
  LEA 190–3
political context 23–4, 147–51, 236, 240–1
  schooling 8–11
  teaching methods 11–13
  see also government intervention
Poole, J. 166, 180r
Popper, K. 7, 21r
practical work 104–5, 2223, 225–9
  aims for 227
  assessment 228–9
  see also apparatus
preconceptions 19
Presst, B. 140, 157r, 162, 180r
private school *see* public schools
Project Technology *see* Schools Council Project Technology
PSSC physics 86, 93, 97, 103, 115r, 164
public schools 13, 33–6, 75
  assisted places 35, 74, 208, 251
  case study 195, 207–13
  Nuffield physics and 33
Public Schools Commission 34

Public Understanding of Science, The 121
publications
  ASE 139–41
  Institute of Physics 125, 127, 129–35
  text books 159–63, 224, 253
publicity drives 69–71
pupils
  4th and 5th formers 56–60
  11–13 years 54–6
  gender differences 36, 37–8, 39, 45, 119, 199
  LAMP 46. 60, 140, 141, 147
  middle ability group 47
  mixed ability classes 145–6
  numbers in maintained schools 27–8
  numbers in secondary schools 40
  science subjects studied 39
  talented 120, 123
  university entrants 44

question books, Nuffield 99–100, 104

Ravetz, J. 257r
Raynor, D.G. 180, 194r
Raynor, J. 10, 21r, 168, 180r
Raynor study 188
Read, Gill 214–5
reconstruction 18
recruitment drives 69–71
Reduced Content 16+ Syllabus in Physics, A 119
reductionism 18–19
Reed, T.J. 234, 257r
Richie, W.R. (Bill) 97, 118
Riverside School 195, 201–7
Robbins expansion 44
Robertson, I.D.S. 154
Robertson, I.J. 179r, 256r
Rogers, Prof Eric 17, 97–8, 99, 102, 103, 104, 105, 115r, 164, 172, 173, 180r, 238
Rogers, John 208
Rosen, H. 106, 114r, 178r
Rowell, P.M. 235, 257r
Rowntree, Peter 94, 108
Royal Institution 10

Royal Society 3, 6, 7, 21, 65, 67, 68, 72, 74, 117–23, 136r, 186, 249, 254
  Scientific Research in Schools 117
Rutherford, Lord 29

St Joan, Sister 89, 95, 102, 118
salary *see* pay
Salter, B.G. 62r
Sampson, A. 15, 21r
SATIS Project (Holman) 141
SATRO movement 125
Savage, Sir graham 86, 92
Saville, Sheila 125
Savory, M.J. 121, 155, 240
SCDC *see* School Curriculum Development Committee *or* Schools Curriculum Development Council
Schofield, Beta 240
Schofield, Roy 1, 7, 21r, 82, 86, 115r, 129, 130, 154, 155, 156, 157r, 238
School Curriculum, The (DES) 184
School Curriculum Development Committee 15, 18, 182
School Science and General Education (ASE) 144
School Science Review (ASE) 85, 139–40
School Technology 51
Schooling of Science, The (Young) 10
schools
  comprehensivization 9–10, 30–2
  Nuffield and non-Nuffield 54
  sixth form colleges 74, 218–21
  tripartite system 30, 31
  see also direct grant, grammar *and* public schools
Schools Council 7, 14, 15, 54, 55, 108, 112, 115r, 181, 249
Schools Council Integrated Science Project 46, 59–60, 82, 112–14, 172, 189, 191
Schools Council Project Technology 49, 51, 52
School Maths Project 56
Schools Science and Technology Committee 49
Schwab, J.J. 257r
Science 5–13 (Schools Council) 56, 112
Science 5–16 (DES) 146, 151, 245

science advisers 190–3, 249–50
Science and General Education (ASE) 145
Science and Society (LEWIS) 241
Science and Technology Education, Journal of 82
Science and the Organization of Schools in England – Implications for the needs of talented children 120, 123
Science at Work 46, 60, 61
Science Education 11–18 in England and Wales 120–1
Science for the 13–16 Age Group 145–6
Science for the 70s 56
Science for the People (Layton) 45
Science for the Under Thirteens (ASE) 145, 146, 148
Science for the Young School Leaver 108
Science in Schools (green paper) 81, 86
Science in Secondary Schols (HMI) 89, 108
Science in Society (Lewis) 141
Science in the Middle Years 140, 146
Science Masters Association 6, 7, 21r, 33, 85, 86, 137, 144, 157r, 246, 257r
  curriculum changes and 87–91
  Modern Physical Sciences sub-committee 89, 96, 164, 165
  Physical Science Apparatus Committee 89
  Physical Science sub-committee 238
  Science and Education sub-committee 87–8, 154
  Science Teaching sub-committee 87
Scientific Research in Schools Committee 117
SCISP *see* Schools Council Integrated Science Project
Scott, Donald 82, 124, 127, 128, 136r, 238
Scott, Peter 240
Scottish Advisory Committee on Physics Teaching 95
Scottish Education Department 96, 115r
Scottish Physics Syllabus, new 160
SCUE *see* Standing Conference on University Entrance
Secondary Examinations Council (SEC) 7, 14, 21r, 88, 169, 172, 177, 178, 180r, 182, 230, 242
  National Criteria 169, 171, 173, 177, 253

Index

Secondary Schools Examination Council 88
secondary science 59, 60
  see also general science; Nuffield secondary science
Secondary Science Curriculum Review 82, 151–3, 157r, 192, 194r, 242
sex *see* gender differences
Sharples, Ken 126
Shayer, M. 103, 112, 115r
Short, A.J. 114r
Shortage of Science and Maths Teachers in Schools 68
Siddle, J. 140, 157r
Simon, B. 252, 257r
SisCON in Schools 141
Sister St Joan *see* St Joan, Sister
sixth form colleges 74, 218–21
Skevington, J.H. 178, 180r
Slade, J.A. 73, 83r
SMA *see* Science Masters Association
Smith, G. 193r
Smith, L.G. 108
Smith, Michael 92
SMP maths 56
SNIPPETS magazine 125
social context 10, 25–6, 141, 147–9
Solomon, Joan 141, 157r
Spears, T. 193, 194r
Spurgin, C.B. 119, 127, 128, 136r, 172,
Squires, A. 140, 146, 157r
SSCR *see* Secondary Science Curriculum Reviews
SSTC *see* Schools Science and Technology Committee
Standing Conference on University Entrance 7, 21r, 119, 136r
Steadman, S.D. 55, 59, 61r
STEP exercises 78
Stevens, P. 106, 115r, 228, 257r
Stevenson, Will 216
Stewart, Prof 120
Stone, Roger 96, 102
Sturgess, L.M. 140, 157r
Sugden, Professor 120
Sutton, C.R. 78, 83r
Swann, Lord 121
Swartz, C.E. 228, 257r

Swift, Jonathan 23–4
syllabus content 173
  see also courses; curriculum; examinations

talented children 120, 123
Tall, G. 58, 62r, 111, 115r
Tapper, E.W. 90, 118, 137, 155
TAPS assessment scheme 228
Tawney, D.A. 179r
Taylor, Prof Charles 126, 238
teachers 65–83
  changes and 230–2, 237–42, 252–4
  desertion and wastage 69, 71
  differential salary 71, 230
  future supply 73–5
  job satisfaction 72
  mature students 70
  MEP training 53
  'Nuffield' 58–9
  numbers 67, 68
  physicists first 5
  professional qualifications 67
  recruitment and publicity 69–71
  supply 65–72
  training 75–82
teaching
  11–13 years 54–6
  pyramid 36–8
  trends *see* changes
  see also political context
Teaching of Physics, The (Warren) 162
Teaching Physics for Understanding 104
Tebbutt, Maurice J. 56, 62r, 82
Technical and Vocational Education Initiative 26, 30, 53, 74, 153, 245, 248, 251
  apparatus
technology 151, 200, 212, 220
  across general curriculum 51
  Callaghan and 14, 43, 183
  engineering sciences 49–50
  low status of 10, 11, 13
  national developments 48–53
  see also Craft, Design and Technology
text books 159–63, 224, 253

268

Thatcher, Margaret 10, 14, 15, 31–2, 250
Thatcher government 26, 35, 120, 188
Thomas, D.E. 227, 257r
Thomas, F.H. 228, 257r
Thompson, Jeff J. 146, 147, 155, 157r, 225, 227, 240, 257r
Thompson, Norman 73, 83r, 126, 127, 128, 136r, 171, 180r, 238
Thompson, Prof J.J. 98
Thomson Report 65
Times Educational Supplement 32, 169, 170
Times Higher Education Supplement 250, 251, 257r
Tippett, Mr 170
Todd, Sir Alexander 90
Topping, Dr J. 126
training
  initial courses 77–80
  tutors 75–7, 80–2
Training of Graduate Science Teachers (Scott) 124, 136r
Tricker, B.J.K. 194r
Tricker, R.A.R. 88–9, 92, 104, 164, 165, 166, 187, 189, 194r, 226, 254
Trotter, A.W. (Bill) 126, 155, 226, 238
Tuff, S.M. 226, 257r
Tunley, Harold 88
tutors 75–7
  influence of 80–2
TVEI *see* Technical and Vocational Education Initiative
Tyndale affair 14, 32, 182

UBET 81
UCET 67, 81
UDE *see* University Departments of Education
UEI examinations 202, 203
unemployment 25–6
UNESCO conference, Hamburg 87
University Departments of Education
  tutors 75–7, 80–2
  see also training
university entrants 44
  core syllabus for 119

Verow, Graham 238
Vinen, Prof W.F. 118

vocational aims 26
  see also Technical and Vocational Education Initiative

Walford, G. 163, 180r
Walker, D.L. 114r
Walker, R. 52, 62r, 109, 115r, 191, 194r
Waring, Mary 87, 98, 115r, 164, 180r, 225, 257r
Warren, John 162, 180r
wastage rates 69, 71
Wedderburn, Prof Dorothy 121
Wellington, J.J. 53, 62r
Wenham, E.J. (Ted) 89, 92, 96, 98, 102, 103, 115r, 118, 126, 169, 170, 238
West, R.W. (Dick) 146, 147, 149, 150, 151–2, 155–6, 157r, 240, 241, 242, 253
Weston, Dame Margaret 121
Weston, R.A.J. 179r, 1256r
Whinnerah, John B. 186, 194r
Whitehead, Jack 12, 21r
Wiener, Martin 13, 49, 62r
Wild, Ken 111
Wilde, O. 8, 21r
Wilkinson, Bill 82
William Tyndale School 14, 32, 182
Williams, Shirley 147
Wilmott, A.S. 180r
Wilson, C. 242, 257r
Wilson, Sir Harold 9
Wilson government 25–6, 31, 34
Windmill Hill School 195, 213–18
Winkley, D. 191, 194r
Wood, Sir Alan 120
Woolnough, B.E. 43, 50, 61r, 62r, 63r, 80, 83r, 173, 180r, 225, 226, 227, 228, 229, 244, 256r, 257r
World of Physics, The (Avison) 161

Yates, A. 30, 63r
Young, Brian 111
Young, Michael F.D. 10, 11, 12, 21r, 147, 236, 244, 257r

Ziman, Prof John 121
zoology 45
Zuckerman, Sir Solly 86